CW00430564

The Power of Narrative in E
Networks

American and Comparative Environmental Policy
Sheldon Kamieniecki and Michael E. Kraft, series editors

For a complete list of books in the series, please see the back of the book.

The Power of Narrative in Environmental Networks

Raul Lejano, Mrill Ingram, and Helen Ingram

The MIT Press
Cambridge, Massachusetts
London, England

© 2013 Massachusetts Institute of Technology

All rights reserved. No part of this book may be reproduced in any form by any electronic or mechanical means (including photocopying, recording, or information storage and retrieval) without permission in writing from the publisher.

MIT Press books may be purchased at special quantity discounts for business or sales promotional use. For information, please email special_sales@mitpress.mit.edu or write to Special Sales Department, The MIT Press, 55 Hayward Street, Cambridge, MA 02142.

This book was set in Sabon by Toppan Best-set Premedia Limited, Hong Kong. Printed and bound in the United States of America.

Library of Congress Cataloging-in-Publication Data

Lejano, Raul P., 1961–
The power of narrative in environmental networks / Raul Lejano, Mrill Ingram, and Helen Ingram.
    pages cm.—(American and comparative environmental policy)
Includes bibliographical references and index.
ISBN 978-0-262-01937-8 (hardcover : alk. paper)—ISBN 978-0-262-51957-1 (pbk. : alk. paper)
1. Environmentalism. 2. Environmental policy. 3. Policy sciences. 4. Social networks. I. Title.
GE195.L43   2013
333.72—dc23
                                    2012048926

10   9   8   7   6   5   4   3   2   1

Contents

Series Foreword

Much of contemporary scholarship on environmental policy and politics centers on empirical analysis of policymaking processes, often rooted in well-developed theories of public policy, such as the factors shaping issue framing and agenda setting or the influence of organized groups on policy decisions. As an offshoot of research on agenda setting and the interaction of citizens and groups in the policy process, political scientists and other social scientists increasingly have turned to analysis of networks. In some ways, this approach dates back to the idea of issue networks that Hugh Heclo developed in the late 1970s to capture the often fluid interactions of policy actors within discrete areas of public policy, such as transportation planning, health care financing, and environmental protection.

In many ways, Heclo's ideas about the importance and operation of issue networks were further refined in later analyses of the agenda-setting process, particularly by John Kingdon in his seminal *Agendas, Alternatives, and Public Policies*. More recently, other scholars have devoted considerable attention to the phenomenon of issue framing—or the use of carefully developed language and communication strategies to affect how policy ideas are conveyed to pertinent publics—which, in turn, shapes the way those ideas are understood and draw political support or opposition. Part of this process, as Deborah Stone argued so well in her book *Policy Paradox*, involves narratives or storytelling that can capture the public's imagination and shape both political discourse and policymaking. The effect is often quite different from what one might expect based solely on the merits of scientific or economic analysis. There are endless examples of the phenomenon in contemporary policy debates, from disputes over the urgency of climate change and appropriate policy actions to how best to reform health care or Social Security.

This new work by Lejano, Ingram, and Ingram draws from the rich conceptual heritage of research on agenda setting, issue framing, issue networks, and nonhuman geographies among other scholarship, to develop and apply a new and exciting approach to the study of environmental policy and politics. It focuses on the operation of environmental networks and the narrative discourses that one finds in debates concerning how best to resolve conflicts over natural resources and their use. As the authors state, their book is about how environmental stories "shape how we behave." They argue that by paying attention to these stories, we can improve our understanding of environmental behavior and possibly change that behavior in a way that promotes improved governance of natural resources. This illuminates the need to be aware of the use of language and the stories that are told by participants in environmental discourses.

Understanding human behavior with respect to the environment also requires that we understand the role of networks, or the relationships that people have with one another and with their environments. In particular, many decisions over the use of natural resources involve the way people think about nature or the environment, such as how we exploit the economic potential of resource use, and preserve or protect the environment against the risks posed by developing such resources, be they freshwater supplies, oil and natural gas reserves, or forest, fishery, and agricultural resources. In contrast to the prevailing understanding of social and political networks, the authors argue that the networks of concern here are exceptionally heterogeneous and may include animals, plants, and other "characters" of the environment playing active roles. These networks often span national boundaries and involve many different kinds of interactions, including how groups of people develop relationships with their environments, how they organize themselves, and how they take action that affects the use of natural resources. Narrative analysis can be used to clarify how such networks help bridge multiple perspectives, focus attention on shared goals, and resolve disputes over resource use.

The authors apply this analytical framework of narrative discourse and network operations to the assessment of three significant cases: protection of an ecologically rich and endangered Sonoran Desert between the United States and Mexico, protection of the Turtle Islands marine turtle rookery, and the development of organic agricultural production in the United States. In the last chapter, they compare insights from each of the three cases to reflect on the broader implications of the book's assessment of environmental networks and their importance for democracy, environmental governance, and social science research.

The book illustrates well the goals of the MIT Press series in American and Comparative Environmental Policy. We encourage work that examines a broad range of environmental policy issues. We are particularly interested in volumes that incorporate interdisciplinary research and focus on the linkages between public policy and environmental problems and issues both within the United States and in cross-national settings. We welcome contributions that analyze the policy dimensions of relationships between humans and the environment from either a theoretical or empirical perspective. At a time when environmental policies are increasingly seen as controversial and new approaches are being implemented widely, we especially encourage studies that assess policy successes and failures, evaluate new institutional arrangements and policy tools, and clarify new directions for environmental politics and policy. The books in this series are written for a wide audience that includes academics, policymakers, environmental scientists and professionals, business and labor leaders, environmental activists, and students concerned with environmental issues. We hope they contribute to public understanding of environmental problems, issues, and policies of concern today and also suggest promising actions for the future.

Sheldon Kamieniecki, University California, Santa Cruz
Michael Kraft, University of Wisconsin-Green Bay
American and Comparative Environmental Policy series editors

Preface and Acknowledgments

This book is a product of an extended conversation between a geographer and two policy scholars. We all share an interest in networks and relationality because these ideas help analyze environmental governance. Our individual scholarship has revolved around the opening up of the complex combinations of personal, community, and public forces and structures that inform the decisions people make, or try to make, about the environment. We were all attracted by the power of networks to describe this complexity but also interested in developing analytical tools sensitive to the heterogeneity of networks of environmental governance that we were all studying. How could we grasp some of this diversity in a way that helps explain innovation, or lack of it, regarding environmental governance? We all saw potential in the power of story and in tools offered by literary theory and analysis to capture the diversity of personal and public, affective and institutional dimensions. We sought a way to describe narratives not as good, just, hapless, and ineffective, but instead as reflecting the concerns, hesitations, and ambitions of people as they react to, shape, and are shaped by their environment.

Coming from different disciplinary backgrounds, and informed by different literature, it took time (over two years) to create a common framework and to develop an analytic that appeared robust and useful to all of us. In working toward this goal, we were enabled by many other people and have benefited greatly from their advice and input. Early inspiration stemmed in part from the participation of one author (Mrill Ingram) in a faculty seminar at the University of Wisconsin-Madison on narratives, networks, and the HBO series *The Wire*. The motivation behind the seminar, held in the fall of 2009, came from a collaboration between UW sociology professor Lew Friedland, who has worked extensively with networks, and Caroline Levine, professor of English, an authority on narrative.

Early work on narrative and policy traces back to the collaboration of another member of the team (Raul Lejano) with Anne Taufen Wessells in 2006 on exploring community development narratives and, subsequently, with Ching Leong in 2009, on the study of controversies surrounding water reuse. Even prior to this was an exploration of the use of hermeneutics in explaining community-based resource management regimes, where Lejano collaborated with fishers' groups in the Philippines. Most recently, he began digging deeper into integrative modes of policy analysis and design, stemming from conversations with Dan Stokols, John Hipp, Michael Howlett, and others, and exploring the role of narrative in climate action with Fikret Berkes and Joana Tavares. Many ideas on integrating ecology and society, which resonate in this book, trace back to these sundry interactions.

Very early in the conception of the book, Helen Ingram brought up the question of why it was that social networks had become such a favored concept in the literature's turn from government to governance. Explanations of the "magic" of such networks, and analyses of why they succeed, seemed to us as sometimes less than complete. We sought a new approach through which we might better describe why one network endures and another does not, why one seems to bind its members tightly and others do not. The approach that evolved took the form of narrative analysis and concepts from narratology. Looking back, it now seems to us that our turn to narrative (to describe and explain the power of networks) was perhaps inevitable. When interviewing policy actors and community members about the groups and initiatives they formed, we invariably found our richest material in the extended stories that people would share with us—the more elaborate, the better.

In the process of exploring the use of narrative as a descriptive and analytic device for the study of networks, we gained a deeper realization of the extent to which these narratives were, in fact, constitutive of the networks themselves for its members. This was especially evident with nonformalized network arrangements where structure and organization drew directly from the narrative. And this led us to formulate the notion of the "narrative-network," which we hope will be a useful contribution to the literature. As we discuss in the book, in this framework, networks are, literally and no pun intended, communities that narrate themselves into existence. And this has implications for how we study these networks and, presumably, how they themselves function.

In conceptualizing the book, our immediate audience comprised two communities: first, those interested in the potential of social networks as an alternative institutional mode of governance and, second, those interested in the management of ecological habitat and biota. But, as it turns out, these two communities encompass a broad swath of disciplines and scholarly groups—not just public policy scholars and geographers, but researchers and practitioners in the areas of sustainability and resilience, conservationists and biologists, social network analysts, new institutionalists, sociologists, political scientists and political economists, marine scientists, planners, and scholars of public administration.

When we speak of new networks as being products of the ecological imagination, we do not invoke an idea of ecological democracy as if it were inevitable or even definable. We merely were intrigued by the possibilities of, within sometimes novel network arrangements, communities of actors discovering new patterns of human-environmental relationships, as we observed in three case studies that we take up in this book. Of course, networks are not just instruments of democracy—indeed, they precede and preexist whatever teleological reasons there are that we read into them. Network arrangements can further entrench dysfunctional social patterns or serve to amend them. Networks do not promise new, more democratic patterns of engagement, but they can, sometimes, help us imagine them.

In this light, the book might be seen as a logical extension of previous works by the authors. The first point of origin was Helen Ingram's book (a collaboration with Anne Schneider), entitled *Policy Design for Democracy*, in which they sought out the democratizing potential of policy instruments and practices. Another was Raul Lejano's book, *Frameworks for Policy Analysis: Merging Text and Context*, where institutions were depicted as a hermeneutic between bodies of text (e.g., narratives) and lifeworlds of context (e.g., persons, places, communities). The most recent necessary ingredient was Mrill Ingram's scholarship on assemblages or actor-networks of humans and nonhumans (especially humans and microbes) redefining the terms by which they coexist—namely, networks are not only social but ecological, too. This is why this book is perhaps unique and why it required three authors.

The collaboration extended beyond the three authors to include others whose contributions we gratefully acknowledge. The authors would like to thank Emma Spiro for her work on the network diagrams that appear as figures 2.1 and 4.3 in the book, and Candy Tong for her help in manuscript preparation and analysis of the Sonoran Desert interviews. Reviews of earlier versions of the manuscript, received from Anne Taufen Wessells, Dave Huitema, Jeremy Schmidt, and Marcela Brugnach, are greatly appreciated. The Sonoran Desert case study was enabled by Wendy (Gwynn) Laird Benner's research collaboration with Helen Ingram. The Southwestern Foundation for Education and Historical Preservation and Dianne Bret Harte provided support for this case. The Turtle Islands case study emerged from Raul Lejano's collaboration with Daniel Torres and Shaoie Agduma. Writing of the book benefited from an SRSS small grant from the National University of Singapore and a leave of absence (for Raul Lejano) from the University of California, Irvine.

We thank David Laird and Wing Kan for proofreading and indexing the final manuscript.

We thank the following for their permission to use the following figures:

Figure 4.1: Gwynn Laird Benner

Figures 4.2 and 4.4: Taylor & Francis for reproduction of a chart that appears in the following article: Raul Lejano, Helen Ingram, John Whiteley, Daniel Torres, and Sharon Agduma. 2007. "The Importance of Context: Integrating Resource Conservation with Local Institutions." *Society & Natural Resources* 20 (2): 1–9.

Last, we express our gratitude for the guidance and suggestions received from Sheldon Kamieniecki and Michael Kraft, editors of the American and Comparative Environmental Policy series, and MIT Press editor Clay Morgan.

1

Introduction: The Stories Environmental Networks Tell Us

The story that most of us typically read, hear, and tell about the environment is a familiar one: across a vast range of ecological settings, we find a diversity of earth's living organisms uniquely adapted to thrive on the local resources, and creating an intricate, multifarious web of relationships with other living things, shaping and shaped by soil, wind, and other elements. Picture humans in this scene, however, and we enter like a giant predatory insect driven by necessity, greed, ignorance, or even good intentions (depending on the twist favored by the storyteller). Humans blunder into the web, rending strands with every move, wreaking the net's destruction, but also hopelessly caught in the gluey strands and unable to escape.

Of course, this is not the only story we hear and tell about people and nature, but sometimes it is difficult to remember that it is not the only story out there. Any day of the week, most of the environmental articles one finds in a newspaper, magazine, web site, or other media outlet are cautionary tales. Human beings will play the role of villain or victim. Accustomed as we are to the portrayal of the commons as tragic, we do not expect to read a comedy or a romance.

The goal of this book is to bring attention to the role of stories in our environmental behavior. We believe that stories shape how we behave, and that by paying attention to our stories we can better understand—and change—our behavior. And we believe that, every day, new stories are being written that are changing the way we live on this planet. This book is about being, to use language from Martha Nussbaum (1990), "finely aware" of these stories and their message of being "richly responsible" for this earth.

This book is also about networks. We are particularly interested in how people understand the relationships that bind them with each other, and with animals, resources, and other elements of the environment. We focus on how groups of people "story" themselves into environmental relations, or how they understand their environmental connections, whether it is to defend or to exploit. If the literature is right, the way we save or despoil the planet is occurring increasingly through boundary-spanning networks for action. We argue that environmental networks and stories, or narratives, are mutually defining. Together, we understand them as "narrative-networks." In order to understand the network, we need to pay attention to the stories told by people about their connections: how they came to be and how they are maintained.

We see the concept of network as fundamental to understanding environmental action: how separate groups of people develop relationships with their environments, organize themselves, and take action to manage change. We argue that networks need stories in order to make sense. Although networks have been a topic of much interest in recent years, and the focus of a wide variety of types of analyses, we see a fundamental gap in how environmental networks are understood.

Stories, or narratives, create the glue that binds people together in networks, providing them with a sense of history, common ground, and future, thus enabling them to persist even in the context of resistance. It is through stories that people both analyze and realize personal relationships with land, animals, rivers, air, and even bacteria as well as new technologies that impact the environment. And we argue that it is through the systematic exploration of story that these networked modes of collective action can best be described and analyzed.

In our science-focused society, the environment is often discussed in scientific terms that can obscure motivations driven by memory, feelings informed by tradition, family, and beauty, and other rationales for behavior that can seem irrational from a technical perspective. Wendell Berry (2012) has described this as "affection" for the land. We suggest that by focusing on the stories people tell about their environments, we can do a better job of understanding what matters to people and why they take action. Perhaps even more important, stories reflect people's visions of how we might foster better relationships with the world. We see stories as reflecting the work people do when they set aside conventional assumptions and think and interact differently with their environment. Stories offer a venue through which we can begin to understand people and environment as "interconnected phenomena, processes and presence" (Lorimer 2006, 506). This might also be described as "learning to be affected"—that is, moved, or put into motion, by other entities, human or nonhuman (Latour 2004b, 205).

An example of the kind of storytelling explored in this book is reflected in the stories that organic and other alternative farmers have been telling about microbes for decades. This example reveals how people imagine and develop new ecological relationships and actions, some of which actually precede the development of supporting environmental science. As we'll describe later in the book, the perusal of organic texts, written recently as well as decades ago, reveals farmers describing the importance of soil microorganisms in some detail, along with various strategies for managing microbial flourishing. Even without the scientific and technical details available today, farmers developed stories about and technologies for managing soil microbes in growing healthy, productive crops. Currently, we are seeing a kind of microbial revolution across the sciences as new technologies for identifying microbial genetics reveal tremendous microbial diversity and influence. However, before much of this science had developed, alternative farmers working in the fields had recognized the significant role of microbes in soil health and "storied" them into material practices such as composting and cover cropping. This was not a discourse and material engagement outside technical information, however, but was built on the science available, extending it beyond what was propounded in land grant colleges and by conventional agricultural suppliers. Thus, we suggest that environmental narratives, and the networks they are inextricably linked to, are important places to look for practical inspiration about new ways of living with the world.

In this book we develop an analytical approach to elucidating and analyzing the stories of three very different environmental networks. Our goals are to show the power of narrative analysis in understanding human environmental behavior and to emphasize the critical role story can play in our environmental future.

Environmental Networks as Solution

In recent years, policymakers, planners, and scholars have been increasingly interested in the capacity of collaborative, participatory, network-type governance to deal with environmental issues. Environmental problems are infamously complex, scientifically indeterminate, and unruly. They are typically characterized by intrinsic uncertainty, and responding to such situations requires the integration of diverse kinds of knowledge. Research on solving environmental problems has described a range of environmental governance networks including public-private partnerships, communities of practice, advocacy coalitions, and boundary organizations, all of which are seen as important complements to top-down command-and-control or market-based approaches to environmental governance and regulation (Dedeurwaerdere 2011; Guston 2001; Haas 2004; Ostrom 2001; Sabatier 1999).

In the context of environmental action and policy, networks have been recognized both as phenomena, resulting from the rooted, complex, and uncertain nature of social-biophysical problems, and as solutions, interconnected but diverse coalitions of people and organizations, closely linked to on-the-ground events, deploying diverse and cross-scale resources for undertaking new types of environmental action. Self-organizing networks initiating direct action in energy and water conservation, local agriculture, recycling of wastes, green consumerism, green infrastructure, and other areas have been credited with addressing significant environmental problems. For example, in 1997 active networks of farmers, food processors, food coops, health food stores, environmentalists, and consumers were able to generate a massive public protest to a flawed attempt by the U.S. federal government to draft rules regulating organic food production (Ingram and Ingram 2005). On another front, informal networks of business entities have also been effective in spurring regulatory reforms in the United States (Kraft and Kamieniecki 2007).

In the classic environmental story of Love Canal, Lois Gibbs (1982) describes a network of neighbors that mobilized with her in response to the adverse health effects of toxic substances buried close to schools and houses near Love Canal. The group refused to accept the official line about cancer and chemicals in the environment. They pushed the issue on the national agenda despite the resistance of state and federal officials and much of the scientific establishment. Other examples of environmental networks in the United States include public-private partnerships that have played a prominent role in setting aside lands for conservation (Fairfax and Guenzler 2001) or in developing restoration and community development projects in the South Bronx (Sze 2007) and pursuing environmental justice in Louisiana's chemical corridor (Allen 2003). Fishermen in the northeastern United States engage in many community management practices even while they operate in a dominant framework that assumes individual behavior is driven by maximum economic yield (St. Martin 2001). Internationally, networks have provided critical resistance to privatization of water utilities (Boelens, Getches, and Geuvara-Gil 2010), and to the construction of large dams in India and elsewhere (Conca 2006; Roy 1999).

Looking beyond environmental governance, networks have been all the rage; a key framework for everything from social life to technology to revolution. Networks are a popular vehicle for understanding the interconnectedness of the world and a conceptual framework for analyzing human behavior. In this book, we work with the basic concept of networks as groups of actors connected by social ties or relationships. These ties are typically informal and flexible, and they can transcend political, institutional, economic, ethnic, and other boundaries. We are particularly interested in networks that appear when people feel they have very few, or very restricted, options through conventional scientific, environmental, and policy channels. A common theme in many environmental networks is the unlikely nature of their emergence. These are networks that arise despite minimal resources, and even very pronounced official resistance, and self-organize in order to accomplish an environmental goal. Networks are often the vanguard of institutional and policy change, framing issues and undertaking collaborative actions that foreshadow later formalization. New networks appear or existing networks expand when people feel that something needs to happen and official institutions are not responding to the need (Day 2001, 2004). A wealth of literature has looked at grassroots movements and other kinds of coalitions in environmental politics (Cawley 1993; Cortner et al. 1999; Fairfax and Guenzler 2001; Hays 1989; Mazmanian and Kraft 1999), yet the nature and persistence of spontaneous environmental networks is not well understood.

We aim to further this discussion on the role of networks in environmental action by arguing that story motivates people with a vision and also pulls them together and creates the ties in a network. Our contention is simple: to understand a network, you must understand its narrative. Narrative provides critical insight into why networks emerge, which specific concerns people have, how networks attract members, and how they persist in adverse situations. We also suggest that narrative offers a useful perspective on the evaluation of networks as democratic projects.

As it is, the voluminous literature on networks seems always in danger of falling into inherent presumptions about their being either a "cure-all" for institutional problems and/or a "universal" phenomenon that we should find everywhere. But, to paraphrase a line from Aaron Wildavsky (1973), if it's everything, then maybe it's nothing. Our work responds to the need to more richly describe networks in ways that differentiate otherwise similar networks from each other, better explain why one network survives and another does not, and more deeply understand why it is that people join and thrive in a particular network. Our approach is to use story, or, as we will define it, narrative, as our mode of network analysis.

Simply put, stories are accounts of a sequence of events, characters, and experiences that convey the meaning of this otherwise disparate assemblage. Moreover, these stories help actors establish their identities vis-à-vis others and their roles as part of a collective. Narrative analysis offers a unique way into understanding people's actions and the tactics through which heterogeneity emerges in networks as people build associations across cultural, disciplinary, organizational, and even species boundaries. We also suggest that such networks emerge when people are struggling to fit into a world for which they have a conflicting or non-workable narrative, and in the process create new ways of understanding, or new stories about their relationships with the world. The literature on social-ecological resilience speaks to how individuals and communities fashion new practices to adapt to a changing environment or to transform human-environment relationships in fundamentally novel ways (Berkes, Colding, and Folke 2003; Folke 2006; Peterson 2010). Our claim is that evidence of such resilience is to be found, first and foremost, in the narratives that people tell about themselves and their surroundings.

In this book we use narrative analysis to elucidate how networks bridge multiple perspectives to forge common collective aims. We trace how networks, often moving against the grain of mainstream policy and practice, sustain themselves and make progress. We move beyond documenting the patterns of ties and relationships in networks, however, to considering why networks form and what holds them together over time. Some of these networks are fleeting, some last for decades; both forms can be very influential.

The importance of story to our understanding of human organizations (Brown 2006), ethics (Nussbaum 1990), and environmental policy (Hajer 1993) is well established. We aim to develop these ideas more concretely by bringing the specific tools of narrative analysis, such as emplotment, characterization, alterity, plurivocity, and breach to bear on networks. These are tools by which narratives are analyzed and described, and, as we suggested earlier, when we understand the narrative behind a collective, we understand the collective itself. These narratives do not simply describe the human dimension of environmental situations but are also able to "emplot" humans along with nonhumans, places, and other things. Narrative has the potential to capture complex ecologies.

Narrative analysis can provide a close-up view of how individuals create the motivation to act. Joining a network can be an act of volition in which people commit time and resources and see themselves as making choices. By their very nature, environmental problems present people with ambiguous, confusing, and often conflicting information. In addition, individuals' experiences and interpretations of the world may differ substantially from dominant ones. We are interested in the alternative stories that emerge, which we view as indicative of a fundamental process of human creativity.

Speaking New Environmental Truths

Conventional environmental discourse, while full of stories about the negative influences of people on nature, has perhaps too few about how people successfully integrate with, actively nurture, and sustain themselves as part of their environment. As our case studies reveal, when people describe their participation in networks, they describe the very specific practices through which they connect with the world around them, revealing their efforts to overcome what is often a very remote, impersonal, technical, or oversimplified portrayal of humans as part of a broader "nature." Thus, the stories that people tell about why they participate in networks reveal the ongoing work of envisioning new and specific ecologies of humans and the rest of the world.

A key piece of our argument is that new environmental networks strive to find an alternative truth, or rationality, about the natural environment. This rationality is not exclusive of scientific knowledge and indeed typically embraces scientific process and facts. In fact, as has been argued, there is no easy dichotomy between science and narrative; both scientists and the public use story in order to make sense of science (Sethi and Briggle 2011; Wickson 2008). Our argument here is that the truths provided by the narratives in environmental networks offer scientific facts *in the context of* personal experiences and ethical considerations, emotions, and values. We see how people frame issues and hear about how they feel, what they have personally experienced, and how that informs their evaluations of problems and solutions. This is, in essence, the illuminating of fact through a discursive process, a weighing of information in an arena informed by personal perspectives and values in order to make decisions under uncertainty.

As our case studies will show, some networks resist the reach of a state that would dictate their relationships with the world around them. Others resist a technical and dualistic portrayal of the natural environment that would both depersonalize and polarize their needs and those of other species. Through story, people can resist the superiority of the outside expert and the idea that the best guidance and decision making can only come from a disinterested party. These stories also reflect a resistance to the treatment of environmental problems as black and white "either/or" scenarios, and instead insist that people tangle with a more complicated idea of rationality, conceived out of contradiction and coexistence. We will see, for example, that turtles can be conceived of as childlike, in need of nurturing, but also as a source of income. In some ways these environmental narratives reflect people working out a "middle ground" between the polarized views of nature as harmony that humans can only disturb, or a barely submerged menace, that must be surveyed and contained with a full complement of chemical and other controls, or a set of resources for human betterment.

This middle ground can reflect democratic potential. We use the term *ecological democracy* in this book in order to capture the possibility provided by this process for sharing information, collaborative action, and grounded policy change. By allowing for more complex understandings of human-environment relationships, these narratives can give voice to those, humans and nonhumans alike, excluded from typical regimes for ecological governance. There are certainly no guarantees about the democratic nature of networks or stories; each one must be evaluated as its own project. We suggest that a focus on story helps illuminate the processes by which people engage in environmental decision making, for example, evaluating a range of possible types of relationships, or describing their rationales for how they negotiate with other species.

In the rest of this chapter, we lay out an argument about the centrality of knowledge in environmental disputes, and how networks offer a key site for emergence of an alternative rationality. We also examine how environmental networks have been understood as social movement, as policy process, and as informal social activity. We suggest that by focusing on the narratives of a network, or the stories that participants tell as they describe the network and explain their participation, we can better understand how networks attract adherents, entertain and legitimize different ways of knowing, and provide new opportunities for people to rethink their relationships with their environment.

Emergent Ecologies

Consider the conundrum of the Asian carp that have invaded the Mississippi River system and, according to many, threaten the Great Lakes. There is little dispute that they were introduced through fish hatcheries, which, when flooded, allowed the fish to escape into natural watercourses. All else is confusion and controversy, especially what to do about the problem. There are four species of Asian carp; the fish process food very rapidly and can grow to be one hundred pounds and sixty inches in length. They have no natural predators and overwhelm any competition with their sheer size and power. They now represent eight out of every ten species of fish in some stretches of the Illinois River. Commercial fishers in the Illinois River regularly catch up to 25,000 pounds of bighead and silver carp per day. Besides feeding on plankton and vegetation, the carp eat eggs of native fish species. Although their impact on native species has yet to be scientifically determined, many people are worried that if the carp makes its way into the Great Lakes basin, it will decimate the region's natural ecology as well as its $7 billion fishing industry. They also endanger people. When frightened (by boat motors, for example), the fish jump up to ten feet into the air. Injuries to boaters have included black eyes, broken bones, and concussions due to collisions with the fish.

Electric barriers have been put in place to prevent the fish from moving into the Great Lakes, but the fish appear to be a step or two ahead of any attempt by people to control them. Environmentalists and the State of Michigan urge that potential entry points into Lake Michigan for Asian carp be closed. There is no simple solution, though, since closing the locks would harm the $30 million-a-year barge industry and is strongly opposed by the City of Chicago. The involvement of multiple states, multiple cities, and the federal government requires collaboration that remains as elusive as solutions that satisfy both commercial and environmental interests (Davey 2010). Meanwhile, the carp continue to adapt and thrive and now support an emerging fishing economy in the region.

This kind of story underscores the need for our political process to acknowledge the limits of impartial scientific understanding—more data alone will not solve this problem—and to embrace processes by which people can explore new environmental scenarios, new ways of relating to and coexisting with other species. Our world seems to abound with stories like these: the reintroduction of wolf packs in Yellowstone

National Park, for example, or the restoration of wolves in Wisconsin has led to the emergence of new (frequently conflicting) networks from wolf watchers to wolf hunters as people try to work out how to coexist with the new residents (Ingram 2010; Treves et al. 2009; Zaffos 2006). Or consider shifting discourses around microbial food contamination. A series of lethal and widespread food safety incidents has exposed the weakness of conventional food production systems and put many consumers on edge. At the same time, emerging knowledge about the complexity of microbial ecology, the inextricable links between the human body and numerous microbial communities, and the benefits of culturing beneficial microbes in order control dangerous ones, challenge the traditional antimicrobial approach to bacteria (Ingram 2010). Clearly, containment is not an option, but what should coexistence look like?

Polarized discussions about the environment as either conservation or exploitation hinder our ability to explore new landscapes of coexistence. We argue that a focus on self-organizing environmental networks and the stories associated with them is a key step toward grasping how people on a variety of spatial scales are creating and managing emerging ecologies. Richard Day has described how some networks explicitly reject conventional rules by creating their own. He explains his idea of "affinity" in new social movements as "a desire to create alternatives to state and corporate forms of social organization, working 'alongside' the existing institutions; proceeding in this via disengagement and reconstruction rather than by reform or revolution" (Day 2001, 740). The end goal, as he describes it, is not creating a new knowable totality (counterhegemony), but "enabling experiments and the emergence of new forms of subjectivity; and . . . inventing new forms of community" (740). While Day's work focuses on indigenous rights and antiglobalization movements, his work argues that we pay attention to ways in which networks might explicitly avoid the conventional policy arena in favor of creating new forms of identity and engagement. In the early decades of the organic farming movement, for example, pioneers developed a new type of farming involving a great range of practical, dependable alternative methods for agricultural production, rather than directly engaging with or changing the mainstream process (Ingram 2007).

Integrating Scientific and Other Knowledge

In this book, we chart how narratives are used to challenge conventional knowledge about complex ecological situations and to provide new frameworks for understanding. What we find is that, increasingly, science is less and less able to provide definitive truths and convince a skeptical public. Or, to put it another way, science and technical work do not suffice to settle debate. In this context of fundamental and often irresolvable uncertainty, the construction of new and integrative narratives can provide direction to a society in search of answers.

As the examples of Asian carp and wolves suggest, ecological complexity escapes the boundaries of environmental institutions and leads to a heightened sense of scientific uncertainty, vulnerability, risk, and confusion. In the public policy arena, uncertainty is often treated as a deficit, a problem that can be solved with more knowledge, rather than as a constant and necessary companion to the scientific process (Gross 2010). Even a cursory review of environmental policy, however, reveals that science seldom produces authoritative truths. Writing about the Endangered Species Act, Holly Doremus notes:

As a society, we hunger for objective, rule-based decision making, especially when the decision pits human interests against those of another species. We worry that decisions lacking a firm, objective basis may be arbitrary, wholly "political," wholly dependent upon the whims of the particular decision maker, or made on the basis of improper motivations. We look to "science" to provide the objectivity we crave . . . Science, however, is not as objective or neutral a basis for decisions as we might hope. In recent years, the uncertainties and gaps in the supposedly "scientific" decision making of the ESA have become increasingly apparent, and increasingly the source of controversy and contention. (Doremus 2004, 400)

Confidence about scientific pronouncements has in recent years come to depend upon who is speaking and with whom they are associated (Funtowicz and Ravetz 1990; Nowotny, Scott, and Gibbons 2001; Wynne 1992). In this case, uncertainty arises not so much as a result of conflicting findings as it does out of a suspicion of particular knowledge communities. This is the "relational" aspect of uncertainty (Brugnach et al. 2008; Brugnach and Ingram 2011; Dewulf et al. 2009). Consider the ways in which uncertainty has been interpreted in the problem of climate change to both justify action and inaction. For climate skeptics, uncertainty is used to justify opposition to Kyoto-type agreements, while for their opponents uncertainty suggests precautionary policies that pursue the least regret and avoid the greatest danger. Uncertainty may be used to bolster arguments skeptical of climate science and to suggest that natural variability best explains climate change rather than human activity (Pielke 2004).

Environmental contention may be more related to emotional and psychological factors than upon the ambiguity of the physical science.

Kari Norgaard found in her study of climate change that emotions play a key role in the denial that has stalled effective action (Norgaard 2011, 9213). Negative emotions can lead to collective helplessness and deflate attempts at innovation and change. Environmental issues typically evoke strong emotional responses, and emotions may unite people in common causes, inform their interpretations of the world, and catalyze the imagination and political power. Emotions can channel efforts to save endangered species and habitat in new and powerful ways—for example, Rosalie Edge's establishment of the Hawk Mountain Sanctuary in defiance of the current logic of the conservation movement at the time (Furmansky 2009). Emotions have shaped perceptions of environmental issues long before climate change took center stage. There is an old saying in the American West, for example, that "whiskey is for drinking and water is for fighting." People have divergent connections with water, and in conflicts, can pull on very different sources of scientific authority and scholarship. Water conceived as a product depends upon the insights of engineering, while water as a commodity is a view heavily influenced by economics. Water as an element in ecology reflects the understandings of ecologists and biologists, and water as a community good is supported by anthropology, history, and philosophy (Blatter and Ingram 2001; Feldman and Ingram 2009b). All these water networks can claim association with sound science, but emotional responses related to value commitments are the driving force. Different sources of authority, backed by the disciplines and values that undergird their divergent approaches, are selected on the grounds of the value positions and emotional appeal. Further, different narratives connect water to emotionally charged ideas such as private property, fairness, justice, and universal human rights.

Narrow and exclusive normative claims can be used to present a particular way of defining a problem and its solution, as if these were the only ones possible, and silencing other ways of thinking and talking. Friend and Blake (2009) illustrate how in the Mekong Basin, where water can and has been variously conceived, water becomes narrowly circumscribed in a resurgent "opportunity narrative" in which the unrealized hydropower potential to create wealth is great and managers can use their technical capacity to make "trade-offs" with fisheries that are acceptable to all concerned. Thus, managerial and technological processes are shortchanging a more fundamental values debate over culturally appropriate development paths that should be taken (Friend and Blake 2009).

Indigenous or traditional knowledge can combine observations or physical phenomena and symbolic and cultural meanings. Traditional knowledge networks have fiercely resisted the division of knowledge along the lines of what is more or less acceptable to dominant culture. One example of such resistance comes from indigenous farmers of the Achamayo River who consistently oppose attempts to install volumetric gauges. They state that it is "fairer to measure irrigation by time [than] by volume." To them, water is a natural flow resource, the irrigation infrastructure was made by "grandparents," and regulators and newcomers lack intimate knowledge (Guevara-Gil 2010, 110). Schmidt and Dowsley (2010) found in their study of Inuit hunting of polar bears that the hunters considered bears to be active partners, able to know and respond to human thoughts, intentions, and actions. What seem to outside resource managers to be efficient and fair quota systems to manage resources were perceived by Inuit as alienating because bears were treated as passive and not engaged in decision making.

Wenger writes of "knowledge in practice" and states that "as a regime of competence every practice is in some sense a form of knowledge, and knowing is participating in that practice" (1998, 141). Knowledge is situated in individuals and communities and emerges through a variety of cognitive and emotional reasoning including authority, intuition, moral reasoning, direct experience, tradition, logic, belief or faith, mysticism, and other ways of comprehending problems. Any of these perceptual lenses may become more or less relevant through continuous discourse, engagement, and learning through social interaction (Feldman et al. 2006; Lejano and Ingram 2009). Knowledge, as it relates to environmental problems, is likely to be continually in flux from the interaction of animate and inanimate objects in the physical and social environment (Brugnach and Ingram 2011). The intertwining of knowledge and practice often works out in complex, informal ways—our framework is sensitive to the informal, "cybernetic" policy processes that work beneath the rational framework of classic environmental policymaking (Kamieniecki and Cohen 2005).

There is a need for integrative analytical frameworks that can better account for the complex social ecology of human-environment relationships (Davies et al. 2012; Lejano 2006; Stokols, Lejano, and Hipp 2012; also Berkes and Folke 1998). In our work, we see networks, and particularly the narratives that bind them, to have the potential for integrating (or, in the terms we will be using, emplotting) the otherwise challenging intermingling of rationality, affect, norms, and culture that characterizes all ecological issues. Conversely, institutional designs and policy analytics that are founded upon narrow utilitarian or rationalist concepts fall short of responding to the complexity of these situations. It is in networks and their narratives that the multiple streams of policy, perhaps and sometimes, come together in new ways.

Research and Critiques of Environmental Networks

Environmental networks, we suggest, offer a way to rethink environmental action as the result of people challenging conventional knowledge and working through new and changing relationships with their world. We are not alone. Self-governing environmental networks, often with established agreements specifying boundaries, membership, decision making, and other rules, have been the focus of a great deal of analysis (Bloomquist, Schlager, and Heikkila 2004). Ostrom (1990) has found common pool natural resources can be well managed by networks of voluntary participants under certain circumstances. Such networks often operate for decades beneath the radar of high-profile politics and policymaking. Networks have also focused attention on neglected issues, set new agendas, and resulted in new laws around recycling, water reuse, and land restoration. Networks have also emerged to engage conflicting parties in standoffs that have frustrated more straightforward implementation of policy. Cortner and Moote observed:

Community-based conservation efforts are said to enhance land use and natural resource management by drawing expertise and input from a wide range of individuals and groups who live in and intimately know the resource base and the local economy. Groups such as the Applegate Partnership and Trout Creek Mountain Working Group in Oregon and the Quincy Library Group in California's Sierra Nevada have gained national acclaim for forging agreements or resource management among local industry, environmental, and agency representatives in areas with a long history of confrontation. (1999, 95–96)

What is common among such networks, as our case studies suggest, is that members are bound together and act according to complex logics (which we will call narratives) that go well beyond, and sometimes defy, the imperatives of individual rationality (for a formal treatment of nonutilitarian logics, see Lejano and Ingram 2012). Our treatment of narratives in networks is an attempt to be faithful to the phenomenon that networks integrate logic, affect, morality, and other complex modes of cognition.

Despite the fact that networks appear to be an inevitable phenomenon of environmental problems, networks as solution have proven problematic in many settings. While they may be flexible, they can also be ephemeral and can disappear when some key actor withdraws or necessary resources become scarce. Defections from networks can occur rapidly if beliefs and incentives change. Critically, networks do not necessarily lead to desirable outcomes. Sally Fairfax and coauthors found that public-private partnerships in land preservation might be more effective in serving the interests of agencies and landowners than in protecting environmentally valuable lands. Some very effective networks can be very unfair. While public/private partnerships succeed in preserving resources of lands of environmental value, such preservation has enriched some at the expense of others and lacked transparency and accountability (Fairfax et al. 2005; Larson and Lach 2010). There is nothing in even bottom-up environmental networks that guarantees a democratic, participatory, and collaborative effort. Networks can perpetuate discrimination and bias in natural resource management (Cooke and Kothari 2001). Similarly, participation of user communities is only weakly associated with positive results for water management on some measures (Meinzen-Dick 2007).

Another broader test of the efficacy of community engagement for environmental protection is even less positive. A meta-analysis of thirty-five cases of participatory governance institutions in North America and Europe suggests that the record is mixed (Fritsch and Newig 2008). In only one-third of all cases in which new perspectives were engaged did information generated or social learning processes initiated lead to better consideration of environmental perspectives in the final agreement. A similar large study by Sabatier et al. of U.S. watershed management that involves networks among diverse users finds: "Collaborative institutions are expensive to implement and maintain and often are extremely time-consuming, requiring as long as four years to achieve effectiveness" (2005, 289–290). These analysts see network-based collaboration as a kind of last resort when more straightforward governance is impossible: "We recommend that the collaborative approach to watershed management be used as a method . . . only when there are high stakes, high social distrust, high governmental distrust and high knowledge uncertainty" (289–290).

Despite the criticisms aimed at environmental networks, numerous studies uphold the potential of bottom-up, informal collaborations for contending with complex natural resource problems. Analyzing a ten-year research program of a range of types of citizen participation, Gaventa and Barrett (2010) report that participation produces positive effects across outcomes such as the construction of citizenship, the accountability of states, and the inclusiveness of society. Susskind, Camacho, and Schenk (2012) report that, despite a paucity of success stories in the area of collaborative adaptive (ecosystem) management, better management of the participatory process, and (in our terms) relationships among policy actors can increase their effectiveness.

Environmental networks have been recognized for their facility in generating and sharing different types of knowledge (Bodin and Crona 2009), for mobilizing resources to accomplish goals (Cash et al. 2003), for creating trust and a shared commitment to specific environmental management efforts (Dietz, Ostrom, and Stern 2003), and even for managing conflict. A study of networks in four estuaries in the United States indicates that networks play an important coordination function (Berardo and Scholz 2008). Networks have proven critical in saving small-scale fisheries in northern Mexico (Basurto and Ostrom 2009). In an article on networked governance of fisheries, Mark Gibbs argues that whatever their merits, networks are here to stay (Gibbs 2008).

The Power of Narrative in Understanding Networks

Much of social network analysis literature focuses on the structure of (formal or informal) networks. As we discuss further in chapter 2, while this approach captures important features like density and frequency of exchange between people, it leaves out qualities of the relationships between and across actors, qualities that determine the strength of the network, the meaning actors find in it, and the kinds of actions that the network engages in. When we say "quality," we refer to the idea that it is not enough to link one actor to another. We need to know *how* they relate to each other. What kind of power or authority does one have over the other? What emerges as a result of that link—is there knowledge exchanged, relationships forged? And what is that relationship that, abstractly, is represented as a link in a network structure? What is the capacity for that relationship to change? Whereas others have written about the strength of these ties as relating to density or structural coverage (e.g., Granovetter 1973, 1985), we are interested in how those ties came to be, how they are maintained over time, and how they represent an added dimension to the network.

Several factors necessitate our focus on the quality of network relationships. One is that we are interested in how people explain their participation in a network. Especially in the context of competition for time and other resources, why are people involved? What motivations do they cite, and what choices do people feel that they have?

Second is the fact that many of the environmental networks we examine are characterized by heterogeneous motivations. One needs to understand the characterization of this diversity. We seek to understand how ties change from actor to actor—there is neither one type of glue that binds, nor one meaning each actor gives to the rest of the network. As chapter 4 will illustrate, Native Americans joined the Sonoran Desert conservation network to protect what they believe to be their patrimony while others become engaged because of a journey of self and aesthetic discovery. And yet, the network is, and it functions, notwithstanding the fact that different members ascribe different purposes to it.

Third, we are interested in how networks challenge a conventional ontology about the relationships people develop with diverse environments. In other words, networks do not occur only between human actors. How are rivers, animals, plants, disease, mountains, water, microbes, and other environmental elements conceived of by humans in a network? How is the interaction mediated? What types of technologies are employed in order to represent and communicate with participants that lack language? How are diverse ways of knowing brought to bear?

Bruno Latour's poststructuralist, agnostic approach to the nature of matter offers a unique perspective on environmental networks. His are "flat," or astructural, but heterogeneous networks in which the potential for agency is distributed throughout (Latour 1993). Every node or "actant" can be influential, from scientists and kings to mice, atmospheric gases, rocks and microbes. Latour's work on Pasteur, for example, revealed how the effectiveness of Pasteur's process was facilitated by a network of humans and objects put into action in order to carry out a new regime of hygiene on dairy farms (Latour 1988). Especially important, he argues, was the activity of hygienists who worked with farmers on farms and with farm animals, which paved the way for the implementation of Pasteur's technique. His notion of network opens the concept up to be a more powerful representation of the multiple, emergent relationships between humans and nonhuman nature (Latour and Weibel 2005).

Importantly, the connections in an environmental network that involves humans and other "things," animate and not, may be represented scientifically. But often, they are not. It is no accident that networks arise around alternative movements that mobilize on the peripheries or interstices of mainstream discourse. It is in these open, heterogeneous spaces that people can articulate different forms of representation, experiment with different ways of understanding their own motivations and views. Alternative views can be presented scientifically, but often network participants will rely on anecdotes from personal experience, stories they have heard from trusted sources, or traditional ways of knowing. Contrast this with contemporary institutional forums for environmental action—mainstream environmental groups, resource agencies, and environmental corporations—where talk is homogenized by consistent scientific categories and measurements. One need only think of the rationalist discourse of coastal zone management authorities, the process chemistry discourse of the pollution control industry, or the taxonomic discourse of many biologists. When specialists encounter people from outside their own epistemic community, the latter have to learn to communicate in their terms or be relegated to subordinate status. In a scientific forum, what one knows and wants to express has to be put in the language of science. In a regulatory forum, one has to talk in the language of rules and regulations. In these conventional arenas, there is a privileged expert, whose mode of knowing and speaking becomes the currency for that institution. New networks allow for new voices to be heard.

A fourth feature we seek regarding our analysis of networks is the ability to grasp multiple constructions of identity and subjectivity. Collective identities related to places and communities are obscured when conventional categories of the self-interested individual are implicitly accepted. Categorizing, naming, and quantifying are not merely descriptive; they are constitutive and enlarge or diminish the power to act. The creation of indicators, audits, scales, and evaluations may create the illusion of objectivity, but are heavily value-laden in ways that are often not transparent. Numbers have social and cultural conditions related to their production contained in them and, especially in contexts where power is being challenged, may poorly capture what is going on with the challengers. Similarly, the methods adopted by researchers are not neutral but instead imply the agency to impose certain control over and distance from the subject. We need new ways of describing networks that allow for the "thick description" of identity.

Posthumanist thought asks us to contend with the decentered individual, a person defined according to multiple and dynamic relations and contexts rather than a neat boundary around a body or a brain. This involves a move away from the assumption of a subject that exists prior to experience toward an examination of the ways in which the subject comes to be in or through experience (Wylie 2005). Our interest is in the ways in which inhuman, nonhuman, and more-than-human forces (Whatmore 2002) contribute to processes of subject formation, place making, and inhabiting the world. Such moves are critical as we rethink our place in the world in the context of challenges like the Asian carp making a new home or wolves returning to land they once roamed (Wolfe 2010).

In the case studies of networks we present in this book, we see the importance of scientific language as it provides people with a sense of legitimacy and access to more powerful networks. But we also see science entertained in the context of very different kinds of discourse such as personal experience, memories, folktales, and morals. A key part of our argument in this book is that this alternative discourse, revealed in the stories people tell, reflects personal relationships, feelings, ethics, practices, and other aspects of our connectedness in the world. Along with the expert testimony, these stories are essential to embrace if we are to make progress on environmental controversies. As Bruno Latour (2011) has put it: "To succeed, an ecological politics must manage to be at least as powerful as the modernizing story of emancipation [from Nature] without imagining that we are emancipating ourselves from Nature. What the emancipation narrative points to as proof of increasing human mastery *over* and freedom *from* Nature—agriculture, fossil energy, technology—can be redescribed as the increasing *attachments* between things and people at an ever-expanding scale." Our method for capturing the attachments of alternative discourse is narrative analysis.

In open, less bounded settings, what comes naturally to us, the common denominator for expressing ideas, is narrative. Not all of us can talk in the terms of finance, or of atmospheric chemistry, but we are each able to tell a story. In these boundary-crossing networks, narratives are the medium of exchange. Knowledge is captured in the group's (possibly multiple) narratives. In the Turtle Islands, the case study examined in chapter 5, we see elders from a traditional ethno-linguistic minority called the Jama Mapun and conservationists and marine biologists coming together into one unique network. We see knowledge shared between them, and this knowledge, in turn, recounted in the form of stories. But it became possible only when the scientists made a commitment to set aside strictly a scientific/regulatory mode of talk and engage the Jama Mapun in storytelling.

So, we make the case that if we want to understand what makes a network hold, what knowledge the network has, and what the network means, it is not so much the structure of the network that we should examine but the narrative.

What holds the members of a network together? Sabatier and colleagues have pointed to the strength of common beliefs as the glue that binds (Sabatier and Jenkins-Smith 1993). Hajer points to narrative storylines that do the task of forging the bond. In Hajer's discourse coalition framework, storylines that interpret or frame events in particular ways are what the members of a coalition share, not beliefs per se (Hajer 1995).

We will take Hajer's reasoning four steps farther. First, narratives are not simply the commonality that members of a network share. Rather, narrative is the means itself by which members become part of the network. *By thinking about an environmental issue or object, and by telling stories to themselves and others, actors literally emplot themselves into the network.* When social media network friends share stories, pictures, and ideas, is that not actors emplotting themselves together? Much as characters in a novel, these actors help weave a group narrative in which they play central roles. Much as an organization chart or a social network diagram is seen to hold the group together structurally, the narrative is the "structure" that holds a group together cognitively and symbolically.

Second, it is not just the story that members share. *Rather, they become and maintain their membership in the group by joining in the act of narration.* This is the distinguishing mark of community and its way of knowing—as opposed to expert discourse wherein the speaker is privileged over the hearer, in a community everyone can be a speaker and hearer. Narratives are passed on, as well as the task of narrating. What makes each a member of a union is their ability to tell the story. Narrating is the mark of membership. Thus, narratives are both shared and individual, with a thread of common plot and many variations.

Third, narratives serve a function beyond that of organization—they are the repositories of what the group knows. *The knowledge that the group seeks to save, the memory of the group, and the foundational history of the group—all that is stored in narrative.* This is easy to see in the case of traditional communities, wherein history is oral history (Berkes 1999). But in urbanized, cosmopolitan societies, what narratives exist that pass knowledge from person to person? Whether in traditional or urbanized communities, narratives abound. From boardroom to boardroom in the corporate world, an annual ritual is reenacted over and over again. Stockholders and boards meet and repeat a common story: these are our goals, this is the company's vision, this is what makes us special. Everyone knows the refrain by heart and, yet, it needs repeating year after year. In every part of the world, Grameen banks, the engine of financing for the poor, start each business day with each member reciting their creed. Their business meetings then revolve around members sharing personal stories about their experience with group financing. To be able to put group knowledge into narrative form is a great advantage—it ensures that such knowledge remains active and intact. Narratives are also the common lingua franca in which all members, widely diverse in training or other orientation, can engage.

And fourth, members of a network do not simply "share" a (common) narrative. In fact, in our interviews members told multiple and varying stories about their group and its mission. It is the power of narrative that it allows for different actors to tell the story in differing ways and still be inclusive of them. It is not necessary for there to be one story in common—rather, the individual stories need only fit together into something coherent. Later on, we explain how narrative allows for such plurivocity.

Envisioning New Ecologies

The environmental movement that burst into public consciousness in the 1970s was profoundly democratic in that it emerged from outside conventional parties, interest groups, and institutions like legislative bodies and government agencies and included adherents from different classes, ideologies, and racial and ethnic groups (Downs 1972). Since that time, environment as a subject matter has been largely mainstreamed. Rather than a consensus subject that once cut across economic, political, and demographic boundaries and species, attitudes about such issues as global climate change and government regulations sharply divide people. Further, the environment has become a technocratic subject that bores and alienates many who would profit from visceral, emotional connection to the environment.

Among the questions to be addressed in this book is whether the narratives of networks reflect a broader ecological imagination that might foster democracy. Ecological democracy suggests deepening the democratic discourse to take into account the ethical consequences of how humans live in and interact with their environment. As already observed, much contemporary discussion takes place in rationalistic terms, with an emphasis on physical, economic causes and effects, and in the absence of emotions or affect. Among the questions we intend to pursue is whether and how narrative networks reflect an increased intensity and penetration of discourse to include the emotional, symbolic, ethical, and cultural aspects of our relationships with the environment. Can such networks and narratives include ecological imaginings that expand the range of choices in democratic and empowering ways (Sandercock 2003)? Certainly, narrative can be constraining as well as empowering, and people can tell stories that end up limiting the options they see available to them (Cope and Latcham 2009). We suggest, either way, that story is a critical place to understand both past behavior and the potential for future change.

To begin with, ecological democracy implies the bridging or joining of matters often separated in contemporary politics. For instance, there is a segregation of the media of air, water, and soil (as found in the disciplines of atmospheric science, coastal and estuarine science, and geophysics). Collaborative governance is supposed to encourage working relationships that reach across established cleavages, yet, as we have noted, they do not always do so. Among the issues we consider in this book is whether networks can span such divisions. Further, can they present alternatives reflecting ecological relationships previously beyond the pale? Such imaginaries embed people in relationships, reflecting how they value, describe, and imagine change with environmental elements around them. Stories individualize members of different species, so that questions change from "how many" to "who." Very different than looking at forecasts or alternatives in an environmental impact statement, this is a search for a personal vision informed by experience.

Layout of the Book

In the following chapters, we lay the conceptual foundations of this book. In chapter 2 we discuss what is missing from conventional ways of analyzing the emergent networks we described earlier. What is missing is the thick description afforded by narrative devices of recounting and examining. We state the fundamental connections, in concept and in practice, between network and narrative. The logical upshot of this is that methods and tools used to analyze narrative should be useful for network analysis. We introduce these tools for narrative analysis in chapter 3 and explain how we employ them in network research.

We then apply these concepts and methods to a set of three case studies in chapters 4–6. Appropriate to the prominence of the themes of inclusion and spanning, we have chosen cases from the margins of environmental politics. The Sonoran Desert case study in chapter 4 addresses the international boundary between the United States and Mexico, which cuts through one of the most ecologically rich and endangered desert regions of the world. Efforts to protect ecologically important lands and species have been active since the 1930s, but recent concerns with border security, drugs, and illegal immigrants have diverted attention from environmental problems and created an atmosphere damaging to collaboration. Nonetheless, some surprising environmental victories are occurring along the border between the U.S. state of Arizona and the Mexican state of Sonora. This case study, based on documents and interviews, argues that the Arizona-Sonora conservation network has managed to persist and make some headway in a time of adversity largely because of a shared ecological narrative that is inclusive and bridges a variety of difference.

The case study examined in chapter 5 is a different kind of story from the margins of environmental action. The Turtle Islands are one of the ten most significant marine turtle rookeries in the world. They also lie in a remote area characterized by a weak government, ethnic conflict, piracy, and illegal trade—just the conditions that should lead to a profligate tragedy of the commons. Instead of setting up a classic marine sanctuary program, the standard blueprint that is usually recommended for the third world, the local conservationists took a different route. An improvised system was negotiated between the members of the network that included regulators and harvesters.

Instead of creating a no-take sanctuary, the regulators (aka PCP, or Pawikan Conservation Program) formalized the culturally accepted practice of the Mapun (harvesters) of harvesting eggs for a number of days (and selling them in nearby Sandakan for income), then allowing the eggs to hatch the rest of the month. The Mapun, in turn, took on some of the practices of the PCP in taking inventory and tracking nests, tagging turtles, and surveying the turtle population. The Mapun we interviewed also described the relationship with the PCP as "pakikisama." The narrative (or plot) we found was mutual accommodation—by the PCP of longstanding practice and livelihood needs of the Mapun, by the Mapun of according the PCP a physical niche in their community. In this case, a shared narrative bridged differences that might well have led to deadlock.

The third case study, the focus of chapter 6, comes from the margins of agriculture, and the development of alternatives seeking to avoid some of environmental and health damage caused by conventional practices. Organic agricultural production in the United States began to develop in the post–Dust Bowl years. The rejection of synthetic pesticides and fertilizers by organic practitioners was initially ridiculed as belonging to an antiquated era in production agriculture, and critics discounted it as regressive and unscientific. Even after strong public and state government interest in organics and the organic market had developed by the 1980s, the federal government dragged its feet for over a decade between the 1990 passage of an organic law, which required that it develop standards for organic production, and the final implementation of the standards in 2002, when the law went into effect. How did support for organic farming develop and sustain itself in the context of this long-term adversity? Research reveals networks that included scientists with connections to credible institutions; publishers who were able to disseminate information through magazines and books, and to organize conferences in order to provide platforms for people to speak; and successful farmers, who not only tested and furthered a large variety of alternative farming practices but also took the time to communicate with others by writing, holding field days, and attending conferences, all in order to spread the word about the advantages of alternative approaches (Ingram 2007).

The basic narrative by which a diverse array of farmers and scientists and consultants find alliance is a common and motivating dictate to "return to nature." Moreover, the pursuit of alternative farming, rather than viewed in contrast to science, is actually argued by network participants to be a more scientific, rational process. This narrative views conventional agricultural science as having been taken over by commercial interests and therefore no longer scientific or trustworthy.

We conclude, in chapter 7, by comparing insights gained in each of the cases and reflecting on the broader implications of this work on networks and their narratives for democracy, environmental governance, and social science research.

Our Choice of Case Studies

We chose our three case study sites for a number of reasons. First, we each have long-term research relationships with these sites and have worked with and talked to numbers of people involved. This allows us, as social scientists, to feel comfortable extrapolating from the great range of individual stories that we heard within each network in order to see a common narrative emerge (we say more about this "plurivocity" in chapter 3). Our case studies are quite different from each other, underscoring the power of narrative analysis in diverse situations.

Our argument that a narrative approach to network analysis has broad utility depends upon testing its application across a range of different settings. One aspect of our case study diversity is reflected in how each network crosses political boundaries. Transcending national frontiers plays a critical role in the Sonoran Desert network that draws from the United States, Mexico, and indigenous communities. The alternative farming case demonstrates the ability of farmers to learn from others in other countries, and its international reach is also key to the longevity and power of the farmer network. In contrast, the Turtle Islands network is very place-specific and localized, although profoundly impacted by government policies at national and international levels.

While none of the case studies are drawn from mainstream environmental action, they exhibit different degrees of marginalization. These networks contrast dramatically in terms of their level of legitimacy in the larger world of environmental discourse. While having a patchwork of parks and monuments, the Sonoran region only now and then becomes a national issue, and even when it is highlighted, it is usually not for reasons environmentalists value. While sea turtles have attracted international attention as an endangered species, the unique relationship between the regulators and harvesters reported in our case study is not recognized (or admitted) outside its local setting. After decades in the shadows, alternative agriculture has emerged as both newsworthy and commercially successful, although depending on who you ask, this success has only occurred as the movement shed many of its core values.

However varied these case studies are, in each of them we find a common aspiration of redefining our human place among a community of beings, human and nonhumans alike, that we refer to as ecology. In the next two chapters, we build the fundamental approach that we will need to explore these cases.

2

A Theory of "More than Social" Networks

The juxtaposition of a review of social networks followed by a discussion of narrative analysis is uncommon. The two concepts have very different research traditions. As Sheldon Kamieniecki and Michael Kraft observe in the foreword, scholarship on networks is firmly rooted in empirical and quantitative analyses, employing approaches and insights from the natural and social sciences, while narrative study can be traced to interpretive policy analysis, political philosophy, and infusions from the humanities. Although some narrative analysts have employed network analysis to gain new insights into how stories are structured, few network scholars reciprocate by considering what stories tell us about the connections we make. Our purpose is to draw together these two threads that make a powerful and promising line of investigation.

In this chapter, we examine some of the intellectual roots of network analysis and underscore the potential of networks for crossing boundaries between people and groups and for being inclusive of heterogeneity. We examine how conventional modes of network analysis provide rich insights in some cases, but inadequate explanation in others, especially those cases of interest to us. This leads to our argument for a narrative theory of networks and our understanding of network as "emplotment." We end this chapter by proposing a narrative definition of the network and suggesting that narrative analysis be recognized as an important tool for network research.

The Structuralist Dilemma

If one takes even a quick dip into the enormous literature on networks, one gets the impression that networks are on the one hand, special, but on the other, ubiquitous. How can they be both universal and particular at the same time? What are networks, how are they different from other forms of organizing, and what power do networks have to motivate collective action?

The literature portrays networks in varying ways. The massive literature in the areas of public administration and organization science began with a portrayal of networks as a "third way," that is, a way of allocating goods and services without conforming to the classic designs of the administrative state or the private market. As Walter Powell describes it: "Networks are 'lighter on their feet' than hierarchies. In network modes of resource allocation, transactions occur neither through discrete exchanges nor by administrative fiat, but through networks of individuals engaged in reciprocal, preferential, mutually supportive actions. Networks can be complex: they involve neither the explicit criteria of the markets nor the familiar paternalism of the hierarchy. A basic assumption of network relationships is that one party is dependent upon resources controlled by another, and that there are gains to be had by the pooling of resources" (Powell 1990, 303).

According to Laurence O'Toole, "Networks are structures of interdependence involving multiple organizations or parts thereof, where one unit is not merely the formal subordinate of the others in some larger hierarchical arrangement. Networks exhibit some structural stability but extend beyond formally established linkages and policy-legitimated ties" (O'Toole 1997, 45). In this (public administration and organizational science) literature, the network is simply "neither market nor state," which leaves open its meaning to a broad continuum or diversity of organizational designs. In the preceding definitions, we see a tendency in this literature to view the network as primarily functional and to describe it in structural terms.

The notion of the social network is even more broadly defined in the sociological literature. First systematically described in the early 1950s, J. A. Barnes claimed that "'the whole of social life' could be seen as 'a set of points some of which are joined by lines' to form a 'total network' of relations" (Barnes 1954, 43). So, essentially, networks are used to describe any set of relationships, formal or informal, existing between two or more individuals or organizations. This literature assumes an absolutely structural notion of the network and defines it as a directed graph, a notion that has strongly influenced the field of network analysis (Wasserman and Faust 1994).

This exceeds even the broad ambit of the notion of the network employed by the organizational scholars. If, in fact, any directed graph found in society can be construed as a network, then networks are almost "everywhere and everything." Networks have been invoked to explicate a great diversity of human organization. In a generic sense, networks typically describe a set of ties linking members across social categories and bounded groups. In the social analysis literature, connections can be local or global, single-stranded or multiplex, densely or sparsely knit, tightly or loosely bounded. There is nothing that is not part of some network. To misquote John Donne, no node is an island.

Consider taking a sampling of people waiting at a bus stop or names from the list of registered voters, and imagine constructing a network based on some notion of ties (e.g., affinity, membership in common organizations, proximity, use of footwear, etc.). We see that we can always draw a network, any time, any place. If we take the network to be the structure or pattern of relationships, then they are universal. If structure is to be always found (where two or more people are), and if each structure is always unique (like snowflakes), then classic network analysis fails to tell us about why one network is more special or meaningful than another, why one lasts while another dissolves, and if and why network members see themselves as part of a network. It is a critique of network analysis that the random assortment of people, drawn from the polling list, would not recognize themselves as part of a network or find any meaning in it. Network analysis answers "what?" before it asks "why?"

The fundamental way networks are understood leads to the primacy of graph theory in describing these networks and, hence, the emphasis on their structural (or geometric) properties. The way networks are understood in major branches of the network literature gives rise to a powerful, positivist mode of analysis that emphasizes pattern and structure and, less so, meaning and identity. We will return to this problem toward the end of the chapter and, using a case from the Sonoran Desert, illustrate how classic network analysis explains only part of the phenomenon of the transboundary network, and how a narrative mode of analysis can make up for this deficit of meaning.

The Power of Networks

Networks have long been invoked both to describe the essential nature of human connection and organization (Grannoveter 1973; Marsden 1990; White 1992) as well as to capture more recent social developments emerging out of expanding worlds of electronic communication and media (Forester 1987). Networks have been invoked to describe "post-bureaucratic" (Heydebrand 1989) social formations that emerge where formal social institutions do not exist (Nohria and Eccles 2000), and in situations where people self-organize in order to solve problems that are not taken care of by existing bureaucracies or organizations (Rycroft 2003). Thus, networks have proven essential for describing basic patterns of human connection as well as particular formations that have emerged as a result of increasingly electronically defined and linked societies (Castells 1996).

This idea of the social network as an alternative way of engaging in collective action, or private action with social dimensions, stems partly out of pure necessity. This occurs during an era in which the failure, or dismantling, of large government-centered initiatives to spur development or quality of life, and the attendant diminishing of faith in the state, has captured the public discourse (see Moran 2002 for a review). The literature on "governance" as a new model of public administration has emphasized the degree to which new constellations of state and nonstate actors are collaborating to carry out functions previously monopolized by the state (de Bruijn and ten Heuvelhof 1995; Klijn and Koppenjan 2000; Kooiman 1993, 2000; Rhodes 1981). The network has been used as both explanation and description of novel, sometimes effective, ways of managing resources and environment. Some also see network thinking as a turn away from the market model as well, since previous experiments in privatization had foundered (see Stiglitz 2002). Even more compellingly, the Great Recession of 2008 caused deepened skepticism over the link, in theory, between the invisible hand of the market and public welfare (see Quiggin 2010). When the state is disempowered and the market deceives, many scholars look to network governance.

Despite this explosion of attention to the concept of networks as a basic social phenomenon, we feel that network analysis is still wanting. The heterogeneity of linked elements, and the quality of the links between different nodes in a network, are usually underdescribed and, in many ways, are still black-boxed by quantitative approaches that focus on frequencies of interactions, for example. Social network analysis has roots in graph theory and is often supported by computer-aided analysis and visualization of the patterns and intensities of human networks. The development of database manipulation technologies and computer visualization has made possible a new comprehension of the extent and complexity of informal human relationships in the world (Freeman 2000). Yet these relations are typically explored in terms of measures of proximity or affinity and frequency of transaction. As some network analysts admit, the significance of network structure is not always conclusive (Bodin and Crona 2009). Emphasis on network structure, as determined from observing transactions between actors, can miss the point of a network.

As we see it, the challenge is to clarify the "why" of networks. Why do they emerge? What does belonging mean to people involved? Why do networks endure and gain influence? As a participant joins a network, what specific physical, cognitive, and emotional elements are significant to creating and maintaining links? Critically for our endeavors here, we seek to understand how people associate themselves with different environmental elements such as an endangered species, an individual animal, a particular piece of land, microbes in soil, or water running in a nearby stream.

What motivates people to join and participate in a network? In the social network literature, there is a strong presumption of strategic, utilitarian, and functional considerations behind the motivation to "network"—for example, the notion of resource dependency and strategic interdependency (O'Toole 1997; Powell 1990). But in our work, and as our subsequent case studies will show, "why" people participate in a network go well beyond any functional or strategic reasons. Or, in Sen's terms, all too often people join not due to individual rationality but due to commitment (Sen 1977, 2005). And the urge toward commitment need not spring only from a sense of normative obligation, but also from affect, aestheticism, or sheer autonomic habituation. Thus, network participation is not primarily the result of "rational" choice that individuals make. Networks emerge around us as we make our way in the world of objects and events, and we connect ourselves to new people and new things. Any single organization or person is likely to be a member of multiple networks, and which takes priority is likely to vary with context.

But this, too, is related to the notion of agency (or volition or self-determination) of those who become part of a network. We have to expand our idea of what the notion of "joining" is as well. Just as membership is not encompassed by the notion of rationality, so too is joining not encompassed by the notion of an autonomous act. Actors' associations are both structured and agentic. The simplest example of this is the truism "one can't choose one's relatives." So, too, in the examples we take up in this book, we will encounter associations that vary from the purely voluntary to the nonvolitional.

Similarly, the essence of trust needs to be understood in a deeper way, in order to capture what binds networks together. In informal arrangements there is most often a necessary element of trust that keeps members from reneging on commitments to the network. Trust is said to be the instrumental element that allows sustained exchanges between members in the absence of contracts, regulatory mandates, or other conventional mechanism. But what generates trust? Most network researchers tend to emphasize utilitarian motivations for joining networks and avoidance of sanctions as motivations for not defecting. For instance, Coleman (1990) argues that information can be gained through networks by people who are not greatly interested in current events by connecting with a friend who pays attention to such matters. If everyone is connected with everyone else in networks, there is less risk. In the organizational and public choice literature, one common assumption is that of reciprocity (whether in the form of reward or sanction). Without the possibility of disapprobation, members of the network renege and get an additional payoff at the others' cost (Burt 2004). More recently, trust is thought to evolve out of learning processes and reputational effects (Dodgson 1993; Sabel 1994) or the reduction of uncertainty through establishment of a norm (Heimer 2001).

When we understand networks as narratives, however, trust is engendered through sharing. We believe there may be less transactional calculation going on in networks and more relational reasoning (in this we agree with Granovetter 1973). When people share a purpose or outlook or enemy or, most generally, a narrative, affirmation of the other members as trustworthy is strengthened to the extent that one affirms one's own identity. One can share one's beliefs and plans with kindred spirits. Members find a story of integrity and authenticity that strengthens their attachment to these networks. Our research examines how affective, emotional ties to others, including nonhuman or inanimate objects, keep people engaged, and are part of their creative process of building relationships with the world, in a sense evoking an understanding of being as intentionality (Husserl [1900] 1970) or identity as tied to place (Casey 1993).

Structural analysis can also emphasize repetition of pattern and homophily. But we feel that the most interesting thing about some network arrangements is their dynamism and heterogeneity. For example, the management literature has suggested that the energy and profitability of Silicon Valley drew from the ability of its network to constantly reinvent itself and adjust to rapidly changing market conditions. We feel that the same can be said for ecological networks, where actors adjust to the constant dynamic of nature and community.

Our interest in heterogeneity is an effort to understand how people relate to the diversity of the world, much of which is nonhuman. How are animals, plants, mountains, water, and other environmental elements conceived of by humans in a network? We are also interested in objects such as dams, windmills, cars, and other technologies surrounded by controversy. How is the interaction mediated? What types of technologies represent and communicate with participants that lack language? The sometimes radical heterogeneity of networks (e.g., including environmentalists, ranchers, cameras, and jaguars) is thought to be key to their power. It is in these diverse associations (e.g., Asian carp, fishers, electric barriers, fish biologists, locks, and insurance companies) that innovative ideas emerge. This echoes insights from the literature on punctuated equilibrium where, despite static, unchanging patterns playing out at the center (i.e., in the traditional, established associations, such as a state agency), innovation constantly occurs at the fringes (see Repetto 2006 for a review of punctuated equilibrium in the environmental field). But this also coheres with Burt's notion that innovation occurs at "structural holes—namely, those interstices between homogenous groups of policy actors where new ideas might be shared, or old ideas might find new life (Burt 2004).

Gary Fine and Brooke Harrington argue for an understanding of society as a web of groups, or "tiny publics." They are interested in the opportunities and challenges afforded by these small groups as defining of civil society, and as a way to move beyond a "dichotomous model of individualism versus associationism" (Fine and Harrington 2004, 343). As McCarthy and Zald (1977) and Snow, Zurcher, and Ekland-Olsen (1980) documented, personal networks may serve as conduits for money, publicity, or materials essential to the survival of civic movements. We see a social movement as a kind of network, typically composed of a number of smaller networks, that is focused on the accomplishment of particular social objectives. The focus on such objectives may be detrimental to the larger network in the long term as the objectives are partially accomplished and some network members drop out while others hold out for more complete victories. Within any social movement, people will often define themselves as belonging to distinct groups within the larger network.

The Power of Narrative in Networks

Policy scholars have long recognized the power of the narrative form. Hajer wrote about coalitions that revolved around the strength of a discourse, the latter defined as "an ensemble of ideas, concepts, and categories through which meaning is given to phenomena" (Hajer 1993, 45). Fischer says it more directly: "It is not the knowledge in belief systems per se that holds the members of such coalitions together, but the 'story lines' that symbolically condense the facts and values basic to a belief system" (Fischer 2003, 102). He writes: "It is through the act of storytelling that individuals assess their social positions in their respective communities, grasp the goals and values of their social groups and communities, internalize their social conventions, and understand who they are vis-à-vis one another" (162). And we might substitute, in place of the word "groups" in this last quotation, the word "networks."

In our work, we strive to advance this reasoning: first, in our depiction of networking as emplotment and, second, in our demonstration of the use of narratology for network analysis. Our third point differs somewhat: it is through narrative that we can conceive of new ways to navigate the relationships between human and nonhuman, material and cognitive—in other words, to form networks of radical heterogeneity. And what allows such heterogeneity to cohere is the plurivocity found in the constituting narrative. Plurivocity, as we will use the term in this book, will refer to the ability of a story to be told in differing ways by different narrators. For example, it is possible for different narrators to tell slightly different versions of the basic story, or to tell the same story but to highlight different aspects more than others. Later in this chapter, we will work these points out more explicitly.

For Harrison C. White, networks are phenomenological realities as well as measurement constructs. He argued for an organic notion of networks and a cumulative structuring of society. Individuals create networks as they pursue unending searches for "self and control" (seeking identity is any action not explicable from biophysical regularities) (White 1992, 5), and this restless, constant effort creates a topology of social spaces that are both means and bar to further social action and control. White views human social order as deriving fundamentally from every person's contradictory efforts to assert control and to belong. While individuals make efforts to take control, they generate stories, which both express perceptions of social process and structure but also conceal things like, for example, failure (13). In White's words: "Identities come to perceive the likelihood of impacts from indirect relations to other identities in some string of ties and stories. The social result is called a network" (65).

This allusion to stories is not incidental. The effort to define one's self, seek out a meaningful negotiation of self and control, takes the form of crafting acceptable narratives of one's self. The human ability to make these complex motivations and reasons fit into a coherent story is what we will refer to as narrativity. Narrativity is used to make sense of our otherwise disparate decisions and actions—later on, we will address how sense making occurs. Another singularly important function of narrativity is the establishment of personal identity. Referring to what he calls our autobiographical selves, Bruner writes: "It is constructed by human beings through active ratiocination, by the same kind of ratiocination through which we construct narratives. When somebody tells you his life—and that is principally what we shall be talking about—it is always a cognitive achievement rather than a through-the-clear-crystal recital of something univocally given. In the end, it is a narrative achievement" (Bruner 1987b, 692–693). Speaking to the normative function of self-narrative, he writes: "In the end, we become the autobiographical narratives by which we 'tell about' our lives" (694). Freeman agrees and suggests that "on some level, narrative is itself the source of the self's identity" (Freeman 2001, 296). It is easy enough to say that we are the story that we tell, and that we decide and act in conformity with that story. And when we associate ourselves with others, we are associating (or, in our words, emplotting) our own stories with their own into a coherent metanarrative.

Thus, identity emerges from narrative, but is also co-constructed. Identity is increasingly understood as dynamic and hybrid, emerging from our relations with others. We become who we are as a result of the multiple and complex relationships we inherit and create (Haraway 1991; Whatmore 2002). A focus on a bounded, independent political subject is replaced with an emphasis on dependence and relationality, even across the species boundary (Barad 2003; Noe 2009). Having a relational and dynamic take on identity offers an important correction because so much of mainstream environmental discourse reflects a homogeneous, unproblematic, ungendered subject. Kate Soper (1995) has argued that "nature" is in fact, a category of human identity, existing to define what is or is not "us" in traditional Western thought.

Just as we use stories to express who we are, so too do we use stories to "model" complex realities around us. There are several strands of such cognitive scholarship. One is identifying certain mental and cultural models that are used to lend coherence to an otherwise bewildering reality

(Kempton, Boster, and Hartley 1995). According to cognitive psychologists, mental models are simplified representations of the world that allow one to interpret observations, generate novel inferences, and solve problems (Gentner and Stevens 1983). Anthropologists have expanded the mental model concept into what is called a cultural model, and defined it as mental models that are shared within a culture or social group (Holland and Quinn 1987). Another branch of literature uses the notion of framing as a mode of reality interpretation. Frames, as Goffman introduced them, are interpretive schemes that selectively highlight aspects of the issue and introduce a specific perspective that then allows one to capture reality in a simpler manner (Goffman 1974; Schön and Rein 1994). Neither models nor frames are as inclusive as narratives.

But seldom found in such research is the explicit recognition that, very often or perhaps generally, these mental models, cultural models, and frames take on the appearance and essence of story. Bruner (1987a) is one of the few to make this explicit connection. As others have expressed it: "Given the amount of uncertainty about the world, people create cause-and-effect stories to fill in the blanks. Frames—also known as mental models, schemas—are essentially such stories" (Wesselink and Warner 2010).

Also relevant is the literature that talks about certain boundary objects that transcend organizational, professional, or cultural boundaries and facilitate conversations across them (Starr and Griesemer 1989). We maintain that (partially) shared narratives can serve as boundary objects that knit together heterogeneous groups of policy actors. Narratives have many properties that make them exemplary instruments for spanning these divides. Turnhout (2009), for example, discusses the need for boundary objects to possess both the ambiguity and flexibility for different groups of actors to employ them in their own ways. As we will discuss in the next chapter, these elements of ambiguity and flexibility are realized as the element of plurivocity in narrative. That is, to the extent that different narrators can tell a story (like Rashomon) in their own ways, yet maintain the shared nature of the basic plot (which we will define in the next chapter as the *fabula*), narratives can serve as objects that bind.

For White stories are "the essential vehicles for elaborating networks" (White 1992, 67n6). The "ties" of a network are stories. Sets of stories, or conventions, emerge over time and lead to different framings and social spaces thus providing the "color" of human social life, according to White, for whom this activity distinguishes human social action from a vertebrate "pecking order." Social networks are always grounded in physical space and time, but survive in a matrix of other stories, or "contending control projects" (214).

Although for White, story is a fundamental process in human organization, he goes no further in terms of analyzing the elements of a story from a literary perspective. Plots do emerge out of repeated, set storylines, but White is not interested in how variations in sequencing in stories, perspective, focalization, plurivocity, or other aspects of narrative can indicate the power of some stories over others, and thus the extent, longevity, or influence of a network. Furthermore, White and most other network theorists have less to say about the complexity and diversity of environmental context. Although he clearly sees the biophysical context as important,[1] he includes only humans as actors in his networks. And yet, if you pay attention to discourse in environmental networks, especially as that discourse can reveal the motivations of people for belonging—it becomes clear that the nonhuman and the biophysical elements of the environment are very active participants.

For that we turn to Bruno Latour.

Latour's world is one of objects and of influences. What is especially remarkable about the networks that Latour proposes is their heterogeneity, both in terms of the wide variety of the participants as well as the diversity of relationships implicated. He does not use networks as a methodological tool for examining the relative strength and weakness of ties between human beings, but casts them out across the whole wide world, providing a metaphysical perspective on the great diversity of objects that populate our lives and the complexity of our relationships with them. His is an inclusive approach to a world traditionally separated by dualistic tensions between human and nature, actor and subject, politics and impulse, conscious and insentient. Latour's "actants" include paint, rocks, drill bits, microbes, presidents, and mass transit systems. Moreover, actants are defined not by core, internal characteristics, but by dynamic, reciprocal, and open-ended relationships that push and pull all elements in a network into various ways of being.

In Latour's, and our, framework, networks are thus "more than social." It is the potentially radical heterogeneity of possible networks that allows us to imagine new kinds of ecological democracy, where nonhuman actants have agency, perhaps (as we will discuss in this chapter), even political representation.

In *We Have Never Been Modern*, a key treatise in Latour's development of his actor-network approach, he begins by listing the diverse characters in a newspaper story on the ozone hole. He traces the dynamic relationships between chlorofluorocarbons, upper-atmosphere chemists, chief executives of Atochem and Monsanto, refrigerator manufacturers, meteorologists, ecologists, future generations, international treaties. "The same article mixes together chemical reactions and political reactions. A single thread links the most esoteric sciences and the most sordid politics, the most distant sky and some factory in the Lyon suburbs, dangers on a global scale and the impending local elections or the next board meeting. The horizons, the stakes, the time frames, the actors—none of these are commensurable, yet there they are, caught up in the same story (Latour 1991, 1). In the interest of exploring these far-reaching and heterogeneous associations, to follow these science, human, nature, politics "imbroglios," Latour offers the notion of network: "More supple than the notion of system, more historical than the notion of structure, more empirical than the notion of complexity, the idea of network is the Ariadne's thread of these interwoven stories" (3).[2]

The network, Latour argues, at once embraces the political, the discursive, and the material thus providing scholars with far more adequate accounts of events in the world than what is afforded by more exclusive sociological theories. For Latour and colleagues, actor-networks are inherently dynamic, needing the constant working and reworking of relationships to maintain the network. But, and here is our insight, the way these actors understand and act within the network also has a performative component—that is, these actions and exchanges in fact frame and define the network. Though Latour did not cast the actor-network in narrative form, we maintain that the network is essentially a story being told and retold by actors in a field of structuration (namely, where actors are both agentic and embedded in structures of relationships).

Isabelle Stengers and Bruno Latour have both devoted considerable effort to rethinking the politics and agency of objects (Latour and Weibel 2005; Stengers 2010). They have argued that our political processes are prohibitive of new solutions to problems because they fail to grapple with the political nature of the nonhuman. Objects are represented by experts, typically scientists, who present the world.

In her "cosmopolitical proposal," Stengers is interested in how people might better contend with the politics of things. What if we were to define nonhumans according to their ability to force thought in humans, she asks. What if what we consider as human isn't thinking (and therefore exceptional) beings, but "humans as spokespersons claiming that it is not their free opinions that matter but what causes them to think and to object, humans who affirm that their freedom lies in their refusal to break this attachment" (Stengers 2010, 5). She concludes, "What makes us human is not ours: it is the relation we are able to entertain with something that is not our creation" (6). Once we understand our humanness as an emergent property of our relationships with objects (even those we create such as technologies) those relationships become fair game for political consideration. We can begin, as Stengers says, to turn the consequences of technology into a political problem (20).

Stengers defines her cosmopolitical assemblages, within which nonhumans have political representation, very much in opposition to a conventional model of political discourse that understands consensus and agreement arising from rational, Habermasian discourse. What she is after is an elusive experience, an "event," when people gather because of a common recognition of their relations to a nonhuman, because of their attachment to something that makes them "hesitate, feel, and think." These attachments need not all be the same, but provoked by their thinking and their unanswered questions, people will gather, insist on better answers, protest. Stengers refers to the "gmo event" in Europe as an example of such an event; both unpredictable—it didn't happen in the United States—and powerful in that it reframed the discourse from a focus on a biological engineering feat capable of feeding the world to a concern with a host of other relationships including gmos as a vehicle for usurping intellectual property rights, capitalist expropriation of agriculture, and disastrous environmental disruption.

Analytically, we are left wondering how we begin to describe, much less analyze, the myriad actors and interrelationships that make up a network or a cosmopolitical event. How does one represent and analyze radically heterogeneous networks, made up of actors that are human, nonhuman, animate, and inanimate? Certainly, classical network analysis, with its penchant for structural representations, is challenged by such networks—for example, how would one represent linkages between human actors and a nonhuman actant such as place? For us, the analytic of choice is the turn to narrative.

Michel Callon (1986) describes the evolution of the network as four phases of translation:

Problematisation: defining a problem that requires joint action and a set of actors who are potentially enmeshed in it.

Interessement: the negotiation of actors' involvement and roles in the initiative.

Enrollment: actors' acceptance and acting out of these roles.

Mobilisation: the expansion of the network to include communities of support.

To us, it is not an accident that the preceding sequence also resembles the exposition of a story's plot—that is, identification of the conflict, description of the setting and cast of characters, and mobilization of action on the characters' part. The description of the network process is not far from the act of emplotment—in fact, for us the two are one and the same.

The idea of network as emplotment also helps us navigate the universality and simultaneous particularity of networks. One can think of them competitively, that is, as a charged field. Because this is a competition, we need to understand why and how people belong to particular networks. It is the particular plot that supports and constitutes a network that explains what is special, motivational, compelling, and affective about it.

Consider two (very simple) networks:

In either case, these two network representations might depict similar things—for example, "boy meets girl" and "girl meets boy." But beyond that, how do we understand this relationship. Simply to depict relationship with a link says nothing about what the relationship is. Are the actors bound by love, blood, history, or commerce? How strong and lasting are the ties that bind? Network analysis can leave us wondering. And, so, we turn toward emplotment, as we explain here. It is in the emplotment—namely, the particular arrangement and assortment of events, character attributes, and relationships, that meaning emerges. It is emplotment that determines whether one network is the tale of Romeo and Juliet and the other that of Tristan and Isolde.

How Networks Explain Heterogeneity

Our main interest in networks is their potential for bringing together and describing heterogeneous groups of actors, some nonhuman and some inanimate, with rich and varied motivations and purposes. And yet, the power of the network to bind together heterogenous sets of actors in often voluntary associations is yet to be explained. The most dominant explanation for what governs social life and collective action is utility. In the model of state-centered governance, the steering mechanism for social exchange is that of authority (or utility in the form of power), while in the marketplace, the steering mechanism is that of money (or utility in the form of a tradable good) (Habermas 1987). But what is the steering mechanism in nonmarket, nonstate, voluntary social networks? The most common explanation, which we do not at all dismiss, is utility. Sometimes, utility is found in solidary benefits, wherein the actor experiences pleasure from joining (Olson 1968). Other times, utility is found in material gain, wherein the actor benefits from the long-run pattern of cooperation that is initiated by their initial commitment to cooperation, as in Ostrom's model of common-pool resources (Ostrom 1990).

The problem with the notion of solidary benefits is that it actually serves as a proxy term for everything that we cannot properly consider individual utility—that is, morality, obligation, obsession, etc. And the notion of long-run benefits, due to repeated cooperation over time, requires some system of property rights and rights to membership in the network. But what of those cases, which we find, in which network actors point neither to the pleasure of group membership, nor formal rights or rules or strategic play, as the basis for their continued participation in the network?

While we find Olson's and Ostrom's explanations for collective action to be compelling, the phenomenon of networks suggests that as or even more important motivations may be found. In his book on community, Marglin attributes the problem of market and state to a common thing: the death of the notion of community (Marglin 2008). In effect, Marglin is saying that, in the state's emphasis on formal lines of authority, and the market's emphasis on individual gain, both models preclude the individual's ability to engage in communitarian activity and to recognize one's self as part of a community. In other words, community (and, by analogy, networks) exist by virtue of giving each actor the ability to consider herself as other than simply a functional cog in an authority-driven organization or a utility-maximizing price taker in a perfectly competitive market.

We see a parallel movement, from the autonomous agent depicted in mainstream liberal political theory and institutionalized in classic state or market-centered modes of governance, to the relationally constituted identities of actors, as subsequently found in networked modes of governance. Social networks allow people to be more of whom they really are, which are relational, as much as individually oriented, beings (Gilligan 1982). People can express who they are by associating with the identity narrative of a network. Somers suggests that perhaps, more than simply being representational, these group narratives can be ontological—that individuals and groups "that people construct identities (however multiple and changing) by locating themselves or being located within a repertoire of emplotted stories" (Somers 1994).

Networks are not necessarily politically progressive. As Dryzek writes: "Networks themselves are not necessarily democratic, and can indeed facilitate escape from accountability to a broader public by hiding power and responsibility" (Dryzek 2008, 199). They bring together diverse groups of actors, some nonhuman and even inanimate, in webs of relationship that are not reduced to simple logics like the profit motivated exchanges of the market or the juridical logic of the state. Let us state the point more clearly: real institutions exist in complex and varied forms that classic institutional models do not capture. Taking an example from Granovetter (1985), the buying and selling of bread is not simply a market, but a complex local culture. Networks are a way of capturing such richness. The network form of description can allow the recognition of the mutual interrelationship of very different kinds of policy actors and their being moved by multiple and varied reasons for action.

But here is part of the dilemma of analysis. Simple, recondite associations allow simple representations. State-centered regimes and corporate bodies are often well depicted by organization charts and formal rules. Markets are even more simply depicted as interlocking supply and demand curves (where individuals are no longer found) and, in its most extreme, represented by a single, scalar price signal. But, in a network where motivations and relationships are complex, what mode of description fits? If we are right, it is the narrative, with its richness of expression, its fullness of description, that best captures the complex motivations and relationships that constitute the network. To best describe a network, we tell a story. Our turn to narrative allows us to understand networks less in structural terms and closer to what Schmidt (2008) characterizes as discursive institutionalism—after all, what is the back-and-forth process of conveying ideas if not a form of storytelling?

An Example of the Structural Dilemma

Let us take a brief look at the data from our study of the Sonoran Desert conservation network to be explored in great detail in chapter 4. The initial list of people to be interviewed was chosen through a snowball method of asking key informants to name other important people in the subject area, an abstract exercise. Then, each person so identified was interviewed and asked about how they got involved in the subject and with whom they worked. This involved a more intimate and relational response as each person wove themselves into a fabric of associates in common experience and endeavor. The names that came up in these open-ended, unbounded statements were then recorded. Thus, the structure of the network illustrated below is a function of the method chosen that encouraged respondents' rambling, free association aimed at capturing who comes to mind in recounting their individualized personal conceptions and experiences. The analysis consists of tabulating these connections, which appear as zeros and ones in a tabular matrix, only a tiny portion of which is shown in table 2.1 for illustrative purposes. (The entire matrix includes 38 people on the vertical axis and 246 on the horizontal axis.) The five people mentioned by Adrianne Rankin in this part of the matrix, reflected as 1s, are mentioned by only a few or none of the others, reflected as 0s. The part of the matrix related only to those interviewed is then translated to a diagram, a depiction of nodes and linkages that is shown in figure 2.1.

We are able to measure the human associations in this network, but only among those we interviewed. The nodes represent people generally regarded as important to the policy arena, even though they are only a fraction of the people who come to mind as significant to each of these people in the course of an hour's conversation. In this diagram, the boundaries of the network are determined by our interview and recording choices. In much of the network analytic literature, it seems almost as if this diagram is by default taken to be the network.

Table 2.1
Excerpt from Sonoran Desert network matrix

	Joe Joachin	Pamela Nagler	Richard Felger	Loraine Eiler	Bill Broyles
Adrianne Rankin	1	1	1	1	1
Alberto Burquez	0	0	1	0	0
Beau McClure	0	0	0	0	0
Bill Shaw	0	0	0	0	1
Susan Anderson	0	0	0	0	0
David Yetman	0	0	1	0	1
Bill Broyles	0	0	0	0	0

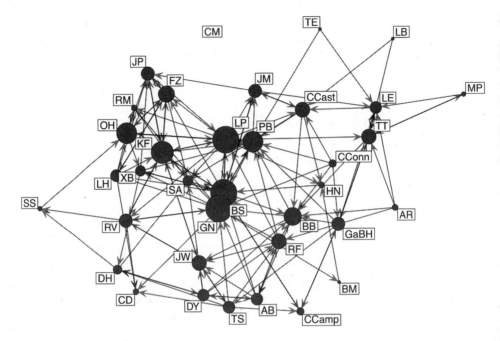

Figure 2.1
Connectivity in the Sonoran Desert conservation network. Size of nodes representing persons interviewed reflects the relative number of nominations of and by other persons. The direction of the arrows indicates whether the person is nominating or nominated

We can assess the properties of this network using figure 2.1, which depicts each mention of one individual interviewee by another interviewee with a line and arrow that shows who mentioned whom. Since the figure depicts the structure of the network, it is no wonder that many of the observations we are invited to make are structural in nature. For example, take the degree of density, which is the proportion to which all possible linkages are actualized. What we see, in the Sonoran Desert network as portrayed, is sparse, low-frequency connections. While all but one of the actors mention at least one of the other people we interviewed, no one mentions or is mentioned by half of the others interviewed. Figure 2.1 portrays an individual's degree of centrality in the network by the size of the node. While some people are more connected than others, there is no clear focal group or center through which most everyone is connected. Knowing the institutional affiliation of more central individuals (the six with the largest nodes) is not very helpful in specifying which institutions are focal since all have multiple affiliations, with three presently at environmental NGOs, and three affiliated with a university, although in very different kinds of positions. This structural portrayal of density and centrality does not give us much insight into why this network has survived changes in context since it is a snapshot of structure at a single point in time, although because those interviewed often reflected on the past, it is likely to be an aggregate of ties that were present at different points in time. The lack of density in its structure does not begin to describe its power to hold its members together with ties that bind for decades and that transcend individual or organizational gain.

The only way we can distinguish one individual from another in this network analysis is in structural terms. Despite the sparsity in terms of overall nominations in the networks, we observe high numbers of mutual ties (i.e., reciprocal nominations). The proportion of ties that are reciprocated is much higher than we might expect given the number of individuals involved and the overall level of activity (nominations). We see that some half a dozen actors are more likely to bridge various other actors and to be a common tie across them and we have no idea why. And what about the other actors—is their place in the overall structure indicative of their marginal significance? Or, is what we are observing a result of cultural differences? For instance, indigenous people may be reluctant to mention names of people who are not present. Perhaps the numbers of others mentioned results in part from the length of an open-ended interview or the train of thought that someone follows. Further, this structural portrayal does not tell us how the actors differ in what they do, what they lend to the network, and how they act. What are their roles, and how do these roles contribute to the life and action of the network?

And, returning to the point about heterogeneity, how does the network diagram capture heterogeneity? Specifying the national and tribal affiliation of members could give us information about the boundary-spanning properties of networks. But, we do not see how the network might include nonhuman actors. For example, if we were to add the Colorado River or the desert pronghorn antelope to the previous matrix, what might be the basis for drawing links between it and the other actors? How could the analysis depict the deep relationships that may exist? How does it capture ties to place?

And so we find that, if the network is consonant with its structure, and structure determined by the observed (or measured) associations, then the analysis fails to tell us what is it about the network that moves people, what is special about this particular network, what keeps this heterogeneous group bound together, and why it exists in the first place. The questions we raise do not go away—in fact, they go to the heart of the overall question of what are networks and what is their magic? And, being persistent researchers, we did what good research requires, which is to bring these questions to the network actors themselves.

In asking these actors these questions, we notice a curious thing. An overarching story tied people together to a much greater extent than people-to-people associations. For example, one of the authors took a blank sheet of paper and asked various parties in the Turtle Islands case study explored in chapter 5 if they would kindly depict their understanding of the network that actually existed on the islands. That is, they were asked to draw nodes and links—a directed graph. The respondents struggled with the request and, in the end, none of them actually drew anything. Rather, they set aside the sheet of paper and began simply telling us what they knew. They each launched into their own story. The storytelling impulse is evident in the other two case studies of the Sonoran Desert alliance in chapter 4 and the organic farming network in chapter 6—people, when asked these fundamental questions about what they are about, what they do, and why they exist, end up telling a story.

The universality of narration as a mode of transmitting information has been established elsewhere—for example, see Berkes's work with traditional communities (Berkes 2009) or Forester's work with city planners (Forester 1999). We find the same patterns and, in fact, people do not just talk about their group and its activities; they often find no other way to represent their network than with the story. In other words, the network is a story. What is most constitutive of the network is the act of emplotment.

The actors do not simply tell a story—rather, almost all of them tell a story that, at least in part, is a story about themselves. These stories do not simply pertain to this group or movement they belong to. Often, their accounts share aspects of their childhood, their experiences, their personal history of encountering this place or that species or this cause. The story of the group is also a knitting together of a set of autobiographies.

And this brings us to a proposition that will guide the rest of our investigation.

Narrative Definition of the Network

Let us propose the following definition of the network:

The *network* is an emplotment of diverse actors (persons, groups, organisms, objects, and places) within a meaningful sequence of events and characters such as to form a coherent system, situated in both material and semiotic space, that has the features of an effective narrative. Actors can engage in narration and, in so doing, bring their own stories to the overall narrative. In essence, the network is a story of stories.

First, what we are saying is that *networks are communities that narrate themselves into existence.* Second, we construe that, in an important sense, *the assemblage that we refer to as an ecology is a type of emplotment.*

The meaning of the network lies in its plot. To the extent that figure 2.1 leaves out the stories that people tell about their Sonoran work and people they work with, we miss the meaning of the Sonoran Desert network. This conceptualization of network as emplotment has considerable significance for how we describe and analyze these networks. Heterogeneity of the network, then, logically follows from the degree of plurivocity of the narrative—but this is a proposition to be tested in the case studies.

Emplotment entails making sense of otherwise disparate events and character—"making sense" being, in this case, connecting parts to produce what Ricoeur (1981) calls an "intelligible whole." As E. M. Forster (1927) put it, plot is not merely one thing after another but things connected by a cause.

When we equate a network with emplotment, we do not, of course, mean to leave out the flesh-and-blood world of people, things, and institutions that make up the network. We do focus attention on the manner by which these real actors and other ingredients are bound into a coherent whole, but we always remind ourselves that the entities we describe as networks exist in a dual, material-semiotic space (also see Stokols, Lejano, and Hipp 2013). At times we will refer to these assemblages with the term *narrative-network*, which evokes the idea that these networks are the product of discursive and organizational strategies. We will have more to say about emplotment and narrative-networks in chapter 3.

If we so define the network as a plot, then logically the way we understand the network is by studying its narrative(s). This suggests particular modes of analysis, to which we next turn.

3

The Turn to Narrative Analysis

The Centrality of Narratives

It is a truism that, to sell something to someone, you have to tell a good story and tell it well. But, in this book, we are not concerned with narrative as a vehicle for "spin-doctoring" (though that is a part of the modern realpolitik). Narratives are much more important than that, especially with regard to the roles they play in networks.

In chapter 2, we ended with the proposition that the network can be understood as an emplotment of diverse characters, objects, and events. In this chapter, we work out how this is so and explain how methods used to analyze narrative (of which plot is an element) can be used to explain what a network is and how it survives. Narratives describe networks not just in terms of structure (as does classic network analysis) but in terms of substance. Just like networks, narratives are everywhere—we are a storytelling species, after all. And a study of narratives in networks can show how the latter can be, like snowflakes, both ubiquitous and unique.

While we do not equate networks with narratives, networks do not exist without them. If, as the considerable organizational literature attests, narratives are the glue that brings members of the group together, then narratives are not primarily about "selling" a movement to the world—rather, narratives form the very foundation of the movement. More than packaging or ornamentation, narrative enables the network to form and function. It is the mode of coordination of the network. Drawing a loose parallel with other institutional designs, we might say that if money is the steering mechanism of the market, and hierarchy the steering mechanism of the state, then *narrative is the steering mechanism of the network*. Narrative is not a surface treatment, it is the underlying logic; not the image, but the reality. When we are able to recount and explain the narrative, to a great degree, we are able to describe and understand the network.

Narrative is one of the key elements that construct a network, as concretely true as a story is a primary (in fact, the most important) element of a novel. It is true, the classic novel would not exist without paper, glue, and binding, but it would not exist without its narrative either (actually, the paper, glue, and binding are becoming more and more optional). There are narratives that actually construct a network, that are not the subject of spin and fabrication. When a member is asked what their network is about, in their heart of hearts, they remind themselves of that narrative they know to be faithful to the organization as they know it. Just as networks exist for society prior to their being purposive, so too do narratives for networks.

As discussed earlier, narratives are also the repository of knowledge in networks. Most of the networks we study in this book have to do with movements that keep alternative knowledge systems alive—whether these are organic farmers, transboundary ecologists, or turtle habitat conservationists. In many cases, these movements arise to challenge a conventional wisdom, an authoritative science, or political hegemony that could not be challenged except through an alternative network. Traditional institutions can privilege the conventional, technocratic wisdom. In these conventional institutions, conventional knowledge takes the form of technical, legal, or other mainstream forms of conveying information. But the alternative networks that challenge them work precisely because they can welcome different points of view and a heterogeneity of knowledge. In these cases, where networks become the home for nonconventional wisdom, narratives are the foremost vehicle for knowledge. As Lyotard (1979) correctly pointed out, while technical knowledge privileges speaker over hearer, narrative knowledge treats all as equals and preserves and builds up community.

Linking Networks and Narratives

What is a narrative? Why is it so important to our study of networks? How do methods for analyzing narratives help us analyze networks? In chapter 2, we described networks as assemblages of ontologically different things (humans, objects, places, events, ideas—things both material and semiotic). We will discuss how the mode of assemblage is none other than emplotment. What this means is that the network understands itself through narrative, and it represents itself through narration.

Bremond defines a narrative in this way: "A narrative consists of a language act by which a succession of events having human interest are integrated into the unity of this same act" (Bremond 1973, 186). This underscores the power of narrative to integrate, and later we will discuss this as the act of emplotment. The definition also points to a coherent sequence of events, as opposed to a list or random assortment of things or truth claims.

As Ryan contends, what constitutes a narrative is a fuzzy, shifting combination of myriad elements, but regardless, its most universally accepted feature is the "representation of a sequence of events" (or actions) as meaningfully connected, and its preferred subject matter the "evolving network of human relations" (Ryan 2007). Most famously, Ricoeur describes it as the most basic representation of human experience: "I take temporality to be that structure of existence that reaches language in narrativity" (Ricoeur 1981b, 169). Quite simply, narrative is the primary means that we have to make sense of the multiple events, actors, and ideas found in life, whether actual or fictional, personal or organizational. These elements are not simply random events, actors, and ideas that appear together coincidentally—rather, they are linked together into a whole in a meaningful way, that way being the narrative. This is why, according to Bruner (1990), when a person is asked to explain who she or he is, the person responds most often by telling a story (as opposed to a laundry list of characteristics or a logical argument). Storytelling and narrative are even important to science. The public uses stories to understand science, and so do scientists, whether they're doing it on purpose or not (Sethi and Briggle 2011).

Readers may recall Aristotle's notion, in *Poetics*, of a plot as something having a beginning, middle, and end. We do not emphasize this, however, as the narratives we study are sometimes very "open-ended." It is hard to call the present moment the end, especially with networks that are in a formative stage. In some cases, these stories are even "open-beginninged." The narrative of climatic change that began with the Industrial Age is one way to begin the story, but it could have begun much earlier (e.g., when Paleolithic humans discovered fire). Rather than a beginning, middle, and end, sometimes the story resembles Deleuze's description of a rhizome that is "open and connectable in all of its dimensions" and links heterogenous elements into one assemblage (Deleuze and Guattari [1980] 1987, 12; also discussed in Hillier 2009). The narrative needs to be coherent, but not compact.

Narratives and Organization

The link between narratives and networks follows this logic. If it is true that narratives are the primary means by which we make meaningful connections between otherwise disparate events and characters in our individual lives, then we might expect narrative to serve a similar role in connecting the different actors, motivations, and actions that come together in a network. This should be especially true in the absence of formal organizational mechanisms, such as rules and contracts, for connecting the various parts of an organization to the whole. But apparently, the need for narrative representations is great even when these formal mechanisms are operative. There is, by now, a considerable amount organizational literature that attests to the constitutive role of narratives.

Early on, there were already good examples of researchers collecting "tales of the field" on the shop floor, in the boardroom, or in other settings of organizational life (e.g., Martin 1982; Mitroff and Kilmann 1975). More recent works in this genre include Boje 1991, Currie and Brown 2003, Czarniawska 1997, Patriotta 2003, and Pentland 1999. A primary focus of this research is to establish how narratives are used to coordinate diverse actions and purposes in organizations. In their research on communities of practice, Brown and Duguid (1991) describe how narratives are used to construct new cross-group coalitions that establish new ways of doing and, in so doing, anticipate much work on cross-boundary networks.

There is another, closely related strand in organizational research, one that goes further by depicting organizations themselves as story making. In Weick's depiction, organizations emerge from joint sense making, most prominently is in the organization's identity narrative (Weick 1995). Since then, a growing number of scholars have begun studying how narratives are not merely functional or descriptive devices, but constitutive of organizations (Boyce 1995; Cooren and Taylor 1997). So much more reason, then, to suspect that the study of narrative will provide new insights into the identity and functioning of boundary-spanning networks.

The most ardent proponents of narrative in organizational theory sometimes contend that organizations are essentially narratives (e.g., Ford 1999). After all, if as Searle says, speech acts create institutional facts that are as objective as material ones, then narratives can enact organizations (Searle 1969). We do not need to make such a strong claim.

Narratives have a recursive relationship with networks but do not necessarily define them.

Pentland and Feldman (2007) envision organizational forms as a series of stories and use the term "narrative networks" to refer to a method for representing and visualizing patterns of technology in use. These authors focus on information and communication technologies and portray them as a point of intersection at which numbers of different stories come together. Our interests transcend the ways in which technologies and organizations are intertwined, as we tap into the ways in which stories or narratives undergird network connections of all kinds, crossing boundaries not just via technologies but through various modes of storytelling. We will, at times, use the term *narrative-networks*, but in a different way, emphasizing our understanding of new movements and coalitions as a discursive-organizational complex, a dialectic between narrating and organization. At the same time, the perspective of the preceding authors is entirely consistent with the theory being developed here.

Narratives, Frames, and Discourses

In developing a theory around the idea of narrative, we invariably encounter the question of how narratives differ from other, closely related concepts—namely frame, discourse, mental model, and others. First of all, we point out that, in some instances, we may find these terms to be used for exactly the same thing. They all refer to ways by which to interpret or render meaning to events and things. So being, when Snow et al. (1986), for example, discusses the importance of framing for successful social movements, very often these frames actually are narratives, as pointed out in Polletta 1998. A populist discourse about illegal immigration very often can be traced to a basic narrative (Newton 2008). But it is possible, in some cases, to make distinctions.

We might begin with Goffman's original conceptualization of frames as "schemata of interpretation" (1959) that provide the "principles of organization" (1974) used to define situations. That these frames can be, and often are, narratives, is inescapable. But consider how the response to the tragedy of 9/11 was framed, initially as a crime but, later on, as a war. Whether as crime or war, the frame provides a basic source for explaining or understanding the event. But, here lies a difference: it comes up short in (or reaches past) narrative. To simply frame it as a war suggests that a compelling story can be told that traces the origin of the event to an act of war and equates the policy actors with combatants—but the story is not yet told. True, the person using or acquiring the frame can construct a story out of it, but that is only potentially true. Indeed, perhaps the most glaring omission with the subsequent framing of the Iraqi conflict around weapons of mass destruction (WMDs) was that it was not cast into a complete enough story, with a logical flow of events and complete characterization. A frame or metaphor or synecdoche need not become a story—in their most rudimentary form, these are potential sources of explanation.

There is one more potential divergence, and that is the degree of cognition of the frame versus the narrative. Frames are sometimes used for cognitive schema that are not consciously applied but remain in the background influencing interpretation in a non-ostensible way (hence the use of the word *frame*, which is closely related to Goffman's notion of the backstage). Not only are narratives consciously employed, they are in fact explicitly told. Narratives are narrated. Later in the book, we will speak of policy actors who tell only part of the story that we might uncover, or who do not tell the whole of the story we think is in place, but to some extent have to tell a story. We use narrative in this book as an action that we can trace back to a narrator.

The notion of discourse is as closely related. Discourse, which is most simply understood as a rhetoric or manner of speaking, has taken on a grander meaning in poststructuralist sociology. Foucault (1969) would refer to discourse as a group of statements forming a valid unity, but in this, he meant entire systems of thought and knowledge governed by (often unspoken or unrecognized) rules about what constitute boundaries of what can be thought and claimed. And again, we see how the term refers to actions (whether in speech or movement or thought) that render meaning to situations and events. But its use, in practice, is very much tied to the uncovering of broad systems of meaning making. And, so, one way to make a fine distinction between discourse and narrative is through the idea of a meaning structure, as Saussure used it, that defined each term within the structure. A discourse is a grand, systemic frame. And, so, a discourse around madness is constituted by everything that can serve to delineate madness from normality. But, to push the analogy further, a linguistic structure is larger than the story, and the story is a specific event allowed by, and occurring within, the structure. A narrative is a coherent unity or sequence linking one specific set of events and actors—it is not a system within which all such coherent sequences can be made. It is a performance that occurs within a performance-enabling structure. As Foucault used the term, a discourse would not seem to be possibly captured in one coherent narrative, in part because not everything in the discourse is actually spoken. But more important, narratives occur within discourse, but the difference seems to lie in how these terms are used in practice. The distinction between narrative and discourse might be likened to how Foucault distinguished archeology from discourse—while discourse establishes what is versus what is not, or what can be accepted versus what cannot, archeology recounts how this state of affairs came to be.

To confuse things further, we can easily say that any discourse or frame can be defined as a certain kind of narrative. True enough, but in this book, we pin down narrative to something more specific and explicit than this. A minimum definition of a narrative is that it is something told by a narrator. Is the story told by Foucault about the discourse of the clinic a narrative? Yes, it in fact is a book. But until that narrator told it in one coherent sequence of events and characters, it was less (or more) than a narrative. To say that "it was framed as a war" or that "hysteria belongs to a whole discourse on madness" is not yet to establish a narrative. For the latter to be a narrative, we need to ask what was the sequence of events that brought us to where we are now, who are the characters who acted out this sequence of events, and what causal or other logic ties these events and characters into a whole? And last, who told this story, and what exactly was told? This is why Foucault chose to call his approach a genealogical one—what he tried to unearth was the story of how an institution evolved over time.

There is something about a frame or a discourse, as formations, that can lie outside myself. But a narrative begins and ends with my telling it. Frames and discourse structure a conversation in a way that governs us all. But there is something about narrative that is both individual and collective. I can tell my own story and, at the same time, tell it in a way that is shared with another. But the narrative does not lie outside its narration.

To cite another example, recall how the Occupy Wall Street movement of 2011 was framed as a reaction of the 99 percent to the greed of the 1 percent. But this is not yet a complete story. What were those actions that the 1 percent committed, and how did these actions hurt the 99 percent? Where did the story begin, and what series of actions (and in what sequence) led to the present moment? And who are those 1 percent anyway—or, to put it in another way, who are the particular characters in this story? How do we know that the actions were motivated by greed and not pure habit or poor intuition? What changes are the protesters hoping to effect by occupying Wall Street? A story cannot simply remain as a concept but has to include specific events and specific characters, fictional or not.

Guiding Principles

The considerable literature on narrative and its role in policy and organization provides a number of key insights that guide our subsequent investigation. These insights motivate us to focus on a number of specific aspects of narrative, as we describe later, in the section on our analytical framework.

The first insight is that narrative is part of the "glue" that binds actors together in a network and enables it to withstand threats and to grow. As Fischer and Hajer pointed out, bodies of discourse, argumentation, and ideas (ideological and otherwise) more so than simple beliefs or ideology, are the root of collectivization in new policy communities (Fischer 1993; Hajer 1995). We extend this line of thought by moving from argument, discourse, and story to narrative, which is text, performative act, and social function. This is not simply to have a reason to be part of a group, like the existence of a material benefit to a person from joining. There are countless other associations a person might form where a rational advantage might be gained, but somehow, this person joins this particular network, out of all the others, and identifies with these particular other actors. Why would a person choose one reasonably rational (i.e., utility improving) action over other reasonably rational actions? The answer perhaps is not in the ethic of rationality per se but in the strength of one narrative versus the other. In fact, though we do not pursue this line of thinking in this book, it is entirely possible to consider the model of rationality to be subsumed under a more encompassing model of narrativity (e.g., see Fisher 1987).

If we were to inquire why someone joins a coalition to save an urban wetlands from infill development, we might hear someone sharing their memories of growing up around the wetlands, walking their dog each evening before dinner, feeling at peace sitting on a rock by the pond, or listening to stories their own grandfather used to tell. We become part of something when it becomes an essential part of the story of who we are (Bruner 1990). Again, organization theory provides us with ample evidence for the binding force of narratives. As Weick describes, there is no organization without an organizational identity narrative (Weick

1995). The social movement literature is replete with accounts of how narratives are used to recruit members to the movement (Polletta 1998). Because Benford and Snow (2000) worked out the importance of framing within social movements, we suggest that narratives are the principal tool for framing. A narrative policy framework is used to analyze advocacy coalitions by some policy scholars (Jones and McBeth 2010; Shanahan, Jones, and McBeth 2011).

The human ability to make these complex motivations and reasons fit into a coherent story—this is what we might refer to as narrativity. The compulsion to narrate is a common feature of public life—for example, this is what lies behind Stone's concepts (1989) of how causal stories arise out of the need to justify public priorities. Another singularly important function of narrativity is the establishment of personal identity. This use of narrative for identity construction is what Bruner means by the term *the autobiographical self* (Bruner 1987b). Freeman agrees and suggests "on some level, narrative is itself the source of the self's identity" (Freeman 2001).

That self-identity, or the autobiographical understanding of one's self, has narrative properties and has been discussed at some length by MacIntyre (1984) and Bruner (1993). But perhaps it is Ricoeur (1992) who most carefully works out why narrative is so essential to identity. In his exposition on narrative identity, Ricoeur describes the use of emplotment as a way to mediate between disparate components of intentions, causes, chance occurrences, and so forth. Narrative is the means by which we bridge the gap between describing (the events in one's life) and prescribing (the aims of a good life). Identity is worked out in the same manner as characterization in a literary piece. In this way, narrative identity is able to encompass, in Ricoeur's terms, both sameness and selfhood. He defines sameness as "the lasting dispositions by which a person is recognized" (Ricoeur 1992, 121). Juxtaposed to this is the concept of selfhood, characterized as self-constancy or "the preservation of faithfulness to a word" (123). Thus, selfhood describes an ethical position wherein one commits to being faithful to a promise, even after one's feelings, original motivations, or disposition have changed. This dialectic helps resolve the conflict of trying to ascertain one's identity in terms of either constancy or essence—in Ricoeur's framework, one is both a bundle of qualities and also a dynamic agency of choice or being. In narrating one's identity as character development, one is able to maintain a fine dichotemy between sameness and selfhood. In this book, we extend this notion of the link between narrative and self-identity from individuals to a network of individuals. In the case studies that follow, and especially in the Sonoran Desert case, we illustrate how a narrative approach helps us more easily see how people's personal identities become integrated into relationships with place and others living in a place (as also discussed in Casey 1993).

The second insight is that, at least in part, the positive features of effective networks—namely, that they bridge, integrate, translate, and generate—can be found in how their constitutive narratives bridge, integrate, translate, and generate. Narratives are plots that tie disparate events, objects, and so forth together. Emplotment is what turns an otherwise random assortment of parts into a coherent whole. Martha Nussbaum, a noted Aristotelian scholar, talks about how complex moral reasoning, often involving multiple ethical considerations, are best captured by narrative forms of representation—most specifically, the novel (Nussbaum 1990). Narratives are able to integrate multiple motivations, contingencies, and ethical principles. In his work on traditional ecological knowledge, Berkes (2009) catalogues rich examples of how, before ecology became a modern science, traditional stories captured the complex nature of ecologies and practices that evolved around them over generations. Narratives are also powerful devices for knitting together communities from hitherto diverse groups of people. Schön and Rein (1994) describe how metanarratives are generated that are used to fuse multiple stakeholder groups with diverse interests and narratives into a working coalition. This is the main defining characteristic of the narrative—its ability to integrate parts, events, or characters into meaningful wholes and, in so doing, make each of its parts meaningful (Prince 1990).

What makes them generative? Primarily, by being fixed as text (through formal or informal processes of institutional "writing"), a narrative then takes on an objective life (Ricoeur 1973) that, rather than fixing meaning, actually frees it up for rich interpretations by different readers—what Barthes called a writerly text (Barthes 1974). Contrary to diffusion theories, narratives do not simply diffuse from one actor to the next but are actively represented, interpreted, and translated into each actor's context. Good stories engage readers in active participation—in this sense, narratives are never merely passively received. Boland describes it as the ability of narratives, as opposed to logical arguments, to bring the noncanonical into relief along with the canonical and, in so doing, build new knowledge within an organization (Boland and Tenkasi 1995). Organizational stories, if they are not to be dominating, need plurivocity (Boje 1995; Thachankary 1992). As Brown (2006) describes, collective orga-

nizational identities are characterized by heterogeneous, sometimes conflicting, narratives.

The third insight is that narratives are crucial to networks that exist
as a challenge to conventional wisdom or political agendas. In these
networks, critical discourse necessarily needs to be inclusive of diverse
perspectives and motivations. It is for these kinds of networks, harboring
diverse modes of knowing, that narratives function so well in capturing
knowledge. We will see this again and again in the ensuing case studies.
So not only is narrative the glue that binds members to a network, it is
also that which is bound by these members, as the latter pool their
thoughts and intentions into the narrative. The narrative is what the
network thinks and knows.

These three insights immediately lead us to a fourth, which follows
logically: that methods for analyzing narratives should be of much use
in analyzing networks. In short, to understand why a network is, what
a network knows, and why the network works the way it does, we
analyze the narratives that represent and are embedded in the network.
We should be clear about why we believe narrative analysis is a crucial
lens for understanding networks. As Fischer wrote: "Without a clear
statement of narrative's relationship to what we normally identify as
policy argumentation or analysis, narrative analysis will only struggle to
gain more than a marginal status in the disciplines" (Fischer 2003, 178).
And so, we emphasize, extant (and empirical) modes for network analysis, which focus on structure and the exchange of material or information, do not capture the complexity of many of the networks we study.
In fact, these modes of analysis do not recognize assemblages of radical
heterogeneity, such as what we observe, to be networks at all. But narrative analysis allows this and, in fact, our knowledge of network complexity and heterogeneity come about only through the narratives we
collect from the actors themselves.

Let us now formulate a framework for analyzing narrative that can
prove instrumental in analyzing the cases we take up later in the book.

A Framework for Narrative Analysis

In this section, we describe the elements of narrative analysis that are
particularly useful in supporting our subsequent investigations of narratives within networks. We will not always employ all of these modes of
description in our analysis of network arrangements, but tailor the
approach to the case at hand.

Narrative analysis, which emerged from the broader field of literary theory and criticism, deals with features of narratives that make them compelling, uncovers layers of meaning embedded in them, and studies the use of literary devices to build a story. We use these analytical methods to delineate special features and deeper meanings of a network's narratives, insights that also help us describe and understand the networks themselves.

One of the barriers to wider use of narrative analysis has been the absence of a commonly agreed upon framework. Narratologists have presented a range of categories they have found helpful in capturing the essence of narratives. Some lists are very parsimonious (as in Aristotle's elements of drama) and others quite numerous, as in Greimas's theory of actants (1966). Our framework draws from this literature and composes dimensions of analysis that are essential, different, and complimentary (see Bal 2009 for a useful review of methods of narrative analysis). We will use this template (not necessarily in the order presented) as a common framework for analyzing our case studies. We also believe the framework will be useful to other researchers.

Emplotment
Plot is the outline of the whole story that, as E. M. Forster (1927) said, makes it not just one event after another but events connected by cause, the making of connections. It is the "intelligible whole" (Ricoeur 1984) that links otherwise disparate events or actions. Plot is the manner by which these disparate things are arranged, related, presented, and articulated so as to connect them and create a meaningful whole. We study the emplotment of a narrative in order to connect the logic of the entire system of elements in the story. When we study the network narrative, we seek to explain the rationale and reasoning by which each action and actant are bound together. We look for the literal juxtaposing of different elements as a way to understand how people make connections. For example, the juxtaposition of accounts of a tragic heat wave that struck France in 2003 with ensuing deliberations of the Intergovernmental Panel on Climate Change (IPCC), created the outline of a whole story that connects scientific deliberations, the weather, and human well-being.

Emplotment is about how the story is constructed out of disparate events and actions into a sequence that has its own compelling logic that may be cause-and-effect, the working out of fate, the application of patterns of moral reasoning, or other schema. That is, narratives are not simply lists of factors or objects or claims, but a congruent sequence of events, a coherent unity. For instance the narrative may revolve around history of settlement, common association with prominent features such as a hill or lake, the race or culture of inhabitants or many other features around which a common story may be constructed. The sense of the whole is found in their collaboratively constructed plot, storyline, or, as narratologists call it, the *fabula*. The fabula is simply the general (and so, shared) sequence of events and set of characters. This is counterposed with the actual narrating of the story by a particular narrator or character, which has to more to do with the performance of it in real time.

Good plots reflect sequence, which is crucial to narrative unfolding. Where does the story begin? What is the backstory and context? How is history presented? In the Sonoran Desert case, which we will discuss in chapter 4, the narrative of the border environment can begin with animal, plant and human populations moving freely and coexisting for hundreds of years or it can unfold with a wave of illegal aliens invading and despoiling everything. What is the next step in the narrative unfolding? In the Sonoran Desert network narrative, it may be the invention of new ways to connect across formal boundaries, or alternatively, the elimination of border crossers who leave discarded water bottles and other trash in the desert. What is projected into the future? This will depend on what people have said about the past. Being able to describe a network as a temporal sequence can provide a better understanding of its identity. Identity is not static, of course, and narrative is the most proper way of describing it. In *Time and Narrative*, Ricoeur describes how we can link emplotment and identity by studying what elements of the latter remain the same and what elements change as the plot works out over time (Ricoeur 1984). This can provide us a richer way to describe what an organization (or network) is, how it differs from others, and how it is changing. The turn of events or the introduction of new characters at some point in time, for instance, can lead to a change in emplotment.

The recognition of salient plots and storylines has become an intriguing way to understand action in the public realm. Roe (1994) showed how the salience of some policy agendas derive from underlying, classic plots or fables—taking a cue from Propp (1968). A similar point was made by De Neufville and Barton (1987) about the use of myths in bureaucratic decision making.

Effective storylines have been recycled, over the years, to inform (or mislead) the public about environmental issues. Wargo (2009) describes how a common risk-benefit narrative concerning the tangible benefits of risky activities, versus uncertain or diffused costs of the same, surfaces time and again when agencies and corporations find need to justify activities such as nuclear testing, pesticide application, and diesel use.

The fabula can be analyzed any number of ways—one useful schema, from Bremond (1973), posits that any fabula can be understood as a grouping of at least three kinds of events: possibility (of an event or conflict or discovery), the event (realization of a possibility), and the result (or consequence of the event). This elementary sequence is one way by which a narrative creates a unitary whole. In short, if a narrative is to be effective, it should employ these kinds of elementary sequences that create a progression to the story. For instance in one version of the Turtle Islands story presented in chapter 5, the rise of an international biological conservation movement led to the adoption of national standards in Manila that led to the imposition of new (and inappropriate) regulations upon the islands. Generally in this book, we will simply use the term *plot* interchangeably with the term *fabula*.[1]

At the same time, while the plot highlights a common theme, effective narratives can exhibit plurivocity (as Bruner points out), which is that quality of a story that allows different characters or narrators to each tell the general story in their own ways. It is part of the magic of narrative that allows the blending of disparate voices (often coherent and compatible but sometimes dissonant) to come together in one shared story.

In our analysis of the case studies, we seek to distill individual narratives. By being faithful to the stories individuals shared with us, we attempt to depict the situation in the richest and most authentic ways possible. At the same time, we look across the individual narratives and seek out commonalities in theme and plot. This involves thematic analysis as well as an attempt to reconstruct the basic storyline or fabula around which the network revolves. The relationship of the individual story to the plot is akin to the particular to the general. This dialectical relationship between the particular and the general is what we will later refer to as hermeneutics.

The degree to which narrative-networks use emplotment in an inclusive manner can be important from a policy perspective. In a marine turtle sanctuary, is the sole policy actor simply that of the regulatory state, as embodied in the local conservation corps? Or, does the plot include artisanal fishers and other community folk as somehow delegated with the task of turtle conservation? Do tourists and recreational enthusiasts have a role in this plot?

Formal agency plans can be understood as narratives. As an example, Goldstein et al. (2012) examined a redevelopment plan for an economically struggling downtown area and noted how the plan emplotted agents of change like the development agency, the developer, and future investors, but did not include the residents in any significant way. There were keenly interested stakeholders who found themselves with no significant role in the redevelopment narrative. Interpreting the plan as narrative in this instance helped the researchers comprehend the extent of resentment and protest witnessed among some of the residents. This turn to narrative pursues a line of thinking, stemming from the argumentative turn in policy and planning, that sees public decision making as linguistic acts (Fischer and Forester 1993; Forester 1999).

Characterization

Characters are as essential to narratives as sequence of events. Notwithstanding Aristotle's work on rhetoric, in which he described events as the primary focus of the narrative, it is said that much of modern-day literature has its primary focus on character development. James Joyce's *Ulysses*, which was patterned after Homer's epic story, is less about the physical events in the hero's journey than it is about the unfolding character of its main protagonist, Leopold Bloom. As such, much of the novel moves in Bloom's mind (with the exception of the last chapter, which occurs in Molly's). Effective narratives construct rich characters, which are not simply the general roles they play, such as hero, villain, betrayer, and so forth, but specific, complex, multifaceted personalities.

Characterization is the process of giving actants (abstract role-players) life and basically giving them specific identity. In our employment of narrative approaches, we assume that nonhumans can be characters, too. Thus, we can observe how storytellers perceive and reveal agency to other species, such as bacteria and turtles, and nonanimate objects too, like volcanoes, heat and soil nutrients. When Rachel Carson (1962) transformed our understanding of DDT from benign to potent, she was engaged in the skillful act of characterization.

Characterization involves the simultaneous processes of individuation and categorization. The richer the characterization, the more we are able to distinguish the individually distinctive features of an actant. In works of fiction, individuation is needed to make a story seem real. In networks of reality, individuation reveals the many facets of the relationships that connect humans and others within a network, whether we consider these social constructs or material facts.

At the same time, a process of categorization is carried out. While individual description can produce a set of attributes associated with a character, a laundry list of descriptives does not necessarily create a character. What is needed is a way to bring together these different attributes into a coherent whole. One effective means for this is to assign individuals into classes or categories. Thus, a character becomes a union of general and specific attributes. Categorization is used to make the individual character intelligible.

One method of building a character has to do with focalization. Focalization refers to the perspective(s) from which a narrative is being told or interpreted. It also has to do with those particular elements in the story that the narrator is focusing on. The narrator may be an insider who is part of the story, an outsider who observes the story from the perspective of the author, or an external reader. It is here where plurivocity can be unmistakable, as it is entirely possible to consider multiple perspectives at the same time—in fact, the writing or exteriorization of the text opens it up to multiple perspectives.

Studying how someone or something is characterized is important for policy. To say that a sea turtle is an endangered species does not begin to tap into how actors in a place regard the turtles. Does a local fisher understand the endangered species designation in its legal sense, as simply a recognition of its legal status? Or does the fisher value the turtle as something to be cherished? How the fisher and other actors view the turtle and relate to it has consequences for policy. In one situation, the feeling that the legal designation is simply imposed from outside can lead to very sparing efforts, or even contrary actions, at species conservation. In another, highly motivated actors can seek out the welfare of the turtle in many more ways than simple obedience to a negative edict.

An important element of characterization is how and to what extent characters are given voice. It is one thing to simply recount a person's view or position on a subject, and another, often more meaningful thing, to listen to the person's own voice in her own words. The words of many great orators of the past, such as Demosthenes, have been lost to time, and we can only access their message indirectly. But we play back footage of Martin Luther King Jr. speaking to a packed church in Memphis one night in 1968, and we encounter the character directly, and the person and his message become alive in ways that can move us.

In our narrative research, we seek to identify different ways characters are given voice. Often, we encourage them to speak to us directly, and we transcribe their words and present them to the reader verbatim.

Action, too, is text, as Ricoeur reminds us, and closely observing and recording the actions of a character also helps give it life on the page. When Leopold (1962) observes the dying embers of life in the wolf's eyes, it becomes more than a representative of a genus: an individual. Identity has a relational aspect, too, and so yet another way we are able to characterize something is by studying how others around it are affected by and relate to it. The aspect of relationality is also at work when a narrative moves us. When a character ceases to become merely an actant in a story but a unique individual, we can be taken up by the story and relate to the character in powerful ways. The celebrated primatologist, Jane Goodall, did this when describing her work with chimpanzees: "For more than ten minutes David Graybeard and Goliath sat grooming each other, and then, just before the sun vanished over the horizon behind me, David got up and stood staring at me . . . The moment is etched deep into my memory: the excitement of the first close contact with a wild chimpanzee and the freakish chance that cast my shadow over David even as he seemed to gaze into my eyes" (Goodall 1998, 3). This kind of characterization was especially important for Goodall, who attributed individual personalities and emotions to the chimpanzees she studied.

Characterization is a universal device that can be strategically employed in policy narratives. Consider the talk employed by agencies that deal with regulating harmful chemicals. Invariably, their work involves reducing but not eliminating risk and, at the end of the day, some will be injured. In agency talk, these are referred to as statistical lives—faceless, generic, and universal. Contrast this to the way Lois Gibbs humanized risk talk by bringing out individual testimonies of flesh-and-blood residents of Love Canal or how Cesar Chavez gave voice to farmers and family members whose lives were damaged by pesticide use. Making victims more human enables us to better relate and makes the situation more real to us. Aside from this, characterization matters to us because it is only by going to these levels of rich detail that important aspects of reality might be uncovered.

In our work, we pay special attention to characterizing nonhuman actants, and how human narrators give them "voice." This requires fidelity to observing these nonhuman actants, but also listening to human actors as they, out of their special relationships to these, characterize them in their own rich ways. We pay attention to the processes of individuation and categorization as people create multifaceted nonhuman characters, at the same time being careful not to anthropomorphize these nonhumans (as Goodall herself was accused of). Note, too, that the device of characterization need not apply just to individuals but to organizations, projects, and other entities—for example, Collins, Cooney, and Garlington's discussion (2012) of how social policy can be thought of as possessing personal virtues such as compassion.

An important aspect of characterization is how and to what extent a character is distinguished from a generic class of actants and understood as having unique traits. We seek thick descriptions of situations and characters that capture both general qualities as well as special, individual ones. Thus, we are not interested in riverway green corridor initiatives as just a class of social movement, but also this particular initiative that arose around, say, the Los Angeles River (Goldstein et al. 2012). Characterization can involve moving in between general and particular. In our research, we deliberately seek out descriptions of a network or individuals in it that capture special and unique qualities. This means encouraging interviewees to talk in particulars, recounting specific events and individual encounters. It also entails seeking out particular aspects of networks or individuals that contradict conventional assumptions about such networks and individuals. In the case of river initiatives, one might ask, how is the Los Angeles River project different from those that formed around different rivers?

Part of this work requires that we seek out different perspectives of a story. We seek out respondents from different places in a network and individuals who hold different views of it. When examining the foundational narrative of a network, it matters much in whose voice the narrative is being told, and whether multiple narratives can be found among network members. In Genette's terms (1980), is the narrative told from a singular, fixed focalization or multiple focalizations? Is it told from an ostensibly official nonfocalized (or, at least in form, objective) perspective, an internal focalization from one of the actors in the story, or an external focalization from a nonactor?

By taking advantage of the inherent plurivocity and focalization of narrative, we hope to capture a story and its characters more richly and deeply.

Alterity and the Other

One of the primary devices that move a narrative along is the introduction of the other—namely, alter egos to the protagonists in a narrative. In analyzing the element of alterity, we are able to better understand what makes a narrative special or innovative, and, in the same manner, the network underlying it.

What is the "other" (i.e., "alter") and how is it treated? Victim? Independent agent? Monster? Predictable? Mysterious? (Nature has been depicted in all of these ways.) As Fludernik (2007) writes, the use of identity versus alterity is an important aspect of all narratives. Identity is constructed against the other. Yet another important literary theme is about encountering and overcoming the unknown.

We find that, to understand a network and its members, it helps us to understand the alter as it is constructed via the network narratives. Some of the movements we study are emergent organizations that are always in some state of ambiguity as they seek to better establish their identity. But we get a sense of what they seek to evolve into by studying the alter that they define themselves against. The other can also exist as a real or imagined threat that gives a movement momentum.

The relationship of self to other offers many possibilities, and we need to seek them out. Is the other directly acknowledged, and do actors distinguish themselves from the other in very direct ways? Does the other loom large in the network's identity narrative, or is it merely a subtext that is implicitly understood? To what extent is the movement driven by fear of or perhaps ideological opposition to the other? And what modes of reconciliation are identified between a narrative-network and its other? Whether a network exists in defiance to or, alternatively, in balance with, the other can affect its design and function.

Breach of Convention

Bruner wrote about how breach of the canonical gives a narrative force. A story is worth telling because it may take a well-known or conventional storyline and put a twist on it. Narrative, writes Herman, involves "disruption of an initial state of equilibrium by an unanticipated and often untoward event or chain of events" (Herman 2007, 83). Polletta, who points out that social movements are more properly analyzed using narratives, not frames, discusses many movements that celebrate deviance as part of their identity (Polletta 1998). In our case studies, we see narratives taking unexpected twists and turns. For instance, the construction of the border wall that would seem to be such a barrier to free movement of people and wildlife becomes the vehicle through which resources become available and a rallying point for opposition.

The unexpected and nonconventional can make for a page-turner of a novel; otherwise, if a story were completely conventional, why bother turning the page? Similarly, we were attracted to the cases later discussed because each of these networks exists in contradiction to the conventional. These networks of practice discovered new ways of doing things, which interests us because of their novelty, but also because we are impressed by how their members are able to maintain these movements in opposition to the more accepted way of doing things. In a way, as a literary critic might seek to explain what makes a novel special and enduring, we seek to understand what makes a network exist in defiance of the conventional. It may be those nonconventional aspects of it that help it endure, since the nonconventional draws those who may be disenchanted with the conventional. It is also in these nonconventional stories or movements that learning occurs. We seek innovative ways of knowing and doing that might bring new solutions to persistently wicked problems.

Good authors can give their stories a dramatic sense of movement by using oppositions to move it along. Barthes, in his analysis of Honoré de Balzac's story "Sarrazine," showed how effective use of antithetical pairs of images build up dramatic tension in a story (Barthes 1974). For example, pairing cold and warm in the same scene lends a sense of transgression, a breach of convention, that drives the story onward and begs resolution. In the cases we studied, part of the drama (and deeper meaning) of the movement arises from tensions with the conventional mode of doing things. Alternative farmers, for example, frequently portray their ideas about soil not only as different from conventional ideas about soil fertility, but in fact more scientific than mainstream practice.

The emplotment of a story can highlight departures from convention. The story of the Cold War is made even more compelling by the unexpected, somewhat inexplicable, opening up of the Soviet Union (glasnost) and the emergence of an individual (Gorbachev) who broke the mold of the stereotypical apparatchik. And, of course, the wide-scale breakup of the Eastern Bloc that followed was so unexpected and improbable that it is often described as a revolution.

Why one network sustains itself over time while others do not, or why one network effects change when others are ineffectual, means that that particular group of people is somehow doing something differently. One way to learn about these is by accessing the narratives the group tells about itself and looking for these interesting turns in the story.

Hermeneutics: Context and Gap

To understand a text of any kind, including a written or unwritten narrative, it is important to relate it to other elements outside itself. This twofold operation, most often likened to a circle, is the art of hermeneu-

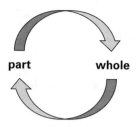

Figure 3.1
Hermeneutic circle

tics or textual interpretation. The hermeneutic circle derives from Gadamer (1975) but was most fully developed by Ricoeur (1981a). In the latter's description, classic analysis involves explanation, which is sitting down with just the text and explaining what it says and how it says it. But texts are never self-contained. Rather, they refer to other texts, which in turn refer to other texts (whether literary or not). They also refer to social and historical circumstances that surround it. Ricoeur refers to the second operation as understanding, which is to interpret the text in relation to the context around it. Figure 3.1 illustrates the hermeneutic circle.

As shown on the right-hand side of the figure, different variations on the hermeneutic circle are possible. It can be treated as the analytic that relates a part (or text) in and by itself, then relates it to a larger whole (or context). The narrative of a group can also be related to other narratives and the entire external reality surrounding it. The point is that deep understanding is necessarily interpretive. What Geertz (1973) called the *thick description* of social phenomena simply means being able to understand it in depth, respecting the complexity of the phenomenon, and not simply relegating the analysis to immediately evident factual observations about a network.

Ricoeur (1976), incorporating an original notion of Frege (1948), talks of the hermeneutic as relating the sense of a narrative to its reference. Sense, in this case, is what we read from the narrative taken in its semantic autonomy. It is here where we analyze the structure, literary devices, and ostensive meanings of the narrative. Reference, on the other hand, involves going outside the text and relating it to the larger discourse or field of institutional life in which it is embedded, what Billig (1996) referred to as examining the rhetoric of a story. The latter includes other texts, history, traditions, and arguments that affect how we understand the primary narrative. Barthes (1974) makes a similar distinction between analyzing elements lying entirely within a text, what he calls a horizontal operation, and analyzing elements that point us outside the text, a vertical operation. An example of the latter is seen in symbolic codes that act like indices to other stories or conditions that inform the text at hand. Allusions and metaphors are classic forms of such codes. In 2009, opponents of climate change science pounced on email, leaked from researchers at the University of East Anglia, which seemed to suggest a selective use of atmospheric data. These critics used the term "Climategate" to describe the situation, a direct allusion to the Watergate scandal of the 1970s that brought down the Nixon administration. Nehrlich (2010) discusses how other allusions, appealing to both science and religion, were used in the social construction of Climategate.

The relationship between part and whole can also be applied to understanding how the local relates to the nonlocal. In each of the case studies, we find a local program that exists sometimes in defiance of a larger political or social reality. We seek to understand this relationship, or hermeneutic, between the local and the general. This means analyzing case studies to determine how the local meanings that evolve in these places, and how these meanings depart from or cohere with more broadly established meanings. Contextualization is especially important for us, and we pay close attention to the localized and special modes of reasoning or ethical motivations that we find in each case. This has to do with motivations that underpin why these local actors keep to the task, and what special meanings the place and its ecology has for them. To the extent that these are differentiated from more conventional or broader rationalities, we better understand what is special about these localized networks and, perhaps, what sustains them even in the face of sometimes discouraging events. So, the first element of the hermeneutic that we seek is context (i.e., the highly contextualized motivations, reasonings, and meanings).

In relating the part of the local to the whole, actors also select what elements of the whole (which we will sometimes refer to as the conventional narrative) seem relevant to them and leave out those that do not. As important to what is linked, revealed, and described in the plot, is what is left out. These narrative gaps are crucial for emplotment because, otherwise, all we would have would be a jumbled assortment of events and actors. It is the selective inclusion and exclusion of elements that gives a story narrative force but also reveals coping strategies of network members.

In this exercise, narrative gaps are crucial, which is important to our work on narratives and networks. Literally, a network cannot contain everyone if it is to work out a narrative—that is, a story of everything appealing to everyone is not meaningful. As large and as comprehensive as the IPCC is, it cannot contain all the atmospheric experts in the world, especially some notable skeptics. Literally, these absences allow the IPCC to function. Likewise, its grand narrative of climate change does not contain all the possibly relevant storylines. People leave out of their narrative those possibilities, details, claims, and subplots that run counter to their cause and cloud the points they want to make or do not know how to cope with. An environmental non-governmental organization (NGO) that is most interested in pursuing carbon mitigation might not include, in its narrative, the possibility that volcanic gases partly contribute to climate change.

Lest the reader suppose that we subscribe to a wholly constructionist notion of narrative, we do not understand the selective use of gaps and presences in narrative to be akin to spin-doctoring or strategic fictionalizing. Not at all. Narrative operations are needed to represent what people recognize and experience as true conditions. Even scientific communication requires that some details, alternative theories, and confusing data be left out of an account. People make sense of complex reality by focusing on what is essential to understand the reality before them. A narrator, trying to capture her experience or situation fashions a story that reflects her strategy for creating a compelling and convincing account and will leave out what she sees as irrelevant or confusing to the reader's understanding. This is different from the narrator who consciously biases the account to convey something other than what he experiences or knows as true, although this, too, is narration (though one geared toward deception).

We pay close attention to the highly contextual meanings that evolve in place. This includes local knowledge and everyday ways of doing. Our task is to uncover not simply that conservationists have a commitment to the environment, but to answer the question, what is it about this specific environment that speaks to each of them in different and often personal ways? A particular interest of ours is the hermeneutic between these local stores of knowledge and a more generalized, scientific body of knowledge and practice. At times, this takes the form of experiential knowledge, in contrast to scientific knowledge. When someone stands up at a public hearing and talks about the difficulties the community has been having with the current drought and the need to plan for a changing climate, that is local knowledge. Local knowledge can sometimes combine affect, beliefs, as well as science. The criticism of local knowledge is precisely that it can differ from the general body of scientific knowledge. The speaker at the public hearing may be told that, scientifically, there is no way to prove that the current drought is due to climate change and, so, his opinion is just factually wrong. For us, it is not as simple as this. First, whether the causal link can be shown or not, the speaker is correctly judging how climate change, decades from now, might be experienced. Moreover, pronouncements of hope, fear, moral outrage, preference, and others constitute important knowledge about what the community experiences. Contextualized knowledge can be a rich combination of all these modes of knowing, and narrative can be an effective vehicle for transmitting such knowledge. The speaker is talking about the kind of knowledge that matters to people. By accessing this knowledge, we gain a better understanding of what moves people.

There is another, more material sense in which the narrative-networks we describe are best understood in hermeneutic fashion. In describing elements of narrative that we can look for in narrative-networks, we have shied away from the obvious question, how does one construct a good narrative-network? Or, in agonistic terms, how does one write a storyline that is sure to win the policy game? This is beyond us, at this point, and it will suffice to simply describe elements of narrative to look for in describing networks, without spelling out how they are optimally employed. The notion of the "best narrative" is problematic, to begin with, because there is an alchemy that has to happen at a specific time and place for the narrative, and its network, to take hold. One reason, we suppose, is related to the fact that one can conceivably read all the how-to books on writing and yet not have the ability to write a good novel. But, more crucially, a narrative for a new movement cannot simply be constructed out of thin air. It is not simply weaving a good story. Rather, the story has to resonate with the persons who would be emplotted by it. The story has to be authentic and has to reflect the everyday contexts and experiences of each of these persons. This is symbolized in figure 3.2 (variations of which appear in Lejano 2006 and Lejano and Shankar 2012).

Figure 3.2 depicts the narrative network as a hermeneutic. It is not simply the storyline that the "authors" of a movement constructed, but also the action of context, which in this case includes subsequent members of the network, the place, and other institutions, that modifies the narrative-network and refines it. Without the modifying action of

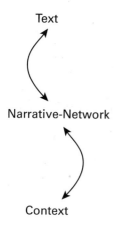

Text

Narrative-Network

Context

Figure 3.2
Narrative-network as hermeneutic

context, including actions of people who do not join the network, the storyline may not reflect the conditions and motivations of people who maintain the network. An example of this is found in Lejano and Ocampo-Salvador 2006, which describes the narrative of a fishers' group that expanded to include the perspectives and interests of rich recreational enthusiasts. The figure reminds us of the need for the narrative-network to be a writerly text, one that allows subsequent members to share in the process of re-narrating the story (Barthes 1974). Narratives have to be told and retold to keep the institution and its shared knowledge alive, and in this process of narration, all members of the community participate (Lyotard 1979). Last, the figure also speaks to the point that we cannot write about what it takes for one to construct a "winning narrative." Narrative becomes a network only if it takes root in a place and in a community, and there are no universals for writing a good network story. To put it another way, text cannot simply be imposed upon a community, it also has to be co-constructed by and from community. Members of the network have to begin living the narrative and, in so doing, they help author and reauthor it. The narrative may need to be coherent with the history of the place and the people it emplots, as the latter understand it.

There is yet another way in which the narrative-network is constituted as a hermeneutic, and that is through the relationship of a text with other texts. When a community takes on a story about its collective aspirations, this merges into a context rich with already existing narratives. When someone joins a network, she brings her own narratives to it. In this sense, if we refer to a narrative as a text, then it necessarily has to find a relationship with other narrative texts. As an example, Lejano and Leong (2012) show how resistance to a water supply project stemmed not just from the negative imagery that the public and the press constructed about the project but also from long-standing stories of the public's disenchantment with the responsible agencies.

We now have a framework for narrative analysis, which consists of evaluating the use of the following narrative elements or devices:

- emplotment
- characterization
- alterity
- breach of convention
- context and gap

Though we do not necessarily analyze these elements in the same sequence, this framework will be used for all three case studies. Figure 3.3 is a convenient mnemonic for describing and encapsulating our narrative analytic framework. In constructing it, we remind the reader that

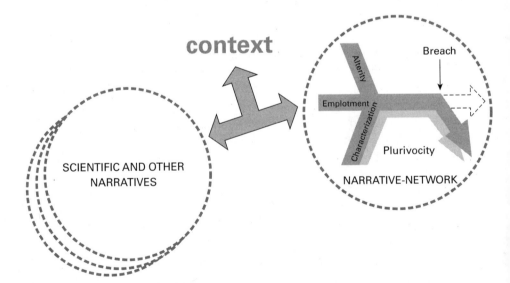

Figure 3.3
Schematic of narrative analysis framework

we have been selective in choosing just some of the elements that narrative scholars use in analysis, and the figure depicts only those that we have found useful for our work.

A Note on Narrative Nomenclature

It will have become apparent, by now, that there is much overlap in the terms that we and other scholars use when talking about narratives. This is unavoidable, because these terms do overlap in meaning and use. For clarity's sake, we will fix the meanings of some of the terms over the remainder of the book. Table 3.1 can be used as a reference. We remind

Table 3.1
Narrative nomenclature used in this book

Individual narrative	Stories and accounts as recounted to us by individuals, most precisely presented using transcripts of their actual words.
Metanarrative	Narratives that are not just individual but shared across individuals. A more specific interpretation is that larger or overall narrative that unites and reconciles differing individual narratives.
Fabula	Narratives that are common to the storylines found in individual narratives. Unlike the metanarrative, which is found in narrators' accounts, the fabula is reconstructed by the analyst and is found wholly only in the reconstruction.
Master or grand narrative	Narratives that provide a worldview; often, hegemonic narratives that are widely adopted in a society. Examples are the depiction of nature as wild and technology as ordering.
Subnarratives	Elements of the metanarrative, but not the whole. Subnarratives can be shared but are only an aspect of the metanarrative.
Counternarrative	Narratives that exist in opposition or as an alternative to master narratives. An example is the idea of capitalism as colonialism, as opposed to the grand narrative that equates capitalism with freedom.
Elemental or mythical narratives	Universal stories that, in their most basic form, can be seen to underpin subsequent narratives, whether individual or grand narrative. An example is the myth of violation of the idyllic, which underlies ecological conservation narratives, children's stories like "Beauty and the Beast," etc.

the reader, however, that these conventions should not be taken as definitive—the authors, like other scholars, in fact, employ these same terms in different ways in other works. Table 3.1 provides working definitions of a number of terms that we will use throughout the book. And the term *narrative* encompasses all of these.

Some examples will be helpful. Propp (1968), in his analysis of the deep (or elemental) structures of folktales, found across all cultures, identified some basic recurring themes. For example, one prototypical theme is the hero wandering far away from home, encountering challenges, and then returning home in triumph. We will use the term *elemental* or *mythical narrative* to refer to these basic plots that can be seen to support and provide universal salience to specific narratives. Corresponding to these deep structures are deeper understandings of character. So being, while the common use of the word *actor* is that of the specific character appearing in a particular narrative, the term *actant* is most often used to refer to the more basic role that the character plays—the elemental or structural function. So, while an industrial polluter might be a character in a story, the same might be thought of as an actant that fills the structural role of the aggressor in the elemental plotline.

A grand narrative, or master narrative as we use it here, is not an elemental story, but a particular, fully specified narrative, but one that is shared so widely across a society or a period that it can often be thought of as hegemonic. For example, the master narrative of the American West is one of unlimited progress and the American spirit for expansion (Merchant 2007). It is the idea of American pioneering, always able to achieve new conquests when encountering an obstacle. When the population time bomb (Ehrlich 1968) was current in the media back in the 1960s and 1970s (and it is gaining currency today), the master narrative of American progress was used to argue instead that innovation and the pioneering spirit (and a Schumpeterian belief in industry) would find solutions when they became necessary. Now, countering such a grand narrative is, inevitably, a counternarrative—for instance, Cronon's alternative history of the American West as progressive ecological and cultural decline (Cronon 1996).

For the authors, what we refer to as an individual narrative is, simply, the story told to us by an individual narrator. These are most faithfully presented in the narrator's actual words. At times, because transcripts can be very long and hard to read, we will either strategically select certain verbatim passages or just summarize the entire text. But whether verbatim or in summary, what we would present is a story that is ostensibly found in what was recounted by the individual.

When we examine a group of individual narratives, however, we invariably encounter differences in the particular stories told, or sometimes, outright contradiction. A metanarrative is thought to be a secondary or subsequent narrative that reconciles these individual differences (Schön and Rein 1994). The metanarrative is thought to be something that the individuals can find themselves in agreement over. Sometimes, the metanarrative can be a schema that includes all the points that are in common across individual narratives, and that leaves out those points over which they clash—in this case, the individuals would agree on such common ground. For example, a story about a common foe can be a basic common denominator—in this instance, community and open-space advocates rallying around an anti-industry position (Lejano and Wessells 2006). Sometimes, a metanarrative can be an acceptable compromise position. At other times, a metanarrative is thought to be a new story that reconciles differences among individuals by appealing to a higher narrative that trumps these individual differences, such as the story about saving the country from the great depression of 2008, which was used to unite budget deficit hawks and Keynesian interventionists around the TARP (Troubled Asset Relief Program). Similarly, a subnarrative, which may also be shared across actors, comprises partial elements of the metanarrative. As an example, if the metanarrative around which a network coalesces involves saving desert wilderness, then a subnarrative might be the subset of actors whose main specific concern is bringing back the pronghorns.

The metanarrative is a story that individual narrators can or do find themselves telling. In contrast, the fabula is an analytical construction. The fabula is the analyst's reconstruction of a common story or plotline that underlies each of the individual narratives. However, the fabula might not actually have been found whole, or actually told by any single narrator. Each narrator may have provided bits and pieces of the larger narrative, and it is the analyst's task to reconstruct the whole. It may require interpretation on the part of the analyst, and the individual narrators may not actually be conscious of the larger narrative or fabula (though, when informed of it, an individual might actually agree with the interpretation).

But this says much about the agency of the analyst, who is not simply a transcriber of things narrated. The notion of a fabula, which the analyst constructs or reconstructs, should not be so elusive a concept. The characters in a novel may not all be written as being aware of the whole story, which the author and reader do know. Similarly, the fabula may exist, in its entirety, only in the construction of the analyst and, always, there is an act of interpretation involved. Even the most bare narrative account requires interpretation on the part of the hearer.

Applying the Narrative-Network Framework

In this chapter and in chapter 2, we have argued that the power of network analysis can be considerably enhanced through the integration of ideas and analytics from narrative analysis. As we move on to the case studies, we remind ourselves of what we hope to gain through the application of narrative-network analysis:

• to more deeply understand how members of a network use narrative to bind (or emplot) themselves into a collective,

• to study how narratives construct and maintain a distinction between the group and the more conventional, dominant, or hegemonic status quo,

• to discover how narratives are used to differently characterize nonhuman actors, reflecting emergent relationships with nonhuman actors, giving them "voice" in public processes, and perhaps suggesting new ways of coexistence with other species,

• to learn how narratives are used to capture, integrate, store, and transmit different kinds of knowledge (scientific, cultural, ethical, experiential, etc.).

4

Narrative, Network, and Conservation on the Arizona-Sonora Border

Introduction

Nearly a hundred, primarily young researchers gathered in April 2012 at the Arizona-Sonora Desert Museum, set in a saguaro forest among volcanic peaks west of Tucson. Their interests were varied, including everything from the middens of pack rats to the language of the Seri Indians. They called themselves The Next Generation Sonoran Desert Researchers (http://nextgensd.com/), and the purpose of their three-day meeting conducted in Spanish and English (with about equal representation of native speakers of each) was to renew face-to-face transborder contacts that existed so strongly thirty years ago and are today being threatened by security barriers and narcotics trafficking violence (Beal 2012). While unified against these common threats that restrict access to research sites, members were attracted by a more positive vision of the Sonoran Desert as a special place. As one local journalist wrote about the meeting, "I listened as a geologist explained to a botanist what clues a hypothetical gold prospector might look for in the rocks before beginning any sampling or exploration. I was regaled with stories of Palma de la Virgen (palm of the Virgin, or *Dioon edule* to botanists)—a beautiful and once prolific plant that fed the dinosaurs more than 65 million years ago and continues to grow in pockets in Sonora. In short, I had my love for natural and cultural history reawakened. I was reminded that every species has a story, and in the desert, many of those stories are dramatic and fascinating" (Hoekenga 2012). This chapter is about the power of shared narrative to forge and sustain network ties in the Arizona-Sonora border desert region.

The Arizona-Sonora border region is an ecologically rare and fragile landscape of desert, freshwater, and marine ecosystems that is increasingly threatened (Felger and Broyles 2007, xi). Iconic cacti such as the saguaro and the organ pipe are famous, but their habitat is far from secure (figure 4.1). A confluence of influences along the border between the U.S. state of Arizona and the Mexican state of Sonora drive change that is mainly negative from environmental and binational cultural perspectives: a Sunbelt growth machine including new residents with little sense of border history or culture; climate change–driven aridity and over-exploitation of water resources; riparian habitat reduction and destruction; species threatened, endangered, and gone extinct; generations-old cross-border migration patterns of native peoples broken up; and environmentally damaging fences, walls, and towers erected. Such transformations call out for collaborative action. Yet, the possibility of formal governmental cooperation would seem to dim in the face of contemporary concern over security and sealing the border against illegal immigration that is strong everywhere, but particularly in U.S. border states. Anti-immigrant sentiment expressed in Arizona state law, partially upheld by the U.S. Supreme Court and which allows law enforcement officers to ask about immigration status, jeopardizes the cordiality of official discourse between Arizona and its southern neighbor state, Sonora, Mexico.

Yet, surprising headway is being made in terms of ecological protection, despite mounting pressures and poor collaborative atmosphere. Among hopeful signs, cross-boundary network efforts have secured water resources to protect the Cienega de Santa Clara in the Colorado River estuary. A reserve has been established with help of U.S. and Mexican actors to protect the jaguar. Native endangered fishes are recovering in the Santa Cruz largely due to the efforts of voluntary water monitors. Historic wetlands are being restored in the Yuma Crossing National Heritage Area (Laird Benner and Ingram 2011).

The goals of this chapter are to establish the applicability and usefulness of the narrative analysis framework introduced in chapter 3 and to show that networked relationships, such as those reflected in the Next Generation meeting and heavily reinforced by narratives, have operated to sustain and increase protection of the border environment in the face of a host of unfavorable forces. After describing the physical and social context, the chapter will detail our method of collecting data about and documenting the network of environmental activists working toward the protection of the Sonoran Desert region. A shared narrative binds the network together, and we employ the framework for narrative analysis to examine the way in which emplotment, characterization, alterity, breach, and context weave a common story. A mutual story or fabula of

Figure 4.1
Sonoran Desert cacti (with permission from Gwynn Laird Benner)

"homecoming" provides acceptance, energy, and perseverance that allow the network to persist and even prosper in the face of apparent adversity. The roles of human and nonhuman characters as they guide the story are examined together with the way in which many voices blend into collective themes. Along a divisive border where people with different national, racial, economic, and ideological backgrounds coexist, alterity or the way the "other" is portrayed can present real challenges to sustained interaction. The chapter examines how benign portrayals of the "other" soften identity conflicts. Even science is made part of the restoration of "home" story since the process of knowledge creation is linked to forging relationships for action. Surprising twists or breaches in the storyline are created as serious impediments to the notion of a common home place, such as the border wall, become points of resistance and opportunities for collaborative research rather than the impermeable barriers probably intended. Not everything important to the existing context becomes part of the fabula however, and some things like the border violence and trash that are central to the hegemonic master or grand narrative are generally underplayed or ignored. Only by turning a blind eye to certain things can the narrative-network project its positive and unifying themes. The chapter concludes with some reflections on what narrative-networks mean for democracy and governance, and what narrative analysis adds to other perspectives.

The Setting: A Place of Contrasts

The physical and social characteristics of the U.S.-Mexico border are so various and divergent that they can supply support for a wide variety of different perspectives and narratives. It is at once a place of riches and opportunity and long-standing poverty. Fortunes have been made in real estate in the growing urban areas like Tucson and retirement communities like Rio Rico. At the same time, border counties are plagued by unemployment and low wages, especially among clusters of rural Hispanics and indigenous peoples (Brown and Ingram 1987; Ingram, Milich, and Varady 1995). A swelling of undocumented migration along this segment of the border caused by a concentration of enforcement in California and Texas that funneled migrants into the Sonoran Desert is associated with increasing deaths due to exposure and dehydration. Yet, twin cities of Nogales, Arizona, and Nogales, Sonora, boast of a mutual sharing of emergency services (Ingram, Laney, and Gillilan 1995; Ingram, Milich, and Varady 1995), and binational, bilingual families have regu-

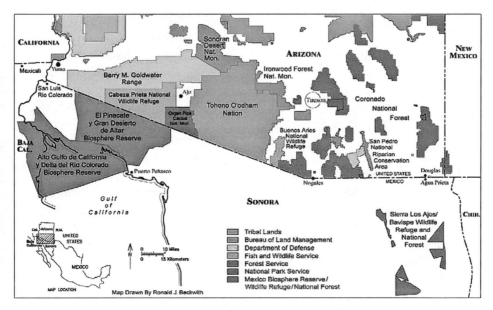

Figure 4.2
Protected federal and tribal lands in the Arizona-Sonora border region (*Source:* Laird Benner and Ingram 2011)

larly and easily moved back and forth across the border (Martinez 1988). Many such families can trace their lineage back many generations to when the area was under Mexican and Spanish dominion. In contrast, the area attracts both snowbirds and retirees who have no roots in the area.

That natural endowment of the area is both scant and plentiful. Very little rain falls on the Sonoran Desert. Yet, the Sea of Cortez (Gulf of California) is rich in biological diversity and supports enormously productive fisheries. The area contains large numbers of reserves and protected areas (see figure 4.2). Even so, fifty-six endangered and threatened species in Arizona continue to struggle—many, like the pronghorn, jaguar, pupfish, and Yuma Clapper Rail, with habitats that cross the border.

Tracing Network Ties

This case study is substantially based on interviews completed in 2010 with Wendy (Gwynn) Laird Benner of forty-seven individuals, from the

United States, Mexico, and Tohono O'odham Nation, who are engaged in one way or another in the pursuit of environmental quality or cultural preservation in the Arizona-Sonora border region. Individuals were identified through a variety of sources: lists of attendees at conferences, newspaper and journal reports of key actors, and main informants' identification of others involved and influential in the region. A diverse group of forty-seven individuals with varying backgrounds were interviewed. Forty-one of these actors have been involved in the area for twenty years or more. Twenty-one are currently affiliated with a variety of non-governmental organizations, fourteen are from academia, and eleven are government agency officials (three of whom have now retired). It must be noted that while these actors have remained focused throughout most of their careers on a given broad topic or geographic region, they have moved among academic, NGO, foundation, and government positions, sometimes working within several settings over the course of their careers (Laird Benner and Ingram 2011).

Our interviews lasted about an hour and were recorded and transcribed. We asked a common set of questions, inviting open-ended responses with follow-up questions. We also probed interviewees to describe their first encounter with borderlands ecology/cultural preservation and who first influenced them during these early years.

We employed network analysis to create figure 2.1, which portrays rather thinly connected relationships among those we interviewed based on one individual mentioning others and others mentioning that individual, but shows five or six people as thickly connected. Figure 4.3 extends the network analysis further by including all of the people identified by those we interviewed as important or influential to their own perspectives and work whether or not they were among those we interviewed. In this analysis, in contrast to figure 2.1, the arrows in figure 4.3 go only one way.[1] The resulting network identifies a central corps of people interwoven with each other (larger dots) and also connected by shared associations to the commonly identified individuals (larger squares) more clearly than figure 2.1 does. While these are one-direction relationships, a degree of bonding may be implied on the basis of direct and indirect connections. The logic is "a friend of a friend is a friend." According to sociologist Carol Heimer (1992), things get done in networks because there is a particular obligation to others in the network and a sensitivity to what others need, feel, and believe.

At the same time, the larger numbers of smaller squares, indicating people selected by only one person we interviewed, show that network

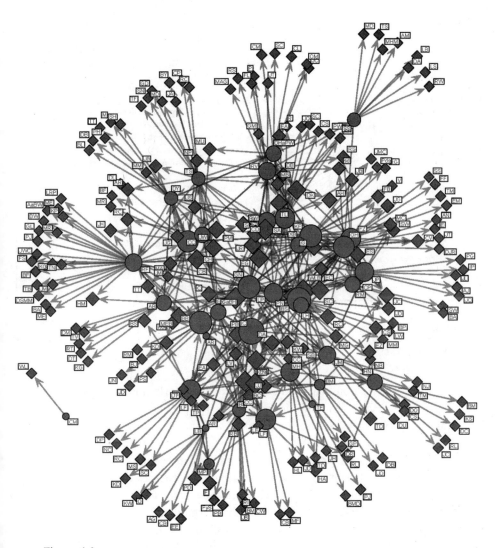

Figure 4.3
Sonoran Desert conservation network ties depict choices of network members
of others as important to them in their work. The dots are people we interviewed.
The squares signify persons identified as significant who were not interviewed.
Size of dots and squares are in proportion to numbers of nominations.

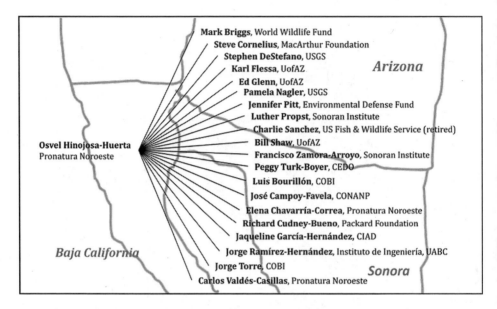

Figure 4.4
Transborder network of Osvel Hinojosa-Huerta (*Source:* Laird Benner and Ingram 2011)

members have a number of outside the core network links. Such associations may serve as bridging ties to specific people, arenas or venues. For instance, data collected from an interview with Osvel Hinojosa-Huerta, employed by a Mexican NGO, Pronatura Oeste, is portrayed in figure 4.4. Hinojosa-Huerta shows up as one of the larger dots designated OH in the figure 4.3. The line drawing in figure 4.4 focuses on the network of Hinojosa-Huerta alone and illustrates each of the twenty actors Hinojosa-Huerta mentioned as important in forging his career and in his current conservation work in the Upper Gulf of California.

Figure 4.4 indicates those individuals from either side of the border (the top half is U.S.-based and the bottom half, Mexico-based). It is notable that Hinojosa-Huerta's ties include as many actors situated in the United States as in Mexico. Some of these individuals are U.S. citizens who head Mexican organizations, while others are Mexican nationals who are now working in U.S. organizations, attesting to the way in which the network bridges international divides.

Seventeen of the twenty relationships Hinojosa-Huerta mentioned are long-standing, extending back to his undergraduate and graduate school days working and researching Upper Gulf conservation issues. These associations, he noted during the interview, have continued despite these individuals having transferred to different positions, having moved to other organizations, or having chosen to study across the border (in either the United States or Mexico). Seventeen of the twenty remain key players today in Upper Gulf/Delta conservation, with two moving and shifting their work focus and one retiring.

While the network analysis assures us that a network of interrelationships among Sonoran Desert conservationists exists, and tells us something of its structure, other issues are not explored. We do not yet know what impulse causes actors to reach out and associate with one another, or how robust and resilient these connections may be. We do not know what role nonhuman actors play in the network. To address such questions, we turn to narrative analysis.

Border Environmental Activists' Narratives

Narrative analysis of what border activists say and which works they cite in the course of the interview adds substantial understanding of the content of the ties that bring people together in working relationships. Narrative analysis involved listening to recorded interviews multiple times in order to identify emplotment, characterizations, and other components of narratives discussed in the last chapter. In addition to interviews, data includes books, reports, web sites, and other information mentioned as significant by interviewees.[2] Such literature includes essays, photography with commentary, and edited volumes of scientific and professional papers. In the section that follows, we apply the framework for narrative analysis set out in the last chapter to responses to questions about how activists got involved in conservation efforts, who they worked with, and what influenced their endeavors. A fuller picture emerges that better explains the network longevity, persistence, and success even under difficult circumstances.

Emplotment

The Arizona-Sonora conservation network has managed to persist and make some headway in a time of adversity largely because of a shared homecoming metanarrative as universal as Homer's *Odyssey*. The story includes the struggle to recover and restore what has been lost. The common metanarrative that unifies the Sonoran Desert conservation network revolves around home in the sense of the place of belonging, including locating home, displacement from home, returning home, and defending home. For Anglos, Native Americans, and Mexicans who consider the Sonoran Desert a home place, it is a matter of magnetic attraction, a force that is impossible to resist.

One anthropologist/activist who has written widely, mentored many students, and served on committees to conserve the Sonoran Desert stated: "As a student at Prescott College, I went to a fiesta in Magdelena. It was just like falling in love. I was infatuated with how things looked, smelled, sounded. After that, whenever I could, I headed South." A federal agency employee who has documented historical and cultural resources on federally managed borderlands observed: "I was one of those people passing through, and when I drove over to Organ Pipe the first time. . . . I got into the monument and I just had this overwhelming feeling that I had come home and I've never left." A writer and naturalist who raised a family on forty acres outside Tucson, and is frequently referenced by others in the network observed in print: "A home is not just a house; it is the natural world around it, and with both his feet well rooted in this a child can look out with confidence to the world of man. Each of them will have its proper measure and proportion. Our home is the desert, and from it will come identity, solace and, yes, Joy, above all, Joy" (Woodin 1984, 247). The director of an important border NGO reflected: "I got here because I was driving down Highway 85 and fell in love with the desert when I saw Crater Ranch, and so I bought a house [in Ajo] the same day." A leading biological authority with more than half a century experience in the region commented about his initiation: "I quickly realized that University of Arizona was geographically the closest to the good stuff and there was plenty of good stuff even here around Tucson. I remember coming here, driving all night to get to University of Arizona registering and that very same day hightailing down to the Sonoran Desert. I kind of thought I was in heaven, and then every so often I had to go to classes."

Home is all of a piece—including animate and inanimate objects, culture as well as nature, economic well-being as well as environmental quality—and transcends political boundaries. Home in this sense is an ecological metanarrative, where everything pertaining to home is inter-related. The metanarrative weaves together human and nonhuman physical and cultural assets that generate and perpetuate commitment. At the same time, the specialness of what is interconnected is extraordinary and worth preserving. Several quotations from interviews and written documents are illustrative:

It is about the environment shared by both countries [U.S. and Mexico] it is about nature, wildlife, ecosystems, and protected natural areas along the border. It is also about ecological connections that drive processes from deep inside each country—such as the nectar-feeding bats that follow the flowering of the giant columnar cacti from Oaxaca to Arizona, the hummingbirds that track the flowers of the ocotillos and the agaves along the slopes of the Sierra Madre, and the river-driven dynamics of the Colorado River Delta. But it is also significantly about the hopes, anxieties, and expectations of human beings who work every day to protect our shared environment. (Ezcurra 2009, xiii)

We talk of the American Southwest and Northern Mexico as this sort of mythical areas full of wonderful places that have magnetic force that pulls you, has enormous open spaces that you do not see in North America any more that makes the place so appealing.

Some places are like touchstones for your soul. The Pinecates are like a giant Zen garden with black lava flows, red cinder cones, white dunes, and splashes of wildflower color. It just really spoke to me.

[The Pinacates] fascinated me more on a kind of aesthetic point of view as much as anything else . . . and it was just a combination that I liked, and other people have said this that from an archeological point of view, everything is visible. It is out there on the ground and the desert is clean, visible and there is a kind of beautiful order to it that I have always been intrigued by. There is a combination of alien, and clean, and you can see the horizon. There is something immediately visceral in nature creating the circular forms of the *tinejas* (natural water tanks).

Not all respondents portray the specialness of the border as beauty, even though nature as Eden is a common environmental grand narrative (Cronon 1996). The juxtaposition of physical attractiveness and discomfort is a key aspect of the emplotment. Frequently people we interviewed admitted that the Sonoran Desert is not for everyone because of punishing summer temperatures and a lack of freshwater, but indicated that the harsh and dramatic landscape is haunting and gets into one's blood and requires a certain emblematic toughness and persistence. For example, several people we interviewed wrote elsewhere:

Even though I did not know it yet, the desert was twisting inside me like a catclaw. (Sheridan 1998, 14)

I came for the first time to the Sierra del Pinacate in August 1980. . . . It was a hot, dry unwelcoming summer. Daytime temperatures were above 50C (122F) . . . . I did not like the place. I found it to be dry, dusty, unfriendly, and dangerous desert, and I returned to Mexico City as soon as I could. My spirit, however, was burning not from the heat of the August sun, but from the fire of nostalgia for the wide, open wilderness. Like a moth subdued by the dangerous light of a flowing fire, a month later I was back in the great desert, El Gran Desierto del Alto. Since then, I have never ceased to return. Swearing and mumbling against heat and drought, I was unwittingly seduced by this wonderful land. (Ezcurra 2007, xi)

Another federal land manager recalled in his interview with us: "I remember popping the cap from a soft drink and telling a friend, I would never live in a hell-hole like this. Ten years later I am still here."

Threats to and loss of home are a part of the plot, although interpreted differently by different people. Repeatedly those we interviewed referred to losses of valued objects including species such as the pronghorn and jaguars and cultural artifacts like native seeds and foodstuffs that once were common. Another important juxtaposition in the plot is that of rich and varied past with a degraded present. For instance, a leader of an influential NGO remarked that the Delta of the Colorado River today has about the same conservation value as a tile floor. He observed: "The Colorado River Delta is probably the most degraded nonurban place in North America, particularly if you look at it today and what it was one hundred years ago."

He contrasted this low-value area with what Aldo Leopold wrote about in *The Sand County Almanac*. He said, "It makes you cry to read what he saw and to see what it is today." Leopold recalled in his writing a trip taken with his brother to the mouth of the Colorado River in 1922:

Dawn on the Delta was whistled in by Gambel quail, which roosted in the mesquites overhanging camp. When the sun peeped over the Sierra Madre, it slanted across a hundred miles of lovely desolation, a vast flat bowl of wilderness rimmed by jagged peaks. On the map, the Delta was bisected by the river, but in fact the river was nowhere and everywhere, for he could not decide which of a hundred green lagoons offered the most pleasant and least speedy path to the Gulf. So, he traveled them all, and so did we. He divided and rejoined, he twisted and turned, he meandered in awesome jungles, he all but ran in circles, he dallied with lovely groves, he got lost and was glad of it, and so were we. For a last word in procrastination, go travel with a river reluctant to lose his freedom to the sea. (Leopold 1962, 141)

Even for physical scientists who could be expected to see the area in dry, laboratory terms, there are expressions of emotional attachments of belonging and a kind of wistfulness about what has been lost.

I asked a colleague of mine here in the department who had just gotten her pilot's license to fly us over the Colorado River Delta and my jaw just dropped. From a geologic perspective it was just a fabulous place. Then I drove down with a graduate student in a Chevy Suburban, getting stuck a couple of times, and hiring a boat. Whole beaches were made of shells of species no longer living in the gulf.

I had one of those duh (as apposed to ah-ha) moments when I recognized that there had been no fresh water flowing through this part of the Delta since the building of the dams. So, we could measure how the Delta was biologically before the dams were built and what had been lost.

Plurivocity or Many Voices

Many voices and subplots exist within the border environmental network, in most important respects telling the same story. As one remarked, "There are people who care about resources who just happen to be on different sides of the border." A U.S. Fish and Wildlife Agency official attached to an organization entitled Sonoran Joint Ventures explained:

We have a wide variety of partners on both sides of the border. Our management board it's made up of representatives from [the] U.S. and Mexico and we alternate our meetings in [the] U.S. and Mexico and they hold the same responsibility in determining the direction of the program and how we spend the money and all our working committees that we have also are binational, have equal representation in [the] U.S. and Mexico and again they alternate between [the] U.S. and Mexico and there's an equality there of both countries determining the priorities of the program and how money are spent in order to address those priorities and so the very unique thing about the Sonoran Joint Venture is it's truly binational.

Most of those interviewed expressed close intellectual and emotional ties with people on the other side of the international boundary. A mutual respect clearly prevails. One prominent Mexican scientist explained:

I have always had face-to-face ties for forty years. Over time, we have started working in more equal relationships. When I first returned to [the] desert, I started reestablishing links to A.S.U. [Arizona State University] and U. of A. [University of Arizona]. Most ecological research then was done in U.S., and if in Mexico, not in Sonora. As I was among the first scientists of environmental era coming from the Sonoran Desert, I got extraordinary support from American colleagues—others ignored us. Without support of people from U.S. institutions, it would have been difficult to work in Sonora. Richard Felger, Larry Venable (from U. of A.), and Paul Martin were very influential. Ray Turner—I did fieldwork with him. Dr. Mink at A.S.U. . . . just meeting and talking [with him] provided inspiration. I learned so much from Paul Martin on a trip to Alamos. Martin was able to change or steer perspectives of young scientists.

One of the collaborators from the United States expressed much the same sentiment: "I would say among people working [in the] Sonoran Desert today, I don't see any difference between the people who come from Mexico and the people right here. There is not any such thing as one side being better. I don't know many people who don't collaborate. There are always people who do their own thing and there is nothing wrong with that. I think as far as research in the Sonoran Desert, it is almost as if the border isn't there."

The differences between Anglos and Native Americans are potentially as stressful to collaboration as those related to working with Mexicans. One anthropologist remarked:

Well collaboration took a lot of time because in the 1970s and 1980s there were some problems with archeologists and tribes and it did blow up. When I started working with the Tohono O'odham Nation, they did not know me all that well. So every day at lunchtime I took my lunch up to the district office and sat with the people. Then, at the end of the day [of collecting], I would bring all of the artifacts and set them out and we would look at them together. Now, we have two O'odham working with me, and that has established trust.

The loss of home metanarrative took on a different kind of resonance in the recollections of a Native American we interviewed, whose lands were displaced in the creation of Organ Pipe Cactus National Monument. She recalled:

You could say that the Sonoran Desert was my playground. I walked all over the place with a bunch of kids. We were all related, very close, and so everybody was very protective. Of course, at that time we had no fear of anything, you know, you just went wherever you wanted to go and stayed there as long as you wanted, as long as you were home before dark. During that time I never carried water because the water tables were very high. There were areas along the washes that we would go and dig, and water would come up, and then that was our water and we would drink. We never feared . . . anything, not rattlesnakes or any kind of bobcats or javalinas. We were just told to shy away from them and don't bother them and they wouldn't bother us.

While she lived in Phoenix for many years and never thought she would come back, images of the desert she had known as a child persisted in her mind. When monetary settlements were negotiated with the federal government, leaving out her community of Native Americans, she became active. She remarked: "I was going to attend whatever there was, whatever type of meeting there was regarding this whole area because it was our area and if anybody has to protect it at least I am there making some kind of noise about it." Another tribal official spoke in a similar vein: "I always felt that the Sonoran Desert and Upper Gulf was our land since the beginning of time. If someone was going to put together a biosphere reserve, I wanted to be involved."

Lack of economic opportunity, for indigenous people and others, is as much a threat to home as is environmental degradation or erosion of culture. The International Sonoran Desert Alliance, which developed a tripartite mission, is a case in point. According to one leader: "We did eventually develop this tagline to make the mission a little more comprehensible that is 'The International Sonoran Desert Alliance—preserving and enriching the environment, culture and the economy of the Sonoran Desert.' The idea is that the preservation of the desert and the environment requires consideration of how humans will be able to live and make an income and support themselves in that environment."

Put to practice in Ajo, Arizona, a former copper mining community close to the border, these ideas included the renovation of Curley School, an architectural treasure. After the shutdown of the mines, jobs disappeared, schools closed and many residents moved away. Under the sponsorship of the International Sonoran Desert Alliance, classrooms were converted into apartments and studios for artists attracted to the community by the beauty of the setting, the culture and affordability.

Common emotional attachments create bridges among people who would seem to be very different. One informant remarked: "There is a thread that runs together. I think it almost looks like a spider web in terms to all the natural resources alliances at work. . . . I think members of the network can be found anywhere and everywhere. In addition to scientists, the native people and ranchers have a lot to contribute. There are also miners."

Irrespective of Anglo, Native American, Mexican, U.S. citizen, alien, or organizational affiliation, border storytellers articulated the homeward journey theme. In other, lesser respects, people told somewhat different subnarratives about specific things. Differences in storylines emphasize various subject matter focuses and nonhuman objects. The Gulf of California provided fodder for a whole subgroup of activists, although other watercourses like the Santa Cruz River were also mentioned by many of the same people. Wildlife managers were apt to refer to pronghorn, and people involved in the Northern Jaguar Project mentioned jaguars.

Characterization and Nonhuman Characters

Just as the mythical narrative of *The Odyssey* revolves around supersized characters, many of them nonhuman, the Arizona-Sonora border story involves nonhuman characters with transformative powers. The Sonoran Desert Pronghorn antelope connects a subset of activists who monitor populations, distribution, captive breeding, and recovery. One federal land manager said:

We have been working with them [pronghorn] really for about forty to fifty years, but more intensively within the last twenty. We had a very long drought, almost a yearlong drought where we had less than an inch of rainfall. The habitat conditions got to be really, really bad for pronghorn and for a lot of other wild-life; we lost about 90 percent of our pronghorn population. Where we got our counts in November 2002, we actually counted only twenty-one animals.

We now have seventy or so out in the wild and seventy in the captive breeding pen and we just did release like twenty pronghorn into the U.S. population this winter. We are looking at in the next year or so starting the second population in other potions of Southern Arizona, and the relationships and the partnerships that exist between federal state and local agencies in this area is absolutely superb, and the ability to be partners and to work on things is quite honestly amazing and if you have asked me in 2002 that we would be talking about establishing a second population in 2010, personally that would be absolutely impossible, and it all goes to the credit of all of these federal state and local groups that are willing to roll of their sleeve and work together to make some-thing happen. I think that is one of the more positive things about this area is that there is a real can-do spirit, and folks do work together and trying to meet broader landscape goals and objectives while still trying to complete local mission requirements.

Jaguars play the same sort of role in linking environmental activists with ranchers in Mexico, and in this case the camera has transformative power. When a big cat is captured on film, the rancher on whose land the cat is photographed gets paid. To lure cats onto their lands and to retain them, ranchers have even engaged in habitat improvement and thereby increased the numbers of jaguars. Further, the photography pro-vides information about population density and range. As one of the founders of the Northern Jaguar Project explains:

After we got [the jaguar] reserve expanded and operating pretty efficiently, we began creating friendships around the reserve, not through the Defenders model of payments for courtesies, nor payments for compensating depredations, but payment for live animals. And so what we got set up were contracts with neigh-boring ranchers and cameras were set out according to the number of acres on their ranch or the number of previous depredations [by jaguars of farm animals]. There was a little bit of flexibility there, but there is a formula for it and what we do is give 5,000 pesos for a photograph of a jaguar and so many thousand pesos for ocelot. And these are ranchers who really depend on the income for their cattle sales for their livelihood. They are not wealthy absentee ranchers who don't care about their livestock. . . . So, people have been incredibly receptive and they love it.

The Northern Jaguar Project founders explained that in the course of the project, they learned a great deal and had to make many adjustments. They preferred to think of their project in network terms rather than as an institution since continuous flexibility and adaptation were required. In the beginning the project was paying several times for the same jaguar as it was repeatedly photographed traversing the same territory. Now there are two cameras in a set, one on each side of the game trail, so that different animals can be identified by distinct spot patterns and compensation is provided only for first sightings of each animal. Of course, refinement of formula for compensation meant negotiation between project personnel and ranchers. One activist recalled: "So, everything is a learning process. I think one of the things about all this stuff of networking, which includes ranchers, is that you quickly pick up what you can advance quickly and what you can't."

Water is an important character in the border desert story. Water scarcity, aridity, and the restorative power of water are very much part of the homecoming metanarrative as many of the previous quotes attest. Portrayals of water go far beyond treating it as a mere resource: it is considered a giver of life. Even a small amount of freshwater can be salvation. El Camino del Diablo or the Devil's Highway is marked by *tinejas*, or bedrock depressions that trap and store storm water, sometimes for an entire year. According to one authority: "Tinejas Altas is a series of nine natural depressions in the southern Tinejas Altas Mountains. Travelers and their animals sometimes died by the dried up lower pools because they were too weak to climb to the upper tanks. More than fifty graves have been found at the mouth of the canyon to Tinejas Altas" (Kresan 2007, 42).

Where fresh and marine waters meet the desert, abundance occurs. Watercourses like the Colorado and Santa Cruz Rivers create habitats where nature and people can flourish, and nutrients carried along sustain valuable fisheries as well as the rare and endangered species of the Upper Gulf including the Yuma clapper rail, totoaba fish, and the vaquita, a species of porpoise called the "little cow." This transformative power of water to restore life to the desert is at the heart of the Colorado River Delta restoration plan. As several scientists whose work has been critical to forging agreements to move water to Mexico for conservation purposes explained: "The simplest solution, of course, is for the United States and Mexico to allocate sufficient water for the Colorado River to reach the sea once again. As we suggest here, a flow of as little as 25 cubic meters (33 cubic yards) per second would have beneficial effects" (Calderon-Aguilera and Flessa 2009, 164). At the same time, the economic and political power related to water is recognized as a reality. One actor remarked, "All of us who care about the Delta know that we are never going to restore the Delta as long as people in San Diego, or Las Vegas, or Denver are short of water. As soon as their taps do not produce water it is our problem."

Human Characters

In the homecoming metanarrative there are pathfinders, who elaborate narratives and inspire action, guides who lead the way to attaching people, issues, and nonhuman actors to the narrative, and mentors who instruct individuals about their relevance to the broader story and network mainly through face-to-face associations. We identified many such highly networked individuals, and they are portrayed as the large circles and squares in figure 4.3. Our interviews tell us more about why and how they inspire and instruct. Osvel Hinajosa-Huerta, whose associations were portrayed in figures 4.3 and 4.4, first met many of his associates in college and graduate school.

People we interviewed spoke of at least two generations of mentors. The first in the 1960s and 1970s included desert specialists like Julian D. Hayden and Paul S. Martin, as well as Gulf of California experts such as Donald A. Thompson and Lloyd T. Findley. The second, contemporary generation of mentors includes ethnobotanist Gary Paul Nabhan, conservation ecologists Karl W. Flessa and William Shaw, and biologist Edward P. Glenn, and Peggy Church Boyer who heads the Intercultural Center for Deserts and Oceans (CEDO). The Next Generation Sonoran Desert Researchers 2012 meeting discussed at the beginning of this chapter made frequent reference to mentors, and five more senior attendees were among people we interviewed. Graduate students and research associates of these mentors are now key participants in the Arizona-Sonora transboundary environmental network. One of the most revered "desert rats" wrote about his mentoring:

Later Paul [Ezell] and I went to the Pinacate together. We'd both read Lumholtz's New Trails in Mexico and Hornaday's Camp-Fires on Desert Lava. We first went to Pagago Tanks (tinajas). I don't think he knew any more about where it was than I did. But I showed him how to "see" or look at things. He did not know anything about the percussion of flake tools, if you like. I got out of the truck. He started looking around, but I started picking up stuff. He said, "What are you doing?" and I said, "I'm picking up tools." He said, "What are you talking about?" "Why," I said, "these are choppers and scraper and cleavers." I showed them how they were made. "My God," he said. "I stood right here and never saw them." I said, "Well Malcolm Rogers showed me. Now I am showing you." (Hayden, Broyles, and Boyer 2011, 167)

Many Sonoran Desert networkers we interviewed were introduced to desert ecology through mentors at an early age where they learned how to tutor as well as how to see. Much of the mentoring took place during fieldwork where much more than scientific information was exchanged.

A deep commitment to place was often mentioned as growing out of these field experiences. One renowned Mexican biologist noted:

At the time when I came here I had the great opportunity of meeting Howard Scott Gentry and it was great talking to him and learning from him. You see, you don't need to work with someone, but if you come close to these people you also get inspiration and motivation through the work and knowing people like Howard Scott Gentry or Paul Martin who was also very important not only in terms of the scholarly work but also in terms of raising basic issues in simple conversation. I learned so much from Paul Martin just from talking to him on a trip to Alamos. . . . In the case of Paul or David [Yetman], the motivation is generosity. They share their knowledge without intending anything else. We just talked about the Sonoran region as a mythical place that is full of wonders that have this magnetic force that pulls you in.

Peggy Church Boyer, who has directed CEDO in Puerto Peñasco on the Gulf of California for a quarter of a century, reflected on the legacy of long-term mentoring:

Yeah. U.S. people, like myself and Lloyd Findley, went to Mexico and we have built, you know. Lloyd built students that began to work. Many became the directors of the conservational organizations as early as ten years ago and many of them are still working in conservation. In my case, I've generated employees because CEDO is not a school, and those employees are off working in different places and some of them are still with me. So we're generating people that just have a passion for this region and we're also doing this in a kind of cultural atmosphere so it's a very collaborative effort that takes advantage of people on both sides of the border with the same passion.

Alterity and the Other

Narrative-networks distinguish themselves by their treatment of the "other." The Sonoran Desert environmental network story treats the other as one of us or someone who might become one of us. Network members display empathy toward people who share the homecoming narrative but are otherwise unlike themselves (from different countries, races, native tongues, agencies, economic levels, roles, etc.) This inclusiveness facilitates boundary-spanning, communication, and interaction that transcends particular geography and persists over time. The staying power of the border environmental conservation network is bolstered by the broad and inclusive identities that characterize the relationships of many network members.

In some cases, individuals transformed themselves rather than just interrelating, and this direct experience nearly erased the distinction between "us" and "them." Recall the situation discussed earlier concerning

Osvel Hinojosa-Huerta and portrayed in figures 4.3 and 4.4. Now working for one of the oldest and most influential environmental groups in Mexico, Hinojosa-Huerta had earlier immersed himself in U.S. culture and customs as a graduate student from Mexico at the University of Arizona. Four other Mexican nationals we interviewed told us similar biographical stories, with two now living in the United States, one as an academic. A reverse path was followed by many of their mentors at the University of Arizona, several of whom spent months and years in Mexico engaging with plant and animal species and communities of resource users. For many of these individuals, the crossing of national boundaries is but one of many bridges traversed, and the distance between academic life and nongovernmental group involvement is small. University faculty, their students, and former students regularly serve as officers and on the advisory boards of conservation-oriented NGOs in both Mexico and the United States. These inclusive identities are part of the biography or individual narrative of individuals, and therefore persist.

The biographical narrative of Exequiel Ezcurra exemplifies the confounding of easy, one-dimensional classifications of identity we encountered among border environmental networkers. Ezcurra has moved practically seamlessly from government-funded universities in both Mexico and the United States, to independent research organizations, to official positions in government. Born in Argentina, Ezcurra moved to Mexico early in life. He completed his higher education at the University College of North Wales, Bangor, where he received a master's degree and a doctorate in plant ecology. His dissertation topic was influenced in part by funding from the Mexican state of Sonora. In 1980, Dr. Samuel Ocaña, a devoted conservationist, became governor of Sonora and was instrumental in initiating planning for a Pinacate biosphere reserve. Ezcurra spent three years developing a master plan for the reserve and using the data collected for his dissertation (Chester 2006, 64). From 1979 to 1987, Ezcurra was housed in a government think tank, the Institute of Ecology in the Mexican Museum of Natural History. He was full professor and head of the Community Ecology Lab in the National Autonomous University of Mexico from 1987 to 1998. In 1992 he was appointed Director General of Natural Resources in the Mexican federal government. His next move to the San Diego Natural History Museum crossed both national and role boundaries. From 1998 to 2008 Ezcurra directed the Biodiversity Research Center of the Californias while becoming a high official of the museum. From this position in a private institution, Ezcurra moved to head up the UC Mexus program at the University of California at Riverside. Thinking like a researcher, administrator, government official, and policy activist comes naturally to Ezcurra, who has identified with all of these things.

Interdisciplinary and intercultural agencies, centers, and offices—often based in universities, frequently housing and often created by border narrative network pathfinders, guides, and mentors—institutionalize and perpetuate connections by sponsoring projects and recruiting binational students. Among such organizations are UC Mexus at the University of California at San Diego, The Southwest Center, and the Udall Center at the University of Arizona.

Common experience and broad identities may facilitate ties within the Sonoran Desert conservation network that share a common "homecoming" metanarrative and similar views of characters. We turn next to relationships with people outside this network who hold dissimilar views of the border and threats related to it. How do the individual narratives portray people with whom sharing identity is difficult?

The Arizona-Sonora border metanarrative avoids any portrayal of the opposition or the other as evildoers. The classic *Odyssey* journey home was delayed and blocked by terrible monsters that may have signified the wicked "other" loose in the world or, interpreted differently, may have reflected human weakness present within us all. The metanarrative of border activists assiduously avoids drawing lines of separation between "us" and "them." Instead, border environmental network activist stress cooperation almost as a sign of protest against more mainstream or grand narratives that portray the border as violent, corrupt.

Since September 11, 2001, violence and war have dominated popular discourse related to the border. Coverage of Mexico by the national press, especially of border cities, has focused on guns, gangs, and drug killings. In Arizona, public officials have conflated this high level of violence with border crossings and undocumented aliens, even though informal crossings back and forth across political boundaries have been ongoing among border residents for more than a century. In Arizona, many political actors have portrayed undocumented border crossers as criminal and malevolent. Governor Jan Brewer has directed a lot of hostile rhetoric toward Mexico including comments that headless bodies were being found in the Sonoran Desert, and that most illegal immigrants are drug smugglers. Unlike the environmental networkers we interviewed, the Arizona governor's grand narrative paints border crossers in highly negative terms. Brewer said, "Well, we all know that the majority of the people that are coming to Arizona and trespassing are now becoming drug mules. They're coming across our borders in huge numbers. The drug cartels have taken control of the immigration" (CNN 2010). Senate Bill 1070 signed into law by Brewer was highly offensive to Mexicans and many U.S. citizens of Mexican descent. The law, partially upheld by the U.S. Supreme Court, allows state and local law enforcement officials to inquire about the immigration status of anyone with whom they have contact and about whose status they have suspicion. Without sufficient evidence or much reflection, county officials and the U.S. press blamed illegal border crossers for wildfires that raged near the border in the summer of 2011. Ultimately, mining company officials admitted that fire resulted from contractor mishap.

Since such negative portrayals of Mexico and Mexicans undercuts border cooperation, and because the border fence and militarization are environmentally quite harmful, one might well expect backlash among border environmental networkers. They might demonize those associated with such negative portrayals and exaggeration of security peril. Instead, a positive orientation toward those not within the network appears to be a form of resistance against the dominant negative imagery. Instead of blaming some alien "other" as the dominant discourse does, less finger pointing is involved in charging misguided policies are at fault. The North American Free Trade Agreement, according to this storyline, undercut the economic viability to small-scale agriculture in Mexico and along with it the vitality of small rural villages. Drug dealers have moved into these villages and now dominate them. Draconian immigration laws and the construction of the border fence have diverted attention away from species conservation. Concern with security has shifted the emphasis in land management agencies away from sustainability toward police work.

While not negatively stereotyping, border environmental networkers do draw the contrast between those who are at home in the desert with all its extremes and those who are not. Another border activist who directed an effective border NGO voiced this notion of contrasting cultures:

It is almost like there are two completely different universes. These two parallel universes. There is what you read in the newspapers about drug wars; there is the drop-off in tourism because of the economy; there are misguided efforts like SB1070 here in Arizona and the vilification by political interests in the United States of Mexico and Mexicans; and, then there is a whole other universe (like two ships passing in the night) of people who are friends with one another, that understand the nuances, that spend a lot of time going back and forth. The first makes it harder on the second, but only in an indirect way.

Other members in the border environmental network simply refuse to see things in negative terms. One old hand observed that the border has always been a bit dangerous and potential violence has always been present "from the time of the Mexican revolution." He noted, it is political and mass cultural attitudes and perceptions, not reality, that has changed.

Land management officials, even outside environmental agencies, are portrayed sympathetically and, at least potentially, as part of the network. The U.S. Air Force has broad power within the testing area designated as the Barry M. Goldwater Range and includes rich cultural and natural resources. As one citizen activist stated:

What we rely on now is the partners' meeting, which is called the Barry M. Goldwater Executive, or something like that. I cannot remember the exact name. The partners don't have any real vote. The military is the one that makes the final decisions on the range. But it listens very carefully to its partner. Partners are, you know, the Bureau of Land Management, Arizona Game and Fish Department, a state historic preservation officer, and others. It goes back to what [the commanding officer] is trying to do out there, getting his people to talk to each other and try to cooperate.

Even the U.S. Border Patrol is afforded some empathy, with damage to fragile habitat inflicted by patrols tolerated as the consequences of ignorance and lack of experience rather than ill will (Laird Benner and Ingram 2011). As an official in a federal wildlife agency stated:

I think what we need to do is to kind of look through the issues that are going on today and try to figure out where there are some potential solutions and where we can work together and to really emphasize those; and also to look where there is perceived conflict and try to work our way through it and try to figure out how we can meet both of these needs. . . . I mean there is a lot of stuff that has been in the press over the last few months that seems to imply that portions of the federal government are basically at loggerheads with each other, either preventing the mission of the Border Patrol from being done or vice versa. I think if you come and actually work with us down here at the field level, you will see that is not the case at all and that we do have these very productive relationships. . . . Because really if Border Patrol is successful in completing their mission, my mission for protecting this wildlife refuge for present and future generations and for this area to be enduring resource of wilderness can get done; if Border Patrol can protect the area, I am meeting my mission goals. There is a strong need to realize that in federal agencies we both have some shared responsibilities here.

There are large numbers of new Border Patrol agents in the Arizona-Sonora section of the border, and agents come and go from the Tucson sector. Several federal officials we interviewed, one who was Mexican

American, resented being stopped and questioned by the Border Patrol about lands over which they have jurisdiction. As he said: "Go through check station once with me as me, and you would know. Drive back and forth to work and get followed by Border Patrol. It is just challenging, because my family sees that, you know, especially when they come and visit. I just wish America was past (judging on appearances), but obviously we are going in different direction." Another reflected upon potential conflicts of missions between the Border Patrol and the Barry M. Goldwater Range:

The Border Patrol does operate on the Goldwater Range. We certainly have guidelines that we ask them to abide by and they include not driving across the desert. But it's difficult to control what they are doing, particularly where we have active training going on. Border Patrol may come on to our range when it is actively being bombed in pursuit of someone, and so we have to shut down our training. That is a different kind of impact than other situations where the Border Patrol affects the environment.

It is not ill will but unfamiliarity with the place and commitment to a different mission that explains some problems with the Border Patrol. As one land manager remarked:

They rotate through very quickly. Maybe every six weeks or so. Even though we have a video for them to watch about the Goldwater Range, it is still difficult to get to rules of engagement. We have a liaison in our office to work with the Border Patrol, but again, it's difficult. We work with two different office of the Border Patrol in this section of the Range. Then, on the northern-most portion of the Range, we also deal with the Casa Grande Office.

When I have been out on the Goldwater Range, I been stopped by the Border Patrol who said to me, as I am seated in the Air Force Vehicle with the Air Force name tag around my neck, "What are you doing out here? We're on this land. . . . There is some difficulty getting through to the Border Patrol that the land that they are patrolling doesn't belong to them.

At the same time, the Border Patrol has become something of a permanent fixture on the border, although the presence is now at historic levels. Long-standing members of the Border Patrol suffer many of the same hardships as other "desert rats" and are recognized by members of the border environmental network as performing important work. For instance, one long-time desert network activist remarked that the Border Patrol may have limited damage:

Change has occurred on some of the most fragile area because they are just being visited too much. Some of the water holes have been hammered. I'm not thinking just the Pinacate, but I'm thinking of both sides of the border, mostly very largely due to traffic and the border fence is a little overdone, but that has really in some ways helped. Of course it stopped the migration of the large animals unable to cross. But there are no longer road-racers across the desert and a lot of that would originate in Pinacate, and so the U.S. Border Patrol has stopped most of that. Of course there is no longer wilderness along the border. But I must say that I have also observed enormous sophistication for the better among the agents on both sides of the border; but especially along the U.S. border; they don't just wantonly drive across the desert the way they used to and there are much more professionalism.

For members of the Arizona-Sonora border environmental network, Border Patrol agents are not the enemy. In the introduction to a book of interviews with Border Patrol agents, one of the coauthors, a prominent environmental network activist, makes the following assessment: "They are common folk doing an uncommon job. Like police work anywhere, days of humdrum patrol and investigation are interspersed with moments of fear and heroics. Shots have been fired here, but the real count is the persons rescued from heat and fatigue, aliens apprehended, and tons of drugs confiscated" (Broyles and Haynes 2010, 19).

Surprising Twists and Breach

Among of the most ironic things about the narrative of the border environmental activists is their refusal to interpret the losses and frustrations in negative terms despite overwhelming evidence that shared values are increasingly endangered. However difficult and arduous the travails of securing home might become, the plot of the metanarrative almost invariably leads to a happy ending. The stories told by those we interviewed were affirmative about overcoming threats to home and restoring home to its appropriate inhabitants. Almost everyone we talked to was positive about the long-term prospects for the Arizona-Sonora border region whether their focus was restoring the City of Ajo or saving jaguars and pronghorn. For instance, one of the activists committed to restoring at least some part of the Colorado River Delta to what it was when the Leopold brothers saw it in 1922 told us: "How can you be in conservation and not be a naïve optimist? Each of us contributes our bit and the Gulf is better off than it otherwise would have been. We are passionate about our patrimony." Another less closely involved in Delta restoration remarked:

I am such an optimist on this stuff. I see the Colorado River Delta as having advanced further than I could ever imagine it would. I am humbled by how much has gotten done. When they had a meeting at Arizona State University and someone said that 140 agencies are involved in whether water will go across the border, I walked out. I said to myself, "We are an hour and a half into this meeting and we hear that water won't flow across the border unless a hundred and forty different water districts and agencies sign on. This will never happen." So, I am proven wrong when I am a cynic. And, I think we are generating such goodwill through the positive projects that happen that kids are growing up expecting that this [a restored Delta] should be possible for them.

The same positive perspective dominated the individual narratives of many others we interviewed who linked identity, networks, and the future of the region:

The land and the people are enormously resilient. We are moving toward more creative and sustainable answers. The stewards of the land are not governments but people who live on the land.

It is about deep patterns of your own that are actually universal but are part of your life. There is something about being rooted in a place. It is a good place that you know. That ought to allow you to go to other places and respond to those places in a deep and profound way because you are a rooted human being. . . .

[We were at a dinner party and the President of a college in the Midwest] was talking about why we tolerate this stuff: immigrants walking down the street, drugs coming through. And I am trying to explain to him there are other realities: there are languages, there are families that camp on both sides, there is the ranching culture, there is history and, by the way, this used to be Mexico, this place where we are actually sitting right now. It is getting harder and harder, so until those things (immigration, drugs) resolve, what we have to do on our end is try harder, work much harder.

The border wall provides a kind of turning point in the border narrative. The border fence or wall was portrayed as a serious environmental problem by most people we interviewed, particularly those concerned with wildlife. One book to which several referred summarizes as follows:

Border walls and roads act as a barrier to wildlife movement, posing risks to species that rely on habitat within both the United States and Mexico including jaguar, black bear, Sonoran pronghorn antelope, Mexican gray wolf, bison, ocelot and cactus ferruginous pygmy owl. In some cases, wall construction will result extirpation of rare wildlife from the United States; for example, biologists believe the extensive wall construction in Arizona will likely preclude jaguar recovery and establishment of a breeding population within the United States. (Segee and Córdova 2009, 247)

The actual physical separation varies a good deal, with solid walls around more populated areas (including, as pictured, parts of a national park) and vehicular barriers, or Normandy fences, in less populated areas (see figure 4.5).

Finally, there are virtual fences, or towers upon which high-tech surveillance mechanisms are mounted. Now partially constructed and can-

Figure 4.5
Border fence and road on southern boundary of Organ Pipe Cactus National Monument (*Source:* Laird Benner and Ingram 2011)

celed, the virtual fence imposes a fairly large footprint, especially when construction roads and now unused power lines are included. Yet the wall and the now canceled but partially constructed virtual fence were reluctantly accepted by some as the price for controlling illegal entry, which, once stopped, would allow managers to return their attention to conservation. Land managers expressed the hope that a beefed-up border would allow interception before illegal traffic and law enforcement penetrated deep within protected lands and caused damage. One land manager explained:

With the infrastructure in place that I talked about before with the technology, the manpower, I think that will really help us. If I am able to recruit and field my twenty law enforcement positions and keep those consistently filled, that will go a long way to enhancing what we are doing. Part of the challenges with any interdiction operation, we can also impact the resource, and especially with the numbers that we just talked about. We talked about the added infrastructure and everything. So, how do we pull all these together and that is one of my huge, huge challenges right now, just to be able to sit across the table from Homeland Security or Border Patrol and just say let me see their operations plan. How are you going to implement your response to all these tower notifications? What is going to be your deterrence strategy along the border?

Others saw the wall as ultimately irrelevant and an object of derision. One head of an environmental NGO remarked:

The wall is such a bad problem, you know, but in twenty years the wall is going to be the biggest transfer of building materials from one country to another since the Marshall Plan. It is already happening. I was talking to the guy who used to own Lukeville. . . . Al showed me where they had built vehicle barriers. The Mexican cartel came along on the south side and sawed the base with a concrete saw and lowered it (think of the *Batman* movies). They rigged it up so that they could drive over it hauling tires [to erase tire tracks] and they put it back up with hinges that you could only see from the south side of the border.

In an even more pronounced twist, the wall is portrayed as an opportunity. Several saw the wall as a kind of symbol or image with actual environmental impacts requiring more study. One university-based border researcher remarked:

It's a border wall but it's kind of a boundary object. Its opening and opportunity for the dialogue and discussion perhaps it's on a national scale in the United States and Mexico. It's refocusing attention to the region. To have Mexico City daily newspapers cover anything we do to ecology or Northwestern Mexico is important. It's new and it's happening and it's probably so much in the forefront of people's mind. What is happening is perhaps more a conversation about symbols and meanings rather than a conversation about the actual environmental impacts generally. It's so much too early to know what the actual impacts are.

To document actual effects requires more of what border networker already like to do. As several scholars write:

Controversy surrounding the wall has . . . helped revitalize the commitment of a growing number of scientists, academics, government officials, and advocates to increase collaboration with their cross-border partners. One example of this cooperation is the recent convergence between a group of U.S. and Mexican conservation leaders seeking to identify the potential impacts of wall construction and designate critical areas for cross-border wildlife movement. . . . This convergence will help ensure a continual binational effort to identify potential impacts of the border wall construction to lands and wildlife, with the goal of proposing defensible alternatives and mitigation strategies. (Segee and Córdova 2009, 249–250)

Context and Gaps

Hermeneutic analysis as described in chapter 3 requires that we interpret the fabula or common storyline with reference to the larger context and master or hegemonic narratives that exist. In our discussion of the setting and elsewhere in this chapter, we have described the context of the Arizona-Sonora border as a place of contrasts and conflicting realities. As our analysis has already established, the networkers we interviewed were adept at picking and choosing what to ignore as well as what to include, and how to emphasize certain aspects while backgrounding others. Application of the framework prompts two additional observations about gaps and modifications, one related to the treatment of trash and violence and the other to knowledge.

As the border wall has funneled undocumented border crossers into more remote desert areas, garbage gets left behind and accumulates. According to news reports, cleanup efforts since 2008 by the Arizona Department of Environmental Quality have included pulling forty-two tons of trash from tribal lands, public lands, and ranches (Gaynor 2012). Anti-immigrant web sites display pictures of desert washes inundated with detritus (www.truthorfiction.com/rumors/a/Arizona-Desert-Trash .htm).

While those we interviewed acknowledge the existence of such trash, it was never treated as meaningfully harmful to the home place. Violence, too, is recognized as a border reality, but not one those we interviewed highlight. A park ranger who was shot when he chose to pursue armed Mexican bandits in Organ Pipe Cactus National Park in 2002 is a case in point. To illustrate the gap between the border narrative-network and the broader context, consider the following excerpt from the *Congressional Record House*. A member of Congress from Colorado stated:

The trash that is distributed throughout the forest is enormous, are enormous, monumental. It is hundreds of thousands of tons of trash discarded by people coming through there, so much so that one would think that Coronado National Forest should be renamed Coronado National Dump because that is what it looks like. Yet, of course, it is interesting we never have seen or even heard the Sierra Club or any other environmental organization take issue with the problem . . . . We spent the next day going to Organ Pipe Cactus National Park, just adjacent to Coronado, also the scene of environmental degradation that is truly disturbing. All of the same problems of Coronado, but it is also the site of the death of a park ranger by the name of Chris Eggle, twenty-eight years old, killed by two Mexicans coming across the border escaping from the crimes they have committed in Mexico. Several other murders that they have committed in relationship to some sort of drug deal, drug situation. (Tancredo 2003, 4508)

What the Arizona-Sonora narrative chooses to relate and wants others to see looks very different from the excerpt in the *Congressional Record House*. One park official we interviewed expressed hope that in the future historical and cultural resources might take their place in interpretive exhibits for visitors that heretofore have mainly been focused on wilderness, natural resources, and the biosphere designation. This, he stated, might be difficult in light of the reminders of border violence now presented to visitors. He said:

What you see when you first drive up to the visitor's center may be a challenge. What is the name of our visitor's center? So it's Chris Eggle. What are the questions that come to mind? It is not the way we like to think about the national park. You made it a destination for whatever reason, and then you get here and then you see the monument, and now you have got the interpretive sign and you start asking questions. And yes, I mean it is a story in time, but again it occurred in 2002. But the thing is what it is. So how do we make the best of it?

While another gap is less dramatic, desert networkers rely in their narrative on knowledge that is distinct from what is created in the broader context or in other places for other purposes. The stories told by desert networkers portray a relational knowledge creation process that profits from the prestige of science but includes a broader spectrum of kinds of localized knowledge and participants. References to the strong science basis of what they do are liberally sprinkled through the transcripts of the interviews conducted among Sonoran Desert conservation networkers. Such reliance upon science is not surprising because a shared knowledge base is a powerful facilitator of sustained networks that successfully recruit new members (Brugnach and Ingram 2012; Feldman and Ingram 2009a). The prestige and credibility of academic science enables knowledge acceptance and transfer. Yet there are forces that discredit academic science in many places and situations. The elitist nature of mainstream science that respects only facts discovered by credentialed scientists following specific procedures is off-putting to people who have experiential or traditional knowledge. The networked process of knowledge creation among Sonoran desert activists is quite different from what is regarded as traditional science.

Knowledge and action are closely associated rather than separated in border environmental work. Only when water testing by the Friends of the Santa Cruz River showed the presence of contaminants dangerous to fish and people was action taken to upgrade waste treatment, and constant monitoring has continued to prod further protection. Scientific studies of species loss in the Upper Gulf of California spawned efforts at restoration that fed back into further research and greater community involvement. As one NGO-based researcher explained:

The key is on the ground actions, you know, because before 2002, there were no restoration projects. We were talking about 'we need to restore this, we need to protect that' but everything was impossible because there was no water in the Colorado River Delta. So, as we increase knowledge about the species, the habitats, water needs for these habitats, understanding evolved. We were able to begin with restoration projects. I think the first one was in 2001, and since then we have more than twelve or thirteen restoration projects. And, at least 80 percent of the staff for such projects [is] from local communities.

Such collaboratively produced, action-oriented knowledge may not get the highest academic respect. Professional sacrifice may flow from such engagement. For instance, one researcher stated the professional disadvantages of site-specific, descriptive cataloguing of plants and animals:

Of course there is this heavy criticism within academia to the taxonomist and the people who make catalogues, like these wonderful books by Richard Felger, and don't understand the deep significance of just providing foundations for further research. We cannot know what we should study if we don't understand things that are there. It is how we can make deeper questions. So, there is heavy criticism of those who do descriptive research versus the hypothesis-driven science. And, of course, many of the issues, going back to the borderlands, are not hypothesis-driven questions that are universal in nature but local processes of description.

The emergence of some more integrative disciplines within the academy, in this case conservation biology, supports the persistent engagement of border conservation networkers within universities. Conservation biology has had considerable influence upon the campaigns to establish international biosphere reserves (Chester 2006; Levesque 2000). One researcher we interviewed, trained as a paleontologist, now describe himself as a conservation biologist. "There is not that much risk in collaborative and action oriented research within the university anymore," he said. He openly embraces collaboration with environmental nongovernmental organizations as well as governmental agencies in his work, such as The Sonoran Institute, Environmental Defense, Defenders of Wildlife, Pronatura, Pacific Institute, and the Center of Biological Diversity. He noted that members of his department had long and strong relationships with energy companies, and he saw no difference in potential conflict of interest by relating to environmental nongovernmental groups. He established an office at the Sonoran Institute during one sabbatical. He likes being able to move between different professional worlds. He said: "It is great being an academic in this business, it is sort of like being Switzerland in international relations."

The knowledge creation process is closely tied to place and local residents, and it integrates researchers into the homecoming metanarrative. The conservation biologist just quoted stated that he hired local people as part of his field crews doing research work. Other researchers in the network place collaboration with locals even more centrally and envision the creation of trust as part of the process. For instance, the head of one research and conservation organization based in Mexico stated:

One of the things that I think has strengthened us over time is the fact that we are still there; the fact that we have weathered criticism, and we have maintained our course and just try to build trust by continuing to do things well and involving more people over time. Kind of related, it is what it is like living in the family. You know, you weathered the good time and the bad and you just trust each other because you survived. And we didn't run away. Had we run away when fishermen were running after us that would have given them a sign that we were doing something wrong, or you know, we are guilty. [The organizations was picketed by trawlers when they learned they were to be excluded from the biosphere reserve.] I remember the day that the fishermen came to protest. I knew they were coming; people had sort of warned me, and I went through in my mind every single thing that we had done for the last few years trying to figure out what we have done wrong and there was very little that I could come up with. The biggest error that I came up with was that we only worked with one group of fishermen, you know. We didn't work with multiple groups, but we really didn't see an opportunity and we had a limited capacity as an organization. . . . So, eventually other fishermen just basically grew to trust us, and it came from them; they told each other that they could trust us. It was because we work with more and more people and they all had good experiences with us. So, I guess that persistence, persistence, is really key.

The intent of knowledge creation in the context of the Sonoran Desert conservation network is to "change not only cognitive structures but normative structures as well" (Levesque 2000, 55). To be guided by science in the individual narratives told by Sonoran Desert informants means integrating science within the network of human relationships. Science facilitates networks not by taking precedence over values and beliefs, but by offering opportunities to collaborate. Similar to the findings from a dissertation about networked relationships on the northern border between the United States and Canada, the role of science in the Sonoran Desert is in part to build grassroots support and collaborative relationships (Levesque 2000).

In summary, the application of the framework for narrative analysis to the case of the Arizona-Sonoran Desert border environment reveals a strong homecoming narrative is woven together by a common plot that has surprising twists that turn defeats into opportunities and simply ignores some aspects of the context. The characters in the narrative include importantly nonhuman actors, and the narrative itself is distinguished by an overall positive portrayal even of opponents.

Implications for Democracy and Governance

"The world is permanently changed and all of this is over," one retired National Park Service official recalled despairing on September 11, 2001, as he reflected upon the future of border environmental cooperation. Prior to the bombing of the World Trade Center, he said, the establishment of international peace parks, regular binational meetings of agencies and NGOs, public/private agreements for the conservation of nature along the U.S.-Mexico border, and other transboundary institution building were patriotic endeavors, regularly occurring. Congress and both parties were supportive. President Vicente Fox of Mexico was the perfect collaborator. President George Bush actually knew personally about binational conservation programs. In a matter of months, the institutional and political context so favorable to negotiating formal agreements and passing protective legislation had vanished and was replaced by disinterest and negative rhetoric at national and state institutional and policy levels.

To what extent do networks compensate for swings in public opinion, and complement or supplement institutions aimed at environmental protection? Is ecological democracy served by the Arizona-Sonora border environment narrative-network and if so, how? It can be argued that the tyranny of the majority and the passions aroused by perceived menace to national security threaten minority rights and marginalize ecological concerns along the Arizona-Sonora border. In the state of Arizona and to a lesser extent in Washington, D.C., policymakers have appeared willing to set aside long-standing environmental and cultural values to fortify barriers between the United States and Mexico. In a myriad of ways, getting across the border has become more difficult for human and nonhuman species. Vigilante groups (themselves a network) have sprung up to patrol against illegal immigrants, imposing additional damage on the fragile desert environment already impacted by stepped-up official border agent patrols and construction activities related to the wall. The application of environmental laws including the Endangered Species Act has been suspended along the border.

Historians suggest that anti-Mexican and anti-immigrant sentiment waxes and wanes in Arizona, and exclusionary periods are often followed by decades of more welcoming practices (Sheridan 2012). It can be argued that networks based on family and community ties, but also including relationships such as those explored here, help alleviate discrimination against people and lessen damage to ecological values. The appealing narrative of homecoming acts to soften the prevailing context of hostility, making a transition to more moderate attitudes in the future less difficult. Democracy would seem to be served by mechanisms that keep alive moderate alternatives and lead away from extremes. Further, networks that give some agency to nonhuman species such as jaguars and prong-horn serve to broaden representation at a time of narrow focus on perceived risk to human security.

Formal institutions are supposed to protect and perpetuate values and missions even after the groundswell of public support that occasioned their establishment has subsided or been reversed. But narrative-networks appear in this case to be more flexible than most institutions and better able to sustain themselves through temporary changes in political climate. Our findings suggest that a metanarrative is essential to maintaining networks that in turn are critical in sustaining boundary-spanning linkages at times when support for institutions weakens or dissolves. An activist in the Northern Jaguar Project explained the advantages of noninstitutionalized networks as follows: "They are nimble, can use money efficiently, have a passionate membership where everyone works; they can choose leaders without political criteria; they can learn cultural differences faster; they can develop a certain ease of trust so that if you screw up, it does not have a lasting effect."

However, other activists pointed with pride at the formal "institutions" established in the past two decades, such as biosphere reserves, parks, monuments, and protected areas. One U.S. scientist working in Mexico noted, "I cannot imagine we would have gotten so far without the [Pinacate and Upper Gulf] Biosphere Reserve." The network members who spoke most eloquently about the role of networks looked toward a formal park or preserve designation as a way to bring certainty and stability to land and habitat preservation. For instance, the ultimate goal of the Northern Jaguar Project, a private effort to fund and acquire habitat land for the large cat, is to obtain a federal decree. Not only does legal recognition provide stability, it also grants stature. A member of the Tohono O'odham Nation regretted the lack of legal status afforded native peoples in Mexico, where he said that "not only do members on the other side of the line lack status they also lack laws that prevent digging in cultural sites without prior consultation with the community" (Laird Benner and Ingram 2011).

Of course there is interaction between institutions and narratives. Common metanarratives support networks that are in turn instrumental in establishing institutions. Past success at creating institutions feeds into perpetuation of positive and optimistic narratives of home that, in turn, sustain networks in difficult times. While administrative and congressional support for collaborative transboundary solutions has weakened, and actions such as the border wall and increased security threaten wildlife and habitats as well as relationships, the metanarrative takes a "happy ending" long-term view that the essential characteristics of home are eternal.

Value Added through Narrative Analysis of a Network

Figure 4.6 employs the narrative analysis schema introduced in the previous chapter to portray the Sonoran Desert conservation narrative. While a lot of the detail of the forgoing analysis is sacrificed in the figure, it

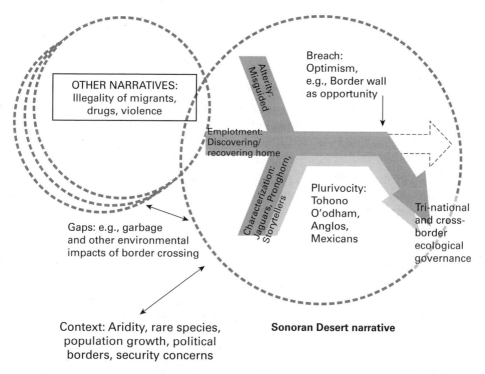

Figure 4.6
Narrative analysis framework applied to Sonoran Desert narrative

illustrates that narrative analysis can be generalized and summarized. Now that the framework is demonstrated as practicable, can it be shown to be useful? Are there significant insights to be gained by taking a narrative analysis approach to the investigation of the Arizona-Sonora border environmental network that might have eluded other approaches?

1. *Narratives are the glue that binds network members together.* Network analysis alone as portrayed in figures 2.1 and figure 4.3 indicates very little about what holds the network together. On the surface these figures might even mislead the analyst to believe the network is weak on the basis of sparse and far-flung connections. On the basis of straightforward documentary history, it might appear that goals like the establishment of biosphere reserves or the restoration of the lower Colorado River draw network members together. Yet narratives preexisted before particular goals emerge and persist after they are thwarted or fulfilled. Examining the stories or individual narratives told by members of the network deepens our insight into how the network gains acceptance and maintains energy even in times where the conservation cause along the border is not popular. How networks, sometimes thought to be ephemeral, manage to persist rather than dissolve when immediate self-interest is not being served is revealed through listening to what members say.

Narrative analysis allows us to understand how people grow into their associations. In the case of the Sonoran Desert, people are strongly attached to place and to other people who share their attachment. Often long-lasting connections began when people were young, in graduate school, doing fieldwork, and being mentored by people who were teaching them not just science but affection for place. The shared metanarrative of being a "desert rat" at home in a harsh landscape and a strange culture creates both bonding and bridging ties that transcend those of organizational or ideological attachment. It is telling that among the forty-seven interviews completed, no one traced their involvement in Sonoran Desert conservation to solicitation by an interest group. In the case of agency officials who are activists, some came to the region for job-related reasons, but those who stayed sensed the place as home. Apropos to these observations, none of the NGO and government network members we interviewed said that notables at national levels were major inspirations or instigators of efforts. .

The Sonoran Desert as "home" has a powerful appeal, at least in part because the harshness of the desert is demanding and seldom merely comfortable. Heat and aridity are ubiquitous, even in the Upper Gulf of

California/Sea of Cortez where the desert meets the ocean. Survival is a challenge in this region, and desert dwellers, were they so inclined, could have many reasons for abandoning their commitments. While the Sonoran Desert is not for everyone, it has a powerful, exotic attraction to those who call it home. As expressed in the individual narratives quoted in this chapter, people are not easily separated from their home place, and they share a sense of home with others in the community despite whatever race, ethnic, economic, professional, or cultural differences exist.

Survival even under extreme conditions is the hallmark of desert dwellers' homecoming metanarrative. Narrative analysis explains why there is little sense of possible defeat among members of the network, and less inclination to give up on it. The natural world will rebound from temporary insults, and long-standing border aesthetics and cultures will persist. Rather than focusing on the passage of a particular law or the establishment of formal organizations as primary goals that can lead to definite loss, striving to protect and restore home is more emotionally difficult to set aside. It is not surprising that, given the metanarrative, activists are not put off by political or legislative reversals.

2. Narratives can facilitate ties that cross boundaries by members of networks. Divisions between the natural, economic, cultural, and scientific blur when it comes to the inclusive *Odyssey* mythical narrative in which home is recovered and restored. Indigenous peoples find themselves in league with Anglos in the preservation of places. Cultural preservationists are part of the same International Sonoran Desert Alliance (ISDA) that also tries to preserve the environment and foster economic development. The inclusiveness of the notion of desert dwellers as people at home in the desert allows people to take different perspectives on various aspects of place. Some network members focus on water for nature, others on species protection, yet others on cultural preservation, to provide only a few examples. Further, the metanarrative transcends international boundaries, agency missions, public and private sectors, and other differences. Individual narrative histories of engagement in the Arizona-Sonora border environment reveal a great deal about the conditions for forging bridging ties. Relationships often began early in life, through field experience, frequently in the company of mentors or informants who mix emotional with informational messages. Walking, talking, and observing in concert reinforce the shared metanarrative. The chapter refers to at least three generations of graduate students who cross international boundaries in their border conservation work so that they become essentially binational people who move easily across national divides. For these people, attachment to home exerts a pull strong enough to overcome divisions of national identity, profession, or organizational loyalty.

Narrative analysis has provided important information about how the Sonoran Desert conservation network established boundaries while not alienating those left out. The people we interviewed were determinately positive, not just about other members of the network with different identities, but also about others whose driving visions and narratives were completely at odds. Being optimistic and constructive, looking at things in the best light, constituted an identity associated with the familial and communal. The network feeds upon positive framing of the border as an affirming place. Even possible negatives like extreme heat, lack of green vegetation, and aridity are treated as positive rites of passage. In particular, the negative portrayals of Mexico and Mexicans, and even the Border Patrol, are explicitly disavowed in a uniformly positive portrayal. There are no "bad guys" in this narrative. The upbeat narrative, reinforced by victories on the ground, sustains the network through what might look from the outside as very bad times.

3. Nonhumans are parts of the narrative and help to bind the network together. Nonhumans such as pronghorn antelope, jaguars, endangered birds and fishes, and rivers are integral parts of the network and focal points for subnarratives. Sometimes they perform the role of "boundary objects" to which different groups of people can relate and contribute. The recovery of the desert pronghorn whose range ignores borders has commanded collaboration of many agents in a variety of jurisdictions. Similarly, the wall and border security erected to discourage the illegal passage of people has badly damaged the environment, and determining how much damage is taking place and how to mitigate it is drawing attention from many quarters. Nonhuman actors can weave themselves into and alter the narrative just as the behavior of the jaguar has dictated the demarcation of reserves and the compensation of private landholders whose property they claim as part of their range. Even species long dead are playing a role. The fossil record of sea life in the Upper Gulf is testimony of the biological riches that disappeared with the damming of the Colorado River and the loss of environmentally sustainable flows in the estuary.

Cultural artifacts are physical objects that are as much a part of the home metanarrative as the natural world. Curley School in Ajo, Arizona, restored by the International Sonoran Desert Alliance, serves to welcome artists, aid economic development, encourage an appreciation of desert culture, and foster, through art, an appreciation of the desert. The natural cisterns that gave sustenance to pioneer travelers on the Devil's Highway taught lessons about the life-giving properties of small amounts of water that are very much part of the contemporary argument for environmental flows to sustain the lower Colorado River.

4. Narrative analysis reveals the knowledge creation processes to be the building of ties and trust and not merely the discovery of facts and development of theory. The knowledge creation process as it has operated in the Arizona-Sonora border conservation network involves scientists, practitioners, resource users, environmentalists, and others to interact. Science is revealed to be relational, allowing members of the network to claim the prestige and credibility of sound science while not separating knowledge creators from those with experiential knowledge and practical experience in resource management. According to their individual narratives, many scientists we interviewed had backgrounds or contemporary experiences with governments and non-governmental organizations. They identified themselves as broad-gauged scientists who were practiced in collaboration and oriented toward action. The role of scientists, as revealed in individual narratives, is often that of conveners and facilitators of collaboration. Narrative analysis shows that persistence on the part of scientists willing to demonstrate through their staying power their commitment to the recovery and protection of "home."

5. Narrative analysis explains how relationships in networks transcend categories and are built upon persistence and longevity. Narrative analysis reveals the ties that bind people together in networks may be at once material and emotional, logical and spiritual, self-interested and other-regarding, and factual and moral. In real life and in relation to things people care about, categories so useful to academic disciplines simply do not serve purposes of understanding or action. Narratives are about making people, things, and events flow together. The parsing of subject matter into bite-sized pieces to facilitate the engagement of expertise does not support a metanarrative that must have a plot, characters, turning points, and other devices to sustain interest.

Narrative analysis in this case illustrates the importance of persistence and time. Relationships are continually reworked as each generation of border activists is succeeded by the next; mentors are recognized as inspirational as well as authority figures; people move from one job to another but carry along previous loyalties and past friendships. The stories of this chapter reveal that staying put, sticking with the task of conservation, and exhibiting dependability and loyalty build confidence and trust. The *Odyssey* homecoming metanarrative that is central to this case takes almost a lifetime to complete and was accomplished only with dogged determination.

5

Narrating the Ethical Landscape of the Turtle Islands

Turtles fascinate us. Why that is, we don't exactly know. They do hardly anything in real time, content to sit there like still lifes in the sand. And yet they draw us to them—how many pictures have we seen of crowds gathering around a giant turtle, probably older than most of the people there, talking and clapping at the sight. We seem drawn by some inner impulse to reach out to this being, notwithstanding its seeming oblivion to our presence, to make a connection and maybe even care for them. In a word, it draws us to relationship.

In this chapter, we take up the story of the Turtle Islands—a system that, despite the simple, almost spartan nature of life on the islands and their rudimentary economy, displays remarkable complexity. The non-traditional mode of ecological management that evolved on the islands is a study of how alternative notions of what a system is can effect deep changes in environmental practice. Later, we describe how this gives rise to an institutional form, the organizing principle of which has been described as an ethic of care (Lejano 2008). It also reflects a richness of ethical and practical ways of knowing that, we claim, can only be done justice by a turn to narrative.

The Turtle Islands are a chain of five islands in the Sulu Sea, found on the Philippine side of this country's maritime boundary with Malaysia. They are just offshore of Sandakan, Malaysia (figure 5.1). They are also one of the most important nesting grounds for marine turtles, primarily the green and hawksbill turtles, in the world. In the 1980s, a team of biologists from the Philippine Department of Environment and Natural Resources (DENR), part of the newly formed Pawikan Conservation Project (PCP), arrived on the islands with the assignment of setting up a turtle conservation project, in part to fulfill its mandate as a signatory to the International Convention on Biological Diversity.

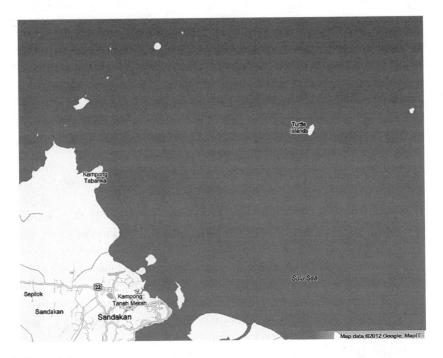

Figure 5.1
The Turtle Islands

What the PCP team found on the islands was an already existing, but informal mode of conservation. To be sure, it in no way resembled the scientific mode of conservation that the PCP was ready to implement, which involved setting up marine sanctuaries and regulating fishing and recreational activities around them. Instead, they found a mixed system of management, involving the harvesting of eggs for income generation for the island residents with rudimentary conservation practices that included the setting aside of periods during the year when turtle nests would be left alone. This coincided with traditional practices that were established over the decades by the original settlers of the island, an ethnolinguistic clan known as the Jama Mapun. The Mapun had cultural practices that involved strict prohibitions on harming sea turtles and limiting activity on two islands, Baguan and Lihiman, which they believed were burial places for two shariff, or Muslim holy men. But this also coincided with the harvesting of eggs, for which buyers in nearby Sandakan, Malaysia, paid a premium, particularly for the larger green turtle eggs. Part of the management system involved the evolution of a group of local experts among the Mapun, known as "egg-probers," who would read turtle tracks, locate nests, and harvest eggs. They already developed means of locating hidden turtle nests, probing for eggs, and noting the relative abundance or scarcity of nets. It was not at all the scientific process of data gathering; to our knowledge, such data was never quantified or formally chronicled (Domantay 1953).

In the discussion that follows, we describe the kind of management system that evolved after the arrival of the PCP. Our interviews with various actors in the Turtle Islands system provided narrative descriptions of this system. In these narratives, we get a glimpse of the nature of the system, as understood and practiced by this network of actors, and better understand how the complex management practices that evolved cohered with this particular understanding of the system. Just as we used narrative accounts to access the meanings of this system, we also find it easiest to use elements of narrative to describe it. In the discussion that follows, we will include some quotations from respondents that are largely translated from the original Tagalog.

Tracing the Narratives

The account we provide relies on a number of sources, including a review of archival records, extended interviews with sixteen stakeholders from the Turtle Islands and Manila, and the author's notes. The open-ended, semistructured interviews initially consisted of having each respondent characterize the turtle management program in his or her own terms (as described in Kvale 1996). The interviewer would then probe further, beyond the formal depictions of the program and into elements of practice. For example, the interviewer would ask the respondent to describe specific instances to illustrate how things were done. In most of the cases, at least two interviews were held with each respondent. Respondents were role-players in the Turtle Islands program, including PCP members from the 1980s to the present, local wardens, management staff from the Philippine Department of Environment and Natural Resources and several external observers. In our interviews, the main goal was to get respondents to tell "their story" and describe how their relationships with other actors evolved.

The set of respondents was limited to those who participated directly in the conservation activities. This is because our main objective was to characterize the PCP's practices. Interviews were taped and transcribed, and these, along with archival documents (reports, briefs, and memoranda) were analyzed using a mode of content analysis around a number of basic themes (following Neuendorf 2001). The primary themes were the formal depictions of the system (i.e., rules, roles) and departures from these formal boundaries. The pooled text was used to characterize both formal and informal program practices. A mode of data triangulation was practiced—for example, when obtaining information from one respondent, we sought to corroborate such information from at least one other respondent or other source.

Emplotment: Making Sense of the Whole

The very first characteristic of a narrative is emplotment. We first discuss one important function of the plot, which is to make sense of the whole and, in fact, to posit the very idea of a whole. When we spoke with some of the islanders about their experience with the PCP program, we heard in their stories an inescapable awareness that what they were talking about was part of a larger reality that made up life on the islands.

When we interviewed some of the Mapun, and other islanders, who were involved in the system, as well as some PCP members, we found descriptions of the ecological system that departed from classic environmental management conventions. Their descriptions did not involve separating compartments or activities, and their accounts showed surprisingly little discussion of inherent conflicts between environment and development. We found, rather, stronger notions of connectedness. The system, as described to us, was a unique representation of what Odum (or, more pertinently, Gilligan) called a web of relationships, which we sometimes refer to as a network (Odum 1953; Gilligan 1982). The mode of description that the respondents used was not to separate out different subsystems and policy actors, but rather to describe the need to understand them together. This mode of emplotment involves allowing each member of the system their place in the islands, attributing to them roles and attributes (i.e., character) as well as action (i.e., agency). Emplotment is not simply the ability to interconnect otherwise disparate elements together in some fashion—more than this, it is the ability to think of them as an intelligible whole.

The system, as the Mapun and others understood it, involved both people and turtles (called *pawikan* in Tagalog), bound together in intimate ways. As some of the egg probers said:

When we talk with islanders there, we talk about how, when we say "sanctuary," we don't mean just the pawikan, but also the people. We just have to assign, just as with our fishing, limits to what we people do. And so, with the pawikan too, they have their limits, which is what sanctuary means. We could not have a sanctuary and say, leave this place, this is for turtles only. This is what we tell people who help us. You are part of the sanctuary.

In the beginning, there were few people on the islands. One could say, the people were there, and the pawikan were there. But there are a lot more people now. Now, the people and the pawikan have to share the place. It is not anymore one or the other. Now they have to live together.

In this case, we see how their notion of the system does not correspond to the environmental management dictum of conservation by separating. In the egg prober's narrative, people and turtles interact and relate to each other not so differently than people interact with each other.

The system, as seen by these network actors, requires the mutual accommodation of a diverse mix of actors. It requires both humans and turtles to respect limits. There is an element of care that goes both ways (the pawikan help the people, but the people also regard pawikan almost like their children, too). This notion of the system was shared by various members of the PCP, who mostly did not approach it from the traditional standpoint of conservation. In almost every interview we had with PCP members, they talked about the crucial need to fit in and not to displace people. In their account, as soon as they arrived on the islands, much of their activity involved finding ways to belong. The need to belong (in Tagalog, *pakikisama*) was evident in the narratives of the egg probers, too, but it was particularly urgent for the PCP:

You see, first of all, in the beginning we would stay in just one place, and we were really strangers there, so we had to learn to belong. Sometimes, they would make requests of us that we were not supposed to do, but we really have to fit in. In the first place, you have to coordinate everything since you are a visitor to the area . . . If we do not engage in PR with people, we do not approach them well. Whatever one may say, this is still their community. So, we made sure to go around and talk with everyone, not just the local government but the local military . . .

When it came to fitting in, we were okay. We were there with them, and we tried not to give them reasons to think we meant ill. For me, though, they way I worked with them, whenever there was any possible source of conflict, we had to give. The minute we did not give, they might have thought worse of us. Even small things, however simple, if they approached you for anything or any request, and you hesitate to help, it would seem like you set yourself apart from them.

So, we tried everything to belong, though sometimes you could not give them what they wanted from you . . . sometimes, we could not immediately decide on their request, especially me as a team leader. So, those times, I ask for their understanding, you just don't know what they will think of us. Just talk, but at least once you approach them for anything, invariably they cannot say no.

We found them willing to support us. On our part, we tried to give whatever we could that was beneficial to the community. This made us conceive of the permit system for the people, since some of them had no livelihood. The mayor knew we were starting to give all the people permits. Personally, I tried to single out the elderly and provide some income. These had no other means. And when we got other project funds, these were blessings to the community as well. Like the owner of the carrier who would sometimes transport us . . . Zyron, okay, we're friends with the mayor, and could we request that you provide us some chairs for the school? Then, we got involved setting up a radio system, that they started to use. If you were on the islands, you would have communication . . . if there were an emergency, the people could use it.

This idea of fitting into the system in place invariably affected the very system the PCP had wanted to set up. This led to a mode of management that departed radically from the classic mode of strict conservation and no-take zones. As one PCP leader recounted:

Brother [the first PCP team leader] was the resource person who set it up. He was the one who worked in the evolution of the initial design. It was renegotiated may times because, you know people, "could you give my family a permit, give us a little bit, I am the son of etc. etc." And out of this evolved the community workshop. They would post a list of permittees before the January to March closed season. Open season is April to December. And they came up with a three-year rotation. Once a family gets a permit, the next time they can get another allocation is only after everybody else is finished.

And what came of the negotiations was a rule system that no one had predicted, involving a hybrid system wherein 30 percent of the eggs would be left in place or transferred to nurseries, 60 percent would be used for income for island residents, and 10 percent would be set aside for the conservation fund. This was a system that, given the already existing NIPAS (National Integrated Protected Areas System Act of 1992) species conservation act in the Philippines, was statutorily inconceivable, and yet it made perfect sense to the PCP and egg wardens, along with the local community. That is, it was intelligible in the context of the narrative that evolved on the islands. On the other hand, a formal conservation program that allows the taking of turtle eggs for income is almost unheard of; the only other such formal program that the authors know about exists in Costa Rica (Campbell 1998).

The system, as the informants recounted it, was more complex than even the PCP, Mapun, local government, and the turtles. It included, in fact, actors on the margins of that community—for example, egg poachers, illegal fishers, and trawler owners who, while openly violating fishing restrictions, would assist the PCP in giving it free transport. It was important to the PCP to be able to coexist with even illegal operators in the area. And it underscored the need to respect the system of relationships in the place, and not simply exercise its mandate (i.e., to apprehend or fine violators). One PCP member recounts how the PCP responded to violators:

I do not think less of the people there . . . but sometimes, they will just not understand us if we simply approached them that way [censure]. So, we would really need to approach not him but his elder brother to work it out. We cannot simply separate out violators and tell them, this is what you did wrong, they are one clan. We cannot violate or punish them, no way. You need to course it through the community . . . you do not own the law. . . . Even the military, they could never simply decide how to deal with criminals since even they have to consult with the elders there.

And when they did censure a violator, the measure of choice was not any formal punishment but asking the elders to make him help the PCP out in its work for a month. Another described his innovative mode of patrolling for egg poachers:

We cannot be in the position of condoning poaching, but we patrol . . . so as not to encounter any poachers. For example, one of my favorite pastimes there was vocalizing [he then demonstrates] . . . I would vocalize until I heard echoes back from the other pocket beaches, till I heard three echoes . . . in the context of these negotiated relationships, they would know that I was coming, because I would project, and they could hide, so I would not see anyone when I passed the area . . . I was telling them "hide," and I will not catch you, because if I do, as a law enforcement agency, we are supposed to apprehend you. If the relationship were otherwise, then people may start bearing arms . . . sometimes it's four of us and twenty of them. . . . We would know when we were going to get hit . . . first, when we hear that there is an upcoming wedding, and you sometimes just need to turn a blind eye . . . and another is during the Hari Raya Puasa [involving the return to one's place of origin] when they need to find funds for travel . . . you learn to understand the culture, their dilemmas.

Emplotment literally gives each actor in the system a place, and what resulted on the islands was a delicate ritual dance in which the PCP and others marked out places for each, avoiding conflict and respecting limits. In turn, the PCP was accorded if not respect at least a sense of belonging on the islands. It is a system of fuzzy, implicit rules, oftentimes not formally acknowledged (except in these confidential interviews). In this case, formal notions of structure such as formal rules and roles and bureaucratic processes do not suffice to describe the system. Where do we find the actual structure of the system described? Nowhere else but in the narrative that emplots, gives each actor a place, and works out a coherent system of meaning. It is only within this complex narrative that many things make sense—for example, the fact that the PCP, while guarding against illegal trawler fishing around the islands, often approach the same trawlers for free passage to and fro, or the fact that it was perfectly normal for the PCP members themselves to "poach" some eggs to help out families who approached them for help. Here is how one of them talked about the trawlers:

Then there are those who would anchor at Baguan (a no-fishing zone) and they would say they would just fish . . . but we would tell them you cannot anchor there by the coral . . . and you cannot fish here . . . because this is covered by municipal waters . . . but sometimes we would go to their boat and fish for a past time . . . sometimes when we run out of food, we would buy some from them, and sometimes they would just give it to us . . . they would ask us to buy some things for them when on our trips to Manila . . . so in turn when we need something it is not embarrassing for us to ask them . . . although we say that these tampasaks are really like that (destroy fishing grounds), how can I tell them you own a tampasak and so you are the cause of these problems in the country . . . how can we say that? Even some of our friends in Malaysia, sometimes they visit us bringing food . . . once they asked us for some eggs, but we could not give them eggs then, we did not want the wardens to see us doing this.

See, with us, we're friends with the trawlers, too . . . so when they come (to our island), they will anchor there, ask us for water, we would give them . . . then they would give us fish, whatever they can give us. So that's where we are . . . we don't even know how much illegal activity they do. But they are the type who share with us . . . whatever favor we ask, they would give. Like one time, there was an emergency, we needed to reach a fishing boat, we turned to them.

Especially the PCP (from Manila), they know that the tampasaks work against the program, but sometimes they hitch a ride with them, they just don't even say "let's go take a tampasak"—no, they would say "tampa" as if they were talking about something else.

It is a narrative of give-and-take, and of fitting in, where respect, suspicion, self-interest, community, and connectedness all figure into the ethic of the system. If there is a balance here, it is not the thermodynamic homeostasis of Odum's ecology, but an improvised ballet of sorts, such as the PCP and poachers' game of regulatory hide-and-seek. What we did not find, in the narratives that they shared with us, was ecological talk: the beauty of wilderness, the inviolate character of species, the aesthetic of nature—whether these were or were not present, they did not appear with any prominence. Rather, the narrative was one of mutual survival and inclusion—literally, in this system, everything and everyone has its proper place (even the improper). One might say, on the islands, ecology exists as a kind of realpolitik.

Emplotment is the action by which islanders take the disparate elements of their everyday lives and make sense of the whole. On the islands, there was not a conservation program on one hand and a separate socioeconomic sphere on the other—rather, these merged together into the same fabric as the local economy. It should not be surprising then (but to us, it was) that egg conservation should then be closely tied to partial harvesting and support of the local economy. There were not, on these islands, an environmental ethic on the one hand, and the local culture on the other. There was only one ethic of place, and that ethic understood the turtles, the islanders, and eventually the PCP members, as simply characters in the greater narrative of the islands.

Another essential function of the narrative is to introduce a logical or coherent sequence of events, whether events are tied by some causal or other logic. So, we look for sequence in the narratives of the islands—this means telling a story that links conditions and events decades ago, to those today, to possible future actions. In fact, the story of the turtle conservation on the islands does not begin with the PCP but decades before, when the Mapun first inhabited the islands and found the shores teaming with nesting turtles (Domantay 1953).

Beyond just establishing a sequence, good narratives make the pattern of events interesting. A good story cannot simply follow an established formula. Rather, it needs to be its own particular story, with a plot that progresses in sometimes unexpected ways. We find all this in the Turtle Islands, where the system of management was not something simply institutionalized and, from that point on, left in place. Rather, it evolved over time, changed shape, took in new actors, and progressed. The plot took twists and turns and led to a system (or narrative) that was unique to the islands—indeed, such a program had not been established elsewhere. An illustration of sequence and progression is seen in figure 5.2.

The lower half of the figure shows, in chronological order, the sequence of key events and actions spanning several decades. It begins with the first colonization of the islands by the Mapun, continues through the arrival of the PCP, and proceeds onward. The lower half presents the basic plot presented as a logical summary or *fabula* of the story. The

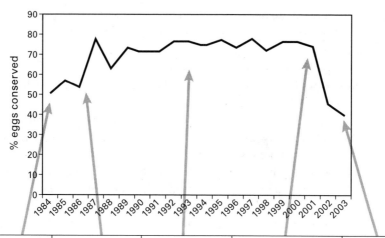

In the 1940s, the Jama Mapun first settled on the Turtle Islands and discovered shores teeming with marine turtles. In the 1950s, they discovered a thriving market for turtle eggs in nearby Sandakan and began harvesting some of the eggs for income. They also evolved cultural practices that had a conservation effect, like having no activity during the first three months of the year, leaving two of the islands untouched, and evolving a local corps of experts (egg probers).	In the early 1980s, the PCP first arrived on the islands with a mandate to create a new conservation program. They felt like intruders at first and sought to integrate themselves into the community first. They found that they could not impose their conservation plan upon the community and instead chose to institutionalize many of the existing practices, including partial harvesting of eggs (which they formalized with a permit system), scientific monitoring, and delegation of the program to the local corps of egg probers.	For more than a decade, the hybrid program was successfully implemented. The PCP became part of the local community, and they participated in many of its activities. During this time, egg conservation increased. The egg permit allocations gave the locals a reliable source of supplementary income. Local government began touting the program to visitors.	After the Philippines signed CITES, its government then passed RA 9147 in 2001, a new law that transferred control of ecologically sensitive areas to the national government, banned all harvest and sale of species and products, and imposed complete conservation practices. The Turtle Islands community was unaware of the new law, until the PCP was asked to deliver a letter to the local mayor. Upon reading the letter, the mayor tore it up, and proceeded to vent his anger at the hapless PCP. One PCP member recalls, after the incident, how a shot was fired in the night, narrowly missing him.	Following the locals' reaction, the PCP stopped implementing the program and kept themselves only on Baguan Island. The little monitoring data since then indicates a sharp drop in egg conservation activity. Hoping to seek reconciliation, the government proposed a moratorium period, during which a formal arrangmenet for turtle conservation would be negotiated. The status of the program still remains uncertain.

Figure 5.2
Egg conservation chart (top) and fabula (bottom) (*Source:* Egg conservation data from Lejano et al. 2007)

upper half of the figure chronicles the degree of effectiveness of conservation over time, as measured by the portion of eggs that were actually conserved. One can see the progression as the PCP and other actors began developing a new system for turtle egg rationing and conservation—in fact, since 1982, the percentage of eggs conserved could be seen to rise steadily. One sees twists and turns in the saga of the management system reflected in the graph.

Figure 5.2 is an interesting comparison of technical discourse with narrative discourse. Taken by itself, the upper half of the figure tells a good enough story, but it is not a rich narrative. When we simply look at the positivist measures of the scientist, we do not learn about the characters in the place, its local ethic, the interesting saga of its history. The lower half provides narrative richness that does not contradict the scientific data but, in fact, helps us understand it more deeply. Now, we see how the fate of the eggs, as measured from year to year, is richly explained by the sequence of events that transpired. When we see the sudden drop in egg conservation, it is not merely the story of the eggs we are looking at—rather, it is now part of the dramatic twists and turns of the narrative, the conflicts and betrayals, the inherent tragedy of it. When we understand the drop in conservation as part of the sequence of events that begins with the mayor tearing up the letter from Manila and throwing it in the PCP member's face and continues to the shot that was fired in the dark at them later on, we have gone beyond mere science to the realm of real-life drama.

The establishment of an entirely unique system of ecological management is something special to this narrative. It is a plot that turns on distinct characters and rich relationships between them. Uniqueness of character is seen not in the nondescript roles of the local government and the PCP, but in the very "personas" taken on the by the turtles.

These twists and turns operate as breaches of canon that maintain a dynamic tension in the narrative. They also correspond to the complex, messy way in which real-life narratives operate. Most significant, in figure 5.2, is the rapid break at the very end of the sequence, which was precipitated by the mayor's indignation at the new conservation regime, and which the figure merely lists as part of the story's fabula.

Characterization: Nonhuman Actants and Conservationists

Narrative also involves character development, and understanding the system involves characterization of the turtles, as the Mapun describe them:

We feel for the pawikan. They help us a lot, in fact, they have given us a livelihood, on our three islands. Permitees (for harvesting) are given a livelihood. . . . For us, we see the pawikan as like our children. Because it's just as hard to raise pawikan. . . . A lot of the pawikan die. There are illegal fish nets, and illegal trawlers. The trawlers catch them. . . . When you look into their eyes (the pawikan), it's as if they are crying. You will feel for them. The same when you hold them . . . We teach (the residents) how to take care of the pawikan, they should care for them since the pawikan help them.

Characterization of the turtle, in this case, involves some element of personification, but perhaps it is not primarily attribution of human elements but the Mapun's understanding of the turtle in the same terms as their interpersonal experience.

The Mapun we interviewed held a certain pathos for the turtles, to the point of personification. The turtles, in this story, followed their own improvised scripts—in this sense, they displayed agency, as a character in a narrative would. In a sense, the delicate ballet of the islands began with the turtle's actions, not directly, but as traces on the sand, which the Mapun would study and follow around the beach. The whole cycle of life on the islands seemed to begin with the pawikan's own dance, a flurry of activity in the deep of night, as she dug into the beach and laid her eggs. The islanders, and later the PCP, would then join in, in their own ritual ballet, which were patterned after the pawikan's. And the progression would end with the hatching of the eggs in the nurseries and the juveniles stumbling their way back into the surf to begin the process again.

Not just the turtles, but the eggs themselves play a part in this sequence. The mayor of the islands described it in this way: "Our life and living, therefore, revolve around turtle eggs as the natural adaptation of our ecosystem . . . And our only hope and solid anchor for our living are the eggs that the Allah-given turtles produce . . . This is a prayer that will define our life and death, demarcate the line between hunger and sustenance, and between living and dying."

The turtles were more than just species to be protected, and the eggs more than just their products. As he said, a whole system of living and social exchange were fitted around the turtles and the eggs they produced. But the talk was not an ecological talk—that is, they did not talk about the turtles as a unique species, as something exotic to be preserved, but rather as just a part of the place like the Mapun.

The way the member of the Mapun described the turtles is important if we are to understand the mode of emplotment that occurred on the islands. The local actors, of course, understood well what it meant, legally, for the turtles to be classified as a protected species. But the deeper characterization of the turtle was as, in a sense, kindred, as co-residents of the island. The turtle was not so much set apart from civilization but an element of the community that inhabited the islands. And this coheres with the type of management system (or, in our terms, the emplotment) that evolved. In this system, all had a place, and nothing was separate. In this manner, the Mapun and other residents shared the islands with the turtles. Aside from one of the islands (Baguan), none of the others featured so-called sanctuaries, on which no habitation was allowed. This stood in contrast to the turtle management program in nearby Sabah, Malaysia, which involved creating a set of ecological parks. On the Philippine Turtle Islands, land was not neatly zoned into settlements and reserves—rather, humans and turtles commingled. Not even poachers and illegal fishers were exiled from this system.

This also helps us understand how it is that the system of partial harvesting of the eggs seemed reasonable to these policy actors. Ecology and economy were not two separate systems, and, similarly, livelihood and conservation were not. It is true this conjunction was contrary to the formal conservation plan, as established by the government, but, as we showed, the management plan that was practiced was done through many nonformalized practices.

The way the PCP characterized itself also helped us comprehend the rationale and meaning of the system it developed. Nearly all of the PCP members we interviewed admitted to a strong awareness that they were, at least initially, outsiders to the islands. They had to deal with mistrust of them by the locals and, in turn, their own apprehensiveness about the islanders. The sense of being different was compounded by the fact that most of the PCP members were Christians, Manila-bred, in contrast to the islanders who were mostly Muslims from the Visayas and Mindanao. They described their position as having to take great care to not be seen as an interloper. In part, this was due to their degree of vulnerability—more than a thousand kilometers from their base in Manila and without any appreciable support in terms of logistics and safety, their choices were getting along or being expelled from the islands. One of the PCP members described the thing they wanted to avoid:

In a traditional view, they're looking at us as the poachers, the outsiders who are taking their resources from them. On our part, (we can claim) this is the Philippines, this is the law, and sea turtles are endangered species, and egg collection is prohibited by the wildlife act. Even traditional forms of livelihood are excluded; no touch, no take. So, from their point of view, we can be the poachers, we are the outsiders, coming in to take their resources. And we can view them as illegal egg collectors. They don't have permits . . . You know, we can always go back to that way of looking at things.

He then went on to describe the waves of settlers onto the islands, beginning from the 1950s and continuing today, then talked about the many activities they had to participate in to become part of the context.

[It's] business in a sense, but it's more of engaging in conversations with people, you exchange things . . . in one place, we talk about fishing methods, then later, they talk with you about using your bunkhouse overnight; in return, they give you ice, fish, information. Then we give them safe anchorage, instead of anchoring in the open ocean. These are easy things to do . . . There is a sense of moral authority that reigns in the area. Sometimes this involves (someone telling another) you're not from here, you weren't born here, and the other says, but I grew up here . . . so, us, we build up some assertion of moral authority, too. We started playing basketball . . . when there's a wedding, they invite us . . . it's like a dance party, but these dances are ritualized.

But some of this understanding remains the sense that part of the PCP's authority was knowledge, but always negotiated within a complex network of community affairs.

Because we have a kind of authority regarding the eggs, we are the ones who can figure out when eggs can be taken. It's based on our computations, semi-scientific. Say (we calculate) only 150 permits a year, but there are 300 families (on the island). How would you handle that. There's always latent conflict. So people would approach us with their needs. They would send "spies." Someone would talk to the wardens, and they would talk to us. The networks of information go from house to house, there are many routes.

Characterization also helps us understand the degree to which the PCP [was] open to accommodating the local ways of doing things, including combining the harvesting and preservation of turtle eggs in the system of management. This does not mean that the PCP members did not see themselves as experts or as having knowledge that the locals did not have—the PCP [was], after all, trained biologists and fisheries experts. But the PCP's openness to local knowledge (and moral authority) is easier to understand when we hear the PCP members characterize themselves as being visiting supplicants—in a sense, the Mapun had primacy of place. They were of the islands, and they knew the islands inside and out. And the PCP members would, at times, express a sense of gratitude to us, when they recalled how the islanders gradually began accepting them. The vulnerability that the PDP members felt coheres with their unwillingness to exert their legal authority and dominate the local agenda. The self-characterization of themselves as sharers of a legacy coheres with the mode of conservation management that shared responsibility and authority with local residents.

The PCP members describe their position vis-à-vis the residents' egg harvesting:

It's like a tradition. Depends on how you look at it . . . they've been there for generations, and this is how they lived, inheriting this way of life from their parents. And then, here you come in from the outside, and you would tell them that they're poaching? No, this is their longstanding tradition. "Poacher" means someone from the outside taking resources from the community. We could be considered the poachers from their point of view . . . They have a fascinating culture . . . they live on an island with limited resources but they survive. How do they do that? This is why there is a lot we can learn from them, how to make use of finite resources. So, my bond (with the local egg probers), it's like they are my mentors. How do you do this? Pa, why does this happen? . . . Pa Iga, I look up to him . . . technically, he is a game warden. I look for these local knowledges and practices, and he coaches me. One fascinating thing I learned (he gets up to get a stick), this is how they probe for eggs . . . so the turtles would lay their eggs there, but when you get there, you don't see any signs on the surface, usually it's 60 centimeters deep, so there is a technique there, you don't just poke into the ground, you have to read it, he taught me how to read it. So he would teach me, here is where the eggs are, based on the signs, here is where the turtle was facing when she laid the eggs, and here is where she climbed back up . . . I was an apprentice.

Alterity and the Other

One theme that often came up in the interviews was the element of the outsider. In the beginning, the PCP's preoccupation was its status as outsiders and its urgent need to start belonging. But the other figured often in these discourses, and the sense one gets is that the life of the islands continued under ever-present threat of encroachment from the other. There are threatening figures in this narrative, and they included the trawlers from Manila, but sometimes from Malaysia and even Taiwan, who could, in a day, despoil the habitat (with their modern equipment) in a way the combined activities of all the locals could not do.

There is the specter of the global community, which regulators are always reminded of by constant reference to the Convention for Biological Diversity and the Convention on the International Trade of Endangered Species, both of which the Philippine government had signed and that drove the writing of the Wildlife Resources Conservation and Protection Act, known as RA 9147. The global norm, which has diffused across the entire global south, considers conservation as a rigid category, separating that which humans despoil from the pristine. Mary Douglas has linked this type of classification system to the same basic ordering impulse that drives taboo and fetish (Douglas 1966). This is aided by the bureaucratic efficiency of such dichotomous classification schemes. What this led to, in practice, is the primacy of concepts such as preserves, no-take zones, marine sanctuaries, and similar instruments. Katrina Brandon has critiqued these zoning schemes, in the context of forest management, for the undue alienation of local community and its means of survival (Brandon, Redford, and Sanderson 1998), and other authors have examined the practice of preserves in general (Brockington, Duffy, and Igoe 2008). But what was being attempted on the Turtle Islands, mixed regimes and partial harvesting, flies in the face of this global norm. The external, in turn, always seemed to be present to the islanders as a nagging if sublimated threat (Lejano and Ingram 2007).

And, most of all, there was Manila. The Turtle Islands, in Tawi-Tawi, were on the extreme southern end of the country, and Manila was on the other. This physical distance served to buffer the islands from the political dynamic of Manila, to a degree, but Manila remained an ever-present figure in the islanders' cognition. The PCP members were wary of the fact that, while the egg probers were considered to be local PCP wardens, they were regarded as Manila-based PCP scientists. Ironically, within the Manila-based DENR, the PCP was considered something of an anomaly too. The PCP was forever a special project of the DENR, not given a set allocation, and its members were hired as contractees, whose contracts had to be reapproved every January.

Manileños were regarded with suspicion. This latent friction between the islanders and Manila came to a head in 2001, however, when the government passed RA 9147, as a response to the Philippines' obligations as a signatory to the Convention on the International Trade of Endangered Species. The act essentially prohibited the sale of wildlife and wildlife by-products. It was understood that the sale of turtle eggs would be banned and that, moreover, the national government would formally have jurisdiction over turtle habitat on the islands. When the mayor was first told of this new policy, he responded in this manner:

This is garbage. This is garbage. [Sound of paper tearing.] These projects of yours . . . they are no good . . . What you want is to destroy our system. We here, we are quiet people. We don't cause trouble to anyone. But you are the ones causing trouble. Okay? Tell them that . . . This is wrong. What you do, little by little, they take. I know your plans. Little by little . . . Better if you just kill us all. But maybe you first. . . . You need to have pity on these people. You have to wake them up. Your visit here is useless. Really useless. Your project is useless. Tell your director. Even the president. You will see.

The mayor's words painted a narrative of intrusion by the outsiders yet again, but this time, to an extreme degree, almost suggesting the physical takeover of the islands by Manila and implying the possibility of an armed response on the part of the islanders. As recounted to us by the PCP members who were there, they simply stood there in shock, not knowing what had transpired. But perhaps the mayor had cause to react in that manner. In the parallel chain of islands in nearby Sandakan, Malaysia, there had also been, years before, a government-initiated movement toward turtle habitat conservation. In that case, what had once been a thriving community of island dwellers is now a set of ecological parks, uninhabitated save for the Malaysian park rangers.

The reaction of the locals, which took the PCP by surprise, was one of indignation over the loss of a source of livelihood and, moreover, a perceived takeover of the entire island system itself. In 2003, the municipal government responded by formally issuing a resolution to keep control of the habitat and essentially take this authority away from the national government (Musilim 2003). The local government's hostile reaction to the PCP resulted in the latter's physical eviction from the islands and unraveling of the PCP program. Even its local counterparts, the conservation wardens, were prevented from implementing conservation and were relegated to observer status on the islands (except for Baguan Island, which was uninhabited). This final breach is reflected in the rightmost portion of figure 5.2 a depiction of the dismantling of the web of relationships that the PCP had been so careful to maintain. (Note: To this day, we cannot obtain updated numbers on egg conservation and, so, the figure tails off at 2004.)

The system, or, in our terms, the narrative that had required a slow process of emplotment over more than a decade, broke down. The social network, which is necessarily maintained by the working and reworking of numerous relationships, crumbled when the PCP's relationships with the islanders were undone by the new mandate from Manila and replaced by a strict conservation regime. The process, to this day, remains a stalemate, as the DENR, realizing the difficulty of instituting a new system in the midst of such conflict, proposed a moratorium on the implementation of RA 9147.

Scholars on community-based resource management, perusing the Turtle Islands case, may point to the lack of so-called cross-scale linkages as a central problem in this institution (e.g., Cudney-Bueno and Basurto 2009). The narratives we heard, however, seem to say otherwise—that insulation was, at least for a time, necessary for the system to survive. As before, eschewing purely structuralist notions, we remind ourselves that such linkages to larger systems of governance are not simply formal ties but relationships. Perhaps the answer lies in the complex nature of these relationships.

Breach of Convention

The nature of emplotment has strong implications for governance. First, the ecology of the system, in the eyes of those interviewed, was not human versus nature, but this nondescript mix of ecology, politics, economy, and culture. The cycle of turtle breeding and survival was integrated into the web of political relationships, even corruption, on the islands. This had consequences for how the system was managed. As one PCP member said: "Yes, we brought (initially) a Western concept . . . like they have the Yellowstone National Park, they have a park setup there, where one cannot live inside a park . . . here, we cannot have a park setup with no one living in it . . . we really had to have different concepts here . . . for example, the permitting system . . . the local concepts, these are not defensible in the scientific world, we just refer to them as local knowledge and tradition."

What they eventually did on the Philippine Turtle Islands stands in stark contrast to the Malaysian Turtle Islands wherein they did create a reserve. Decades ago, the Malaysian government decided to relocate thousands of settlers on the islands and create a park system—today, save for the regular visits by ecotourists, only forest rangers live in the Malaysian Turtle Islands. One former member of the PCP would also contrast the Philippine Turtle Islands with nearby Boracay, a famous tourist spot in Aklan, Philippines. Boracay was, as opposed to an ecological reserve, turned into a tourist paradise. The fear was that ecotourism might bring to the islands the illnesses and crime that they imagined happened to Boracay, the possible preoccupation of locals with tourists instead of their own, and the loss of culture. In the framework of the PCP and other actors on the Turtle Islands, both park and recreational paradise were equally alien concepts. Part of the alienating nature of these concepts was due to cultural factors, but a very real part of it, for the residents we spoke with, was that both of them brought with them the prospect of relocation (as had happened in Malaysia).

Likewise, the establishment of a permit system can be seen, within a rationalist lens, as a system of trade-offs between conservation and local livelihood. However, none of the interviewees used any words or descriptions that evoke the idea of a trade-off or compromise. Rather, the word most often encountered was that of "survival"—a universal consideration that applied equally to turtles, local residents, and the PCP.

At every turn, formal program designs blurred, and what we found were improvised, hybrid designs that were well described in confidential interviews but never recorded in print (Lejano 2008). This contrasts with classic institutional forms involving clear-cut rules and authorities. Perhaps Weber might have described this system as a mix of structure and charisma—however, we understand it better as a mode of practice that is lived more than it is formally institutionalized. In literary terms, narration was accomplished by each actor in the network, and characters worked out their roles and identities in real life, exhibiting both the structuring effect of formal and informal institutions and the dynamic aspects of individual and group agency. These practices are difficult to express as a system of rules. For example, how would we write out the rules behind the practice of sometimes allowing the poaching of eggs and other times disallowing it? We might use ethical principles to reason why the PCP would provide eggs to bereaved families in times of need, but how do we rationalize the fact that the military, to whom the PCP would turn to in serious cases of poaching or illegal fishing, was also the one who most often asked the PCP to give its members turtle eggs for gifts? Rather, these practices were worked out in the dynamic give-and-take of everyday life. But what gave "structure" to these exchanges were the patterns of relationships among the actors and material need for each actor to survive.

The narrative we were most often told about the islands existed in contrast to the larger, conventional narrative of marine conservation. The conventional narrative can be found reflected in various international agreements, especially CITES (the Convention on International Trade in Endangered Species of Wild Fauna and Flora treaty), which was one of the motivating forces behind the Philippines' ecological conservation movement. The latter prohibited the taking of by-products of endangered species or, if allowed, subjected it to formal licensing and approval by an international body.

The Contextuality of Knowledge

What we find is a unique intermingling of aspects of science, local practice, culture, religion, and taboos, and a keen understanding of the political environment. The Mapun had already wrapped their cultural and economic practices around the pawikan.

To be sure, there was no question as to who the privileged scientists were in this community. The locals we interviewed would, almost by habit, talk about how they respected the Manileños and the science they brought. They are the ones who really know, one of them would say. But we also found an openness on the part of the PCP to knowledge possessed by the Mapun, especially the elderly egg probers. The PCP did not refer to this as science or folk wisdom, but simply knowledge or method.

As one PCP member wrote in his journal:

Some local residents have devised methods to locate the eggs in the green turtle nest despite such concealment . . . On a typical early morning, Pa I (alternating with Pa S) treks Baguan's beach, searching for traces of sea turtle activity the night before . . . However, the exact location of the eggs and the depth that these are buried cannot be determined without additional information. To ascertain the location of the egg chamber, Pa I and Pa S use a metal egg probe . . . Pa I and Pa S use the egg probe very sparingly . . . For most nests, they have achieved a skill level that enables them to "perceive" where the egg chamber is located even without resorting to the egg probe . . . During my early fieldwork, Pa I and I would test each other . . . Invariably, Pa I would be correct.

In the preceding description, we see both the respect accorded by the biologist to the egg prober, as well as the care with which the latter went about the search for nests (gingerly using the probe so as not to break any eggs or have the egg chamber collapse).

As was briefly discussed earlier in the chapter, the PCP, in turn, formalized the local practices by giving them a scientific form. The local practice of locating nests and partial storage of eggs in nurseries was made systematic by adding statistical procedures. Egg probers would do extensive accounting of turtles, nests, eggs, and hatchlings. In turn, the PCP would use this information to determine the optimal number of eggs that could be harvested in a year. One PCP member used the term "rationalize" to describe the program they had set up. But this is not simply the displacement of the premodern by the modern; rather, what emerges if an integration of different types of knowledge from different knowledge communities. This seems, to us, to be an important cause and outcome of network ties. When networks are open and relational, even knowledge is transformed.

One of the PCP members described it in these terms: "Your immediate family, the staff, the wardens. In a sense, we look through their eyes to see life on the islands. We listen to them . . . what's happening there, what's up with them."

When we examine the stories these actors tell about how they came upon these stores of knowledge, we realize exactly what it means when scholars describe how social ties and boundary-spanning activities are requisite for building new ways of knowing (Gerlak and Heikkila 2011; Lejano and Ingram 2009).

Value Added through Narrative Analysis

What did we learn from taking a narrative approach to analyzing the Turtle Islands case that we might not have otherwise? The following are a few important insights that other, formal modes of analysis (e.g., network analysis, program evaluation, rational choice, etc.) would not have provided.

1   Institutions as a Web of Relationships

If we try to explain the conservation program that the PCP initiated in the 1980s, we would be hard-pressed to describe it in classic institutional terms. A structural description of the system, such as an organizational chart, would immediately be proven wrong by the complex ways that the program was run. Roles and rules were fuzzy and constantly broken (though we understand these not as "rule-breaking" but "relationship-maintenance"). A policy actor could be conservationist, trader, egg poacher, and other roles all at the same time. The complex mode of accommodating the sometimes urgent need to poach eggs is not something that can be captured by a set of rules. But it is understandable, and adequately described, when we describe the system as a story with characters and relationships and an evolving drama.

Indeed, given the great improvisational latitude taken by the policy actors in going about program implementation (and daily living—there is no break between one and the other), we see that formal structure, rules, and roles can be epiphenomenal to the working and reworking of relationships in the place. And, again, relationships are best described by emplotting them into a rich and coherent story.

The ties that bind one actor to another, and the saga of events that rupture them, are what narrative supplies and (as discussed in chapter 4) what is invisible in a network analysis diagram.

2   Comprehending the Irrational

Seen simply as a conservation program, one can understand the regression of the system to a tragedy of an open commons, but one does not understand the rather extreme actions by the islanders. What would move them to such a hostile attitude, seemingly all of a sudden—in fact, bordering on violence (spoken or attempted)? What would create such a resilient intransigence such that today, years later, the PCP are still hesitant to travel to the islands? It cannot be understood in institutional or programmatic or rational terms. But it can be understood when told as a story of longstanding isolation (by the Mapun), initial suspicion, gradual trust, reconfigured lives, and sudden betrayal.

This points to a curious thing about literature. Rational theories about the rational actor cannot explain heroism and hatred. What would move a zealot to martyrdom? What moved students to give up their lives at Tiananmen Square, or monks to protest on the streets of Rangoon? But when it is written about, whether in a piece of fiction or historical novel, it makes sense to us. These become stories that inspire, not beg disbelief. It is the power of narrative to capture the rich meaning of human action.

But the ethos and pathos of these real-life dramas are, as the ancient Greeks realized, described best through narrative means. Lejano and Leong put it this way: "We hope we have made a case for narrative, as well as the capacity of hermeneutics to elucidate the sometimes impenetrable logic of disenchantment. It is not in the dispassionately rational model of interest-centered pluralism that controversy becomes comprehensible. People mobilize because they care, or have been hurt, and somehow moved. Rather, it is narrative that gets to the heart of the matter" (Lejano and Leong 2012).

3   Institution Building as Narrating

Life on the islands is a story that is constantly being written and rewritten. When the PCP first arrived on the islands, the Mapun had to find ways to integrate them into their everyday round—either that or to alienate them. Literally, the islanders had to be able to re-narrate their everyday existence in a way that included these new arrivals. If it is through narrating that people make sense of the complex and myriad elements of everyday life, then it is through re-narration that they can reconfigure the same.

But it takes time to reconfigure the scheme of everyday life. When we understand institution building through the act of emplotment, perhaps we better understand why it is that the sudden change in conservation regulation could not simply be absorbed by the locals. And, conversely, it helps us understand that the way forward cannot happen overnight.

There is something about narration that speaks to community. Lyotard (1979) wrote about this, in terms of the distance between scientific-technical discourse, where communication goes from expert to nonexpert, and that of narrative discourse, where hearer becomes speaker and communication is shared among all in the community. If narration is a good metaphor for institution building, then we realize that the task of narrating must necessarily include others in the community. All must be able to share in storytelling. The story must have plurivocity, such that others can tell it differently than you. The story of how turtles and humans get along on the islands cannot simply be crafted and told by the PCP or DENR or the international bioconservation coalition—rather, it must be something the islanders can help tell. Narration is, after all, a shared activity.

4   Richness of Ethical Reasoning

What we encounter in the islanders' and PCP's narratives is a richness of normative grounding. One finds it hard to fit the motivations and moral commitments found into neat categories. Classic environmentalism gives way to a mode of understanding environment as not unrelated to poverty, filial relation, power, and tradition. The islanders are perfectly able to reconcile their harvesting of turtle eggs with an understanding of the turtles as kindred beings. Islanders display individually rational behavior. The system does not devolve into a tragedy of the commons even when the system breaks down (i.e., egg conservation continues to some extent even after the PCP program ended) or when monitoring is ineffective (i.e., poaching is not about wealth so much as it is about survival during times of need).

Just consider how one PCP member described how she started being part of the island system:

The way I see it, because I mingle with people, because I meet people when I go from island to island, people seem to respect me . . . no, it's closer to something like family, no? . . . I go around in jeans, in a t-shirt, or a jacket, little by little, I see people starting to dress like me . . . I like Ma'am A's clothes, they would say . . . One really starts to belong. Whatever their custom is, that's what I find myself doing . . . if they invite me to the fiesta or a party, I go even if I'm not in the mood. When I'm there, people come by and give me fruit, so at some point I would feel obliged to bring gifts, too. But they told me, there is a Muslim custom that says you should not reciprocate the giving of a gift, it's not an exchange. When someone gives you a gift, do not give a gift in return . . . It's like you did not appreciate their gift enough. . . . So I am really at ease with them . . . when they eat with their hands, I eat with my hands. . . . One day, someone came, with the flu . . . you know, the one pill I gave, they would pay me back with five kilograms of fish. What I mean is, they respect you.

What we hear is not the classic notion of reciprocity on which collective action is classically based. There is no sense of the tit-for-tat kind of strategic behavior. Rather, it is explained as relationship—namely, that of respect of belonging. In Lejano 2008, this was portrayed as an ethic of care, which was described as a concern not for rule-bound ethical principles so much as enriching the web of relationships, a notion that traces back to the phenomenological idea of intentionality (Brentano 1874; Husserl [1900] 1970) and, more recently, Gilligan's formulation of care (1982). In an ethical system of care, what governs how people act is simply relationship—more than exchange or utility, what governs is how people's identities are mutually constituted by their interaction with others.

Analysis of such ethically complex ground gives us a glimpse into possibilities for institution building. Indeed, if we understand an institution to be a web of relationships, then it should be possible to give a community's rich ethical life institutional form. In Lejano 2008, an attempt was made to trace the foundations of institutional design, in systems such as the Turtle Islands, to this complex ethical system, which was built around neither the rational nor the deontological but the relational—namely, around an ethic of care. Collins, Cooney, and Garlington (2012) similarly talk about the need to institutionalize compassion. The abstract becomes real when ethics transmute into relationships, and relationships take on the life of an institution.

We see how our study of narratives around turtle conservation lets us understand the intricate modes of integration that allow the islanders to blend and act upon science, value, tradition, economy, culture, and identity. These islanders are rational, utility-seeking actors, but they are not simply so. They act according to ethics of tribe, friendship, and fairness, but their motivations are not simply circumscribed by them. If they exhibit topophilia, it is wrapped up in other aspects of quality of life (e.g., Ogunseitan 2005), where love, fear, longing, anger, and hope are all imbued in their sense of place. It all comes together (imperfectly so, to be sure) in talk and in action. We might extend our understanding of narration as also including practice. When we asked an elder Mapun to describe his mode of surveillance for eggs, at some point, he takes his stick and, like a mime, goes through the motions for us. Storytellers are allowed, when words fail them, to act out their story. The crucial aspect is sharing in the meaning of things.

5   Organizing Principle

What we found on the Turtle Islands is a complex management scheme, involving formal and informal elements, that defied classification. Indeed, there are attempts in the literature on community-based coastal resource management that do attempt richer ways of classifying these "co-management" schemes (e.g., Campbell et al. 2009; Christie and White 2006). But typologies and schema can describe only so much, and at some point, these new, sometimes innovative management, programs cannot be described well with classification systems. To simply call such a program a co-management scheme begs more questions than it can answer. What does co-management mean in this particular instance, and how is it practiced? How are responsibilities divided among the different actors, and to what extent are these duties routinized? Questions like these can only be answered through rich narratives. The literature on governance cannot stay content with simplistic classification schemes— to wit: state versus market versus community (and combinations thereof) and, at some point, it needs to make increasing use of narrative and other richly descriptive tools for analysis.

How might we characterize the locally grounded ways of management that evolved on the islands? It was not a classic conservation program with its rule-based behavior. Nor was it a classic open commons, where individually rationalistic behavior ruled. As one PCP member put it, while he was describing the bond between PCP and locals, a fine line exists between complete integration and separateness that has always been maintained:

So, if you don't have a bond with these people, if you don't have a concern for them (apart from your program), you have no business being with them, you might not stay there more than two weeks. They were hesitant (with me) at first, but now when I am there, we are family. But like relationships with other people, even my own family, you cannot share everything . . . A limitation is I don't want to tread too much on their lives, and I don't want them to overindulge with me. These limitations, like respect, you always have to maintain these. Although you bond, there is still the maintaining of respect.

These constant adjustments and readjustments, evidenced in so much of the story told by the PCP, seemed to the author to be tending toward, but never finding, equilibrium. That there never was an equilibrium is seen in the rate of egg conservation, which gradually rose over time, until it reached a peak of above 85 percent in the late 1990s.

And all of these relationships revolved around and extended to the turtles themselves. As a Mapun told one of this book's authors, "We consider the turtles as if they were brothers. Sometimes, I can tell if one of them is crying. You know they give much to the Mapun, they give a part of themselves. And we have learned to take care of them." Another refers to these as "Allah-given." And he proceeds to describe how, when they release newly hatched turtles, they make them crawl across a stretch of beach before they enter the water, so the turtles feel and remember home. The PCP's tagging activities confirmed this. If we were to create an organization chart of this network (which was difficult for the people we interviewed to conceive of), at the center of it would be the turtle and her nest of eggs. How does the turtle exhibit agency in this case— that is, how does she emplot herself into the narrative? Most simply, by returning to her home, struggling up the beach, continuing to make nests and lay eggs. And her ritual dance brings out a ritual dance among the Mapun and, from them, to the PCP. When we describe this coordinated set of practices, we describe the institution. It was a ritual dance, not in any aesthetic sense, but in the sense of the flesh-and-blood realpolitik of daily survival.

If there was an organizing principle, it was the impromptu dance of mutual accommodation, affinity, suspicion, trust, and survival. Perhaps the closest concepts in the literature to this are those of the logic of fit (March and Olsen 1989) and institutional ecology (Hannan and Freeman 1977). But we prefer to describe this as care, which is the mutual accommodation, responsiveness to the other, and the everyday working and reworking of hopefully enduring relationships. This was a community struggling for daily survival, and survival required the give-and-take of relationship and a finely tuned improvisation. But we would not have learned of any of these were we not told stories by the PCP and residents of the Turtle Islands.

6

Narratives of Nature and Science in Alternative Farming Networks

In light of the widespread presence of organic agricultural products and the expansion of organic acreage over the last three decades[1] it is perhaps easy to overlook the extent to which, until fairly recently, organic and other forms of alternative agriculture were marginalized and actively denigrated by mainstream practice. Proponents of organic farming began to broadcast their ideas in the United States, Great Britain, and other countries over seventy years ago, but gained hard won territory in terms of market share and political representation only within the last three decades. In the United States, "mainstreaming" of organic agriculture has included the passage of the federal National Organic Program in 1990 regulating organic production (Ingram and Ingram 2005), the wide-spread distribution of organic products in outlets such as Safeway and Walmart, and the creation of government funding programs for organic research and outreach such as the USDA Sustainable Agriculture Research and Education (SARE) program.

These diverse indicators of interest and support are a radical change from thirty years ago. Commonly held attitudes about organic farming are well represented by a 1971 comment from former Secretary of Agriculture Earl Butz: "We can go back to organic farming if we must—we know how to do it. However, before we move in that direction, someone must decide which 50 million of our people will starve" (Butz 1971). Butz's comment reveals not only the disparaging attitude held by government officials and many agricultural practitioners toward alternative agriculture, but also a still-common notion that organic agriculture, because it is "natural," is already something that we know how to do, and that no particular special skills or training are necessary. Despite burgeoning scientific and practitioner-based literatures on organic agriculture, the idea that the practice requires little technical development and sophistication or educational investment continues to be common.

A 2001 article in the journal *Nature* described organic as "urban myth," "ideology," and "widespread belief" (Trewavas 2001). The article states that organic production rests on "very little science," giving rise "to a great deal of illogicality and confusion."

These comments represent a history of deep and institutionalized resistance to alternative agricultural practice, which has challenged mainstream agriculture by eschewing industrially produced fertilizers and forms of pest control, advocating for a more ecologically informed approach to building soil, managing pests, and increasing yields. Forms of organic and other ecological approaches to agriculture began to emerge concomitant with the advent of chemical fertilizers and pesticides in agriculture in the 1940s (some emerged even earlier). Many of these early ideas form the basis for practices that continue in the present and are now foundational to organic production and market expansion (Fairfax et al. 2012).

To comprehend specifically how organic agriculture has emerged as a viable practice on the ground, therefore, we have to look at the networks that developed and sustained it for over fifty years before it was even considered a candidate for government support. The narrative-networks of alternative agriculture are key to appreciating the technical and ecological sophistication of alternative agriculture, and the strategies via which people developed and shared these ideas in a context of resistance. A closer look at the farming networks behind organic and other forms of alternative agriculture reveals an organized set of research and education efforts that formed around durable, sophisticated theories about the farm environment (Ingram 2007). Alternative farming networks have been how farmers have learned from each other, and how they support newcomers in turning away from conventional approaches to seek out different modes of production.

Consider this comment from a New York organic farmer describing the importance of alternative farmer network support as she and her partner made the switch from conventional to organic during the 1990s:

The most disillusioning thing (about transitioning) was the social environment. Neighbors were always critically examining fields and taking over failing neighbors' farms to get bigger. When you are a potential takeover prospect, your neighbors don't want you to succeed. There was a loss of community and information sharing. But the organic community was more supportive. With the NYOCIA (New York Organic Certification and Inspection Association), we were not alone. And a cluster of organic growers attracts buyers. We are part of eight contiguous organic farms now. (Howell-Martens 2001)

Farming networks have played a key role in the ongoing circulation of information by offering field days, workshops, and conferences, and keeping in print books and articles that contain information about farming techniques. The alternative agricultural community has developed what Bruno Latour has termed "immutable mobiles," which are (for him, scientific) ideas that travel across time and space and act at a distance (Latour 1987). In other words, alternative farmers have produced ideas and models of practice that can be shared and provide predictable results in more than one place. Central to the development of these ideas and models have been networks of publishers, scientists, farmer-authors, and other "nodes" in the network, who have collaborated to develop, test, and distribute techniques to a broader farming audience.

Elucidating Farmer Narrative-Networks

The development of organic agriculture, as well as other forms of alternative agriculture such as biodynamic farming (described here), is an international phenomenon. While specific countries, and regions within countries, have been especially active in developing practices and creating institutions to support alternative farming, an international network has also been critical to the sharing and development of common core concepts. In order to appreciate the role of these supporting networks as well as the narratives engaged in by individual farmers as they weave themselves into the network, for this case study we combine historical research on key figures and publications in the alternative farming networks with individual narratives from contemporary farmers. The narratives of farmers involved in alternative agriculture reveal how practitioners share in core agricultural concepts and bring them to life on their own farms. Farmers' stories also illustrate how individuals are motivated to make risky choices against conventional practices and advice, how they learn new approaches, and how they conceive of and negotiate relationships with cows, soil, crops, microbes, and other non-human elements of a farm environment. Narrative analysis also shows that while some of these farming networks hold several very distinctive approaches to the farm environment, they share a common enemy—conventional, industrial agriculture—which many farmers come to see as environmentally and economically corrupt and unsustainable at the level of both the individual farmer and society as a whole. Some alternative farmers view state and federal governments as complicit in allying with industry to push industrial agriculture and in establishing policies biased against small, independent farmers.

The farmer narratives gathered for this research come mainly from the Upper Midwest, home to the largest organic dairy farming cooperative in the nation, Organic Valley, which grew from a tiny cooperative of ten farmers in rural western Wisconsin in the early 1980s to a company posting revenues of over $500 million in 2011 with $12 million profits and representing over 1,700 farmers around the country. While Organic Valley is certainly the most dramatic example of the growth of organic agriculture in the Upper Midwest, the region has been a source of new ideas and home to a diverse range of alternative farmers as well. Community Supported Agriculture, or subscription farms, thrive there, as do farmers' markets, with Madison, Wisconsin, hosting the nation's largest market every Saturday throughout the growing season. Farmer narratives were gathered from interviews with thirty individuals, by attending conferences such as the annual Upper Midwest Organic Farming Conference and the Acres U.S.A. conferences, and by going to field days on farms in Wisconsin and Iowa.

These personal narratives and conference presentations provided a number of contemporary and historical figures, from both the United States and other countries, from whom farmers say they learned important ideas and practices. Thus, we "read" individual farmer narratives in the company of a number of books, most of which can be found for sale in the exhibition hall of farming conferences, as well as from alternative farming periodicals such as *Organic Gardening and Farming*, published by Rodale Press, and *Acres U.S.A.*, a monthly newsmagazine put out by a publisher of the same name. As a former director of the nonprofit sustainable farming group, Michael Fields Agricultural Institute, stated in 2001, "The alternative agriculture information network is structured in terms of subsets that really vary. Some are politically driven, some socially. Some are farmer-led, some academic. They can be allies, but the driving forces differ, as well as the structures of information sharing and knowledge traditions."[2]

The publications and conferences reveal subgroupings of farming practices according to different takes on farm ecology—in particular, soil fertility, or what elements of the soil are critical for a farmer to manage in order to be successful (Ingram 2007; table 6.1). For example, a focus on organic matter and soil building via biological processes such as composting and cover cropping is a salient feature of organic farming practice. Early proponents of organic practice include Sir Albert Howard, an imperial botanist for England working in India in the 1930s. His experiences working on plantations and with Indian peasant farmers, along with his reading of books such as Charles Darwin's treatise on earthworms, F. H. King's *Farmers of Forty Centuries*, and S. A. Waksman's 1938 volume on the importance of soil organic matter, *Humus: Origin, Chemical Composition, and Importance in Nature*, convinced him of the importance of "life" in the soil. Many of Howard's ideas were disseminated in the United States by the publisher J. I. Rodale, who was attracted by the connection Howard made between soil and human health. Rodale published numerous foundational books and periodicals on organic farming and gardening, which found avid audiences during and after World War II. Rodale foresaw the emerging concerns of Americans with personal health issues, especially in response to food safety concerns. He helped lay the groundwork for burgeoning public interest in gardening and in the connections between food and personal health.

Approaches associated with "ecoagriculture" complement this focus on organic matter with a dominant focus on the chemical makeup of soil and the addition and management of a wide variety of "trace" soil elements, such as calcium and magnesium, rarely discussed in mainstream agriculture. A founding figure in this network was University of Missouri soil scientist William A. Albrecht, who wrote a great deal between 1950 and 1970 about the importance of micronutrients. In his overview of alternative agriculture written in 1978, Garth Youngberg drew a "rough" division between ecoagriculture (what he called ecofarmers) and organic, and described them this way:[3]

Organic farmers normally manage smaller and much more labor-intensive operations and tend to eschew commercial soil amendments favoring, instead, compost and manures for organic matter. By contrasts, ecofarmers, although sympathetic to many traditional organic concepts, are far more willing to adopt various new soil amendments or natural "fertilizers" such as rock product minerals, humates, seaweed derivatives and bacterial soil activators, and even limited amounts of synthetic fertilizers and pesticides. Large-scale farmers or those wishing to expand operations are drawn to these expanding sources of organic matter. In an ideological sense, the smaller-scale organic farmer and especially the organic gardener are more attuned to the ideology of Robert Rodale of *Organic Gardening and Farming* magazine. Ecofarmers find greater wisdom and ideological guidance in Charles Walters, Jr., of *Acres U.S.A.*, the man often credited with coining the term ecoagriculture to indicate that farming can be both ecologically sensitive and economically profitable. (Youngberg 1978, 228)

Albrecht joined the soil science department at the University of Missouri after receiving his doctorate there in 1919. He made a name for

Table 6.1
Timeline of significant events in the development of three alternative agricultural networks in the United States between 1910 and 2000, and compared with nationwide agricultural events

Decade	Farming network	Year/Event
1910s		1911: F. H. King publishes *Farmers of Forty Centuries: Permanent Agriculture in China, Korea and Japan.* 1914: Smith-Lever Act establishes co-op extension. 1919: *The War Garden Victorious* by Charles Lathrop Pack.
	Biodynamic	1913: Rudolf Steiner separates from the Theosophic Society and founds Anthroposophical Society.
	Ecoagriculture	1918: William Albrecht joins the faculty of the University of Missouri and begins publishing work on the importance of organic matter and nitrogen in soil.
1920s		
	Organic	1920s–1930s: Sir Albert Howard, British imperial botanist, begins agricultural research in India and learns about composting from peasant farmers.
	Biodynamic	1923: Rudolf Steiner gives his agricultural course on biodynamics in Koberwitz. Dies later that year.
1930s		USDA establishes the Soil & Conservation Service. 1938: USDA publishes *Soils and Men Agricultural Yearbook 1938*, which includes a chapter by William Albrecht on organic matter in soil as "our most important national resource." 1939: USDA Agricultural Yearbook, *Food and Life*.
	Biodynamic	Ehrenfried Pfeiffer establishes biodynamic research lab in Spring Valley, New York. In 1938 he begins publication of the *Journal of BIODYNAMICS* and establishes the Biodynamic Association to promote education and practice.

Table 6.1
(continued)

Decade	Farming network	Year/Event
	Ecoagriculture	Albrecht begins publishing work on the importance of calcium in soil fertility, and of connections between livestock health and soil nutrients.
1940s		40 percent of all U.S. vegetables are produced in Victory Gardens.
		1948: U.S. Plant Soil and Nutrition Lab publishes *Factors Affecting the Nutritive Values of Food.*
		1949: Aldo Leopold publishes *Sand County Almanac.*
	Organic	1940: Sir Albert Howard publishes *An Agricultural Testament.*
		1945: J. I. Rodale, editor of recently founded *Organic Gardening and Farming* magazine, publishes *Pay Dirt: Farming and Gardening with Composts*, with an introduction by Howard.
		Soil and Health Foundation founded by J. I. Rodale. Later becomes the Rodale Institute.
	Biodynamic	1942: Ehrenfried Pfeiffer publishes the book *Biodynamic Farming and Gardening.*
		1943: First U.S. biodynamic farm established in southeastern Wisconsin.
	Ecoagriculture	1947: Albrecht publishes "Soil Fertility as a Pattern of Possible Deficiencies," *Journal of the American Academy of Applied Nutrition.*
1950s		
	Biodynamic	Josephine Porter begins thirty years of researching and teaching about biodynamics in Cherry Valley, Pennsylvania.
	Ecoagriculture	Albrecht continues to publish his work on soil micronutrients and health. Charles Walters first reads Albrecht's work.
1960s		1962: Rachel Carlson's *Silent Spring* published, documenting negative consequences of agricultural chemical use.

Table 6.1
(continued)

Decade	Farming network	Year/Event
		Nitrogen, phosphate, and potash use in farming rises from 7.5 million nutrient tons in 1960 to a record 23.7 million tons in 1981. Since then it declines to 18.1 million tons in 1984 due to fewer planted acres. Total nutrient use then resumes an upward trend, totaling 20.6 million tons in 2001.
	Organic	1967: At the Student Garden Project, UC-Santa Cruz, Charles Chadwick introduces French intensive system to the United States, inspiring John Jeavons and "biointensive" gardening movement.
		1967: British Soil Association sets its first standards for organic food.
	Biodynamic	Steiner's lectures published in book form and made available to general audiences.
	Ecoagriculture	Walters writes for the National Farmers Organization.
1970s		1970: Nobel Peace prize awarded to Norman Borlaug for his green revolution work in developing high yielding strains of wheat and rice.
		U.S. environmental movement gains momentum; passes the Clean Water Act in 1972.
	Organic	1971: Maine Organic Farmers & Gardeners Association.
		1973: California Certified Organic Farmers the first organization to certify organic farms in North America.
		1974: Oregon passes first state law defining organic standards.
		1977: First International Federation of Organic Agriculture Movements (IFOAM) meeting in Sissach, Switzerland.
	Ecoagriculture	1971: Walters founds Acres U.S.A. and begins publishing magazine of the same name and hosting the annual Ecoagriculture conference, which is still held each year. Walters begins a series of in-person interviews with Albrecht about the scientist's work and publishes the collection *The Albrecht Papers* in 1975.

Table 6.1
(continued)

Decade	Farming network	Year/Event
1980s		1988: USDA's Sustainable Agriculture Research and Education program is established, providing competitive grants to support sustainable and organic research. Funded at $3.8 million.
		1989: The "Alar scare" involving chemical residues on apples leads the Center for Science in the Public Interest to gather a petition of some 236,000 signatures asking federal legislature to pass a federal organic law.
	Organic	1980: California passes state organic standards.
		1981: Rodale Institute begins long-term research on organic with the Organic Farming System Trails.
		1984: Organic Foods Production Association of North America, later the Organic Trade Association, established to represent growing organic commercial sector.
		1988: Washington becomes the first state to develop organic standards *and* implement a certification program.
	Biodynamic	1982: Demeter Association, Inc. (the U.S. branch) certifies its first biodynamic farm.
		1984: Michael Fields Agricultural Institute founded in Wisconsin to promote research and education of biodynamic agriculture.
		1985: Josephine Porter Institute founded in Woolwine, Virginia, to carry on her work on biodynamics.
1990s		1994: FDA approves genetically engineered bovine growth hormone to increase milk production.
		1997: FDA approves food irradiation (ionizing radiation) as a method for killing bacteria in beef.
	Organic	1990: Organic retail sales reach $1 billion in the United States. By 2000, thirteen states have their own organic standards.
		1990: Passage of the National Organic Foods Production Act requiring USDA to develop national-level standards and regulations for organically produced agricultural products.

Table 6.1
(continued)

Decade	Farming network	Year/Event
		1997: USDA releases rules to guide the implementation of the National Organic Program (NOP) and receives a record 275,000 comments voicing considerable opposition to three practices allowing genetic engineering, irradiation, and sewage sludge in organic production.
	Biodynamic	Biodynamic method of cultivating wine grapes becomes popular in Mendocino County, California.
2000s		
	Organic	2000: USDA releases the second proposed NOP rule, with the "big three" removed. The national rule is implemented in 2001.
	Biodynamic	According to the certifier Demeter International, over 142,450 biodynamic agricultural hectares exist across forty-seven countries by the end of the decade.

himself through work on soil inoculation for legumes, and then went on to research the importance of the relationship between mineral elements, particularly calcium, in soil fertility. He was a pioneer of the "cation-balance," or "base saturation" theory of soil fertility, which focuses on the need for particular ratios or balances between nutrients in the soil, especially calcium, magnesium, and potassium. For Albrecht the presence of these nutrients and their balance was fundamental—no addition of compost or humus would improve soil fertility if these basic requirements had not been met.

Thus, while the majority of the agricultural world was increasingly focused on managing soil by adding industrial "NPK" (nitrogen, phosphorous, and potassium), Albrecht worked hard to champion the trace elements such as calcium, magnesium, iron, cobalt, boron, and sulfur. His articles, written over more than four decades, repeatedly argue for the correct balance of these elements in soil, and their relation to farm animal and human health. This focus on soil chemistry provides a contrasting subnarrative to Sir Albert Howard's concentration on organic matter. Albrecht was not a supporter of what he called "the organic cult," arguing firmly that chemical soil amendments were necessary in order to avoid mining the soil. He also did not distinguish between organic and chemical fertilizers, a point that would keep his work from being published later by Rodale Press. Albrecht's work was instead championed by agriculture journalist and publisher Charles Walters Jr., who coined the term "ecoagriculture" to describe a combination of farming approaches that he believed would guide farmers to success. Since 1970 his publishing enterprise, Acres U.S.A., and the newsmagazine of the same name have provided a platform for the airing of Albrecht's writings along with a wide variety of other, sometimes unorthodox, theories and practices. Articles in *Acres* often discuss soil "energetics," created by different ratios of soil nutrients, for example. Energetics, according to supporters, works much like a low-level magnetic field influencing plant health, and can be managed by administering various chemical nutrients or organic matter to the soil.

A third network, biodynamic agriculture employs organic techniques, but uses these and other methods in the context of a "spiritual" focus on agriculture, which involves the manipulation of seasonal and celestial forces in order to enliven the soil and encourage biological activity. Biodynamic agriculture methods are built on a set of lectures given in Koberwitz, Poland, in 1924 by Rudolf Steiner, whose work on natural science and spirituality was inspired in part by Goethe. Steiner referred to his work as "spiritual science," and he elaborated on a wide range of topics including medicine, art, architecture, education (he developed the Waldorf educational model), and agriculture. Steiner approached spirituality as involving predictable, natural forces, which he described as cosmic, ethereal, and astral, that guide and shape physical and emotional form. "People will think you are quite childish if you believe that the cause [of a compass] is inherent in the needle," Steiner said in his lectures. "But it is equally childish to believe that what you see in a plant depends on what science discovers in the immediate surroundings of that plant. In fact, the whole starry heaven is involved in the growth of plants" (1924 [1993], 11). Biodynamic farmers manipulate natural forces through various herbal preparations, which, once administered, will promote growth and fruiting in crop plants, for example, or the processes of digestion and decay in a compost pile. In contrast to those espousing ecoagriculture, biodynamic farmers work to create a contained farm "organism" and to minimize off-farm outputs. Adherents of biodynamics also often view their farms as ethical undertakings and a way to heal a damaged earth, both by producing nutritious food in a nurturing manner, and by engaging in partnerships with schools, health facilities, or other community organizations.

These are three of the more organized subgroups (biodynamic and organic agriculture both involve national and international certification programs, for example) among a great diversity of theories and techniques in alternative agriculture. Approaches also vary in terms of longevity and number of participants. In farmer's narratives, we find definite overlap, and farmers' stories reveal them moving freely between these approaches, employing ideas, citing authors, and referencing other farmer experiences. For example, in sharing the story of his transition to biodynamic farming, one farmer describes the usefulness of knowledge from Albrecht, who was associated with the ecoagriculture network, as well as Steiner and a University of Nebraska professor:

I highly recommend that the soil research work of Albrecht be incorporated with the spiritual-scientific research that Rudolf Steiner presents in the Agriculture lectures. Then include the 50+ years of research that James E. Weaver, professor of Plant Ecology at the University of Nebraska, did investigating the tall grass prairie and Great Plains grasslands of the Midwest. The work of these three men gives one a total picture, a blending of material and spiritual science. (Morgan 2002)

While the distinguishing features of these networks are interesting, what is perhaps more important in understanding the historical development of alternative farming practices is how participants of these groups have created common ground, identifying with each other as they share a path of discovery (and often recovery), sensitive to a whole world of ecological beings and elements ignored by the mainstream agricultural community, and sharing a common enemy in industrial agriculture. The elements of their narratives reveal how farmers place themselves in relation to their farms, and also how they include themselves as part of a larger "alternative" farming movement.

Emplotment in Alternative Farming Networks

What emerges from a broad reading of individual narratives is a common "salvation" story in which farmers have lost their way, often by following conventional agricultural practice, and have ended up in debt or with severe environmental problems. The solution, the story goes, is to turn away from the overly centralized and technological world of conventional, industrial agriculture, and to learn how to heed the complex and subtle natural farm environment, the sensitive and frugal management of which will result in farming success.

This alternative salvation story reflects a journey in which farmers make their figurative way out of a land of ignorance. A common pitfall is presented by conventional practice, which promises quick, easy returns but risks long-term degradation of the farm, principally, the soil. As a conventional corn and bean farmer related his story in *Acres*, "It's sad when one family can't survive on land that three families used to survive on . . . I was contemplating quitting. We were searching for answers. We had to change or we weren't going to survive" (Olson 2003, 1).

Paul Olson, who is now president of the National Farmers Organization, laments the common disregard for the importance of cultivating soil organisms: "I see the latest implement a lot of farmers are starting to use are the deep-tillage rippers, and they have to get a bigger tractor to pull them. Well, why are they using them? Because their ground is turning to concrete. There is no life in the soil. The earthworms are gone. The angle worms are gone. All the life has been completely destroyed" (Olson 2003, 1). A common element in many farmer narratives is a particular event, or turning point, that marks a moment of awakening or the beginning of a transition toward more sustainable practice. Olson describes his: "A good friend of mine lost a bunch of heifers that spring [1973] because he was planting corn, and he had spilled some insecticide in the back of his pickup. He loaded the pickup with corn silage and hauled it out to the bunk and fed the heifers. They died, and he traced the source back. I haven't used any insecticide since."

Albrecht, years before, similarly argued that contemporary forces to modernize agriculture had pushed farming off track, and that to correct the course, farmers needed to be sensitive to the farm as a dynamic, biological system:

We are apt to forget that agriculture is first a natural biological performance, and second a financial transaction . . . if we have lost sight of the life of agriculture in our management of it, should we not anticipate considerable bad health and disaster when we are concerned with only its economics and the technologies applied to it? . . . Our attempt to put a biotic performance by nature under industrial economics is the real reason for what is said to be the agricultural problem. (Albrecht 1975 171)

Although an established scientist, Sir Albert Howard emphasized in his writings that while science is a powerful tool, it must not be used with the expectation of ultimately capturing the entirety of natural processes—some aspects of which involve the mystery of life: "The insistence on quantitative results . . . has profoundly influenced agricultural research . . . Many of the things that matter on the land, such as soil fertility, tilth, soil management, the quality of produce, the bloom and health of animals, the general management of live stock, the working relations between master and man, the *esprit de corps* of the farm as a whole, cannot be weighed or measured. Nevertheless their presence is everything . . . why, in a subject like this, should there be so much insistence on . . . the statistical interpretation of figures?" (Howard 1940, 197).

Farmer transition stories often center on questioning perceived alliances between business and agricultural science. As a dairy farmer at a 2001 biodynamics workshop held in Random Lakes, Wisconsin, put it:

I converted from strictly conventional confinement dairying at fifty years old. I was fully learned in conventional practice and financially very capable—sent my kids to college. I consider what I do now biological agriculture. I'm skeptical about biodynamics, but I am excited by these approaches—it's minds on. It's part of a negative reaction to the technology of the mainstream. I was really upset about [the growth hormone] somatotrophin—it was so obviously research in the interest of industry and not farmers. I put a sign up saying "not on my farm," and quit donating money to my alma mater. Now I don't go to extension meetings anymore—it's too technological.

Sometimes the awakening is a more extended process, like that of Rich Bennet, a corn and soybean farmer from Ohio. "We were only concerned about producing more bushels, not more profit," he states, describing his early attitude toward farming. "One year, I got a recommendation from my fertilizer dealer that cost me $25,000 on our 300 acres. My dad always used rye cover crops after row crops and a mix of red clover and sweet clover after wheat to keep the soil from blowing. But I thought they were a big nuisance and got rid of them as soon as I could" (SARE 2005). Conventional tillage machinery was not adapted to shredding and burying cover crops, and Bennett was also trying to find time for hog farming and for off-farm work as a commissioner for Henry County, Ohio. The hog operation helped them pay the bills, but in the mid-1980s Bennett realized that his farm could not support them unless they started doing things differently. He decided to attend a sustainable farming workshop sponsored by the Rodale Institute. "I only registered for the first day," Bennett remembers. "But I came back for the second. The workshop helped me get the confidence to try to cut back on my fertilizer rates." He tried reducing his phosphorous and potassium applications on a few acres at first. He saw no difference in yields, and soon trimmed applications on his whole farm. "Today I spend about the same on fertilizer as I did before I cut back," he says. "But now that fertilizer covers six hundred acres instead of three hundred."

In describing his own farming transition, Olson identifies government farm policy as a central culprit in his troubles: "There were several years where we did run quite a bit of land—cash crops, corn and beans, space for the cattle, and we were raising hogs at that time. It seems that year after year all we were doing was wearing out the machinery and not getting ahead. This is exactly what the government wanted us to do. The Farm Bill was designed to produce more cheap commodities for someone else to use to make money. So, gradually our thinking started changing" (Olson 2003; 12).

There is of course a great diversity in personal experiences in how different farmers describe their "awakening" to the lessons that farm ecology has to teach. Alternative farmer narratives reveal a tension between the construction of farmer as a tough independent, capable of withstanding peer pressure in the mainstream, and a sensitive, symbiotic human, responding and cooperating with a wide diversity of other beings, the workings of which all together make a farm. Themes within this plurivocity include being stalwart in one's commitments, able to withstand peer-pressure from neighbors, but also sensitive to messages broadcast by nonhuman actors all around on the farm. In the context of this information, a good farmer is envisioned as perceptive, innovative, and thrifty, using these qualities to come up with new, more efficient and self-sufficient processes for managing a farm. Organic farmer and author Eliot Coleman writes, for example: "The secret to success in agriculture is to remove the limiting factors to plant growth . . . by efficiently and economically generating a balanced soil fertility from within the farm rather than importing it from without . . . When chosen carefully and managed perceptively so as to take full advantage of specific aspects of the natural world, these good farming practices are all the farmer needs" (Coleman 1989, 4). Although Coleman's words might sound like an endorsement of a simpler life, the narratives and literature of alternative farming reveal a complex world with dozens of interacting parts exhibiting both pattern and idiosyncrasy. A good farmer must make sense of all of it. Consider this from farmer and author Joel Salatin:

Where in the world does a farmer start? How do we sort through all the products and theories to determine what is the best procedure for us? . . . Although I don't have an answer to that question, I wonder if it is the most important question anyway. Perhaps a better question is this. "What can I do right now, without really spending any money?" Our creativity is bounded by the questions we ask. . . . I would suggest that, to be truly economical and ecological, we should start with what we can do on our own farm, with our own resources. (Salatin 1998, 1)

These words reflect a farmer both independent and relational, withstanding conformist pressures from the world of conventional agriculture but sensitive of her or his dependence on much more subtle shifts and alterations in the farm landscape. These changes can be indicators of connection and influence, offering possible new management strategies for the creative farmer. Being a producer of knowledge through being open to learning from animals, plants and other characters of the environment is a central thread in alternative narratives.

Characterization—Nature as Partner

Generally speaking, alternative agriculture is about observing and working with natural cycles and animal and plant behaviors on the farm. The farm environment, including everything from cows to soil microbes, has internal logics, which if understood and managed correctly, can lead to economic success. How that farm environment is specifically perceived and responded to varies widely across farmer narratives, and each narrative reveals specific processes of individuation and categorization via which plants, animals, soil elements or other players in the farm performance are brought to life as rounded characters with quirks and foibles but also typical behaviors that a farmer can take advantage of.

For example, while much of his work described soil tests, assays, and field experiments around micronutrients, William Albrecht often articulated that farmers could extend their sensitivities to the importance of a farm system and the quality of soil by "following the cow": "We need to start observing and judging the cow as she is a chemist on the hoof guiding her own nutrition. That observation and the subscription to her suggestions may well be exercised in advance of our judging her merely as so much beef carcass . . . Cows must have always been chemists of renowned capabilities to have done so well in keeping the stream of their own lives flowing all these year in spite of us, rather than because of us" (Albrecht 1958, 82). The earliest writers about organic farming began to populate the farming story with a diverse number of natural "characters" that a good farmer heeds, responds to, and nurtures, not just scientifically manages.

Soil fertility, Sir Albert Howard argued, can only be understood if it is considered in relation to "Nature's round" (Howard 1940, 22). In the introduction to *An Agricultural Testament*, he wrote that instead of looking at soil fertility "in piecemeal fashion by the analytical methods of science," a proper investigation must look at the "wheel of life," the processes of growth and decay, and keep them in balance. Nature is Howard's "supreme farmer." An examination of the interactions of humus, mycorrhizae, and plants in a natural setting like the forest, for example, reveals "how the forest manures itself" (25). Later in the book he wrote, "Nature has provided in the forest an example which can be safely copied in transforming wastes into humus—the key to prosperity." He elaborates, "Nature has gone to great pains to perfect the work of the green leaf by the previous digestion of carbohydrates and proteins. We must make the fullest use of this machinery by keeping up the humus content of the soil. When this is done, quality and health appear in the crop and in the livestock" (223).

Sir Albert Howard's writings have inspired generations of organic farmers to see the soil as a living dynamic substance, a community of diverse organisms. We see the soil come alive in statements such as the following: "It must never be forgotten that living organisms and not human beings are the agents which make compost. These organisms exist everywhere . . . and govern what goes on in the compost heap from start to finish" (Howard 1947 (1972), 212). Decades later, Eliot Coleman wrote similarly: "I am an admirer of the intricate cyclical systems of the natural world, and I prefer to study them in order to make less work for myself, not more. Even if I thought I knew everything I would rather let it be done for me by the real experts . . . activities of bacteria, fungi, dilute soil acids, chemical reactions, rhizosphere effects, and countless others we are unaware of" (Coleman 1989, 99). Thus, the farm environment becomes alive in distinctive ways, multiple players emerge, indicators of change and with internal logics that can teach farmers useful information.

In a contemporary narrative, for example, Andrew, Vaughn, and Cindy Pitz relate the story of their farm, Sawmill Hollow in Iowa, one of the few to produce black chokeberries. The farmers acknowledge the importance of their grandparents and the surrounding community to the farm's success. But they also mention the loess hills, the legacy of soil and climate, the interaction of microrrhiza, glucose, rye, bluegrass, and fescue in the cultivation of the "flexible and hardy" aronia, and the family dog, as they relate the processes that result in the creation of a number of products from the berry and an annual festival on their farm (Camillo 2011, 34). A diagram of the environmental actors invoked in their story reveals the interconnected narrative-network of influential actors with various roles in the success of the farm, and to which the chokeberry itself is fundamental (figure 6.1).

Looking across narrative-networks reveals the diverse ways that people characterize nature on the farm—for example, a biological emphasis on organic matter, a chemistry-oriented focus on trace amounts of soil nutrients, or a concentration on spiritual forces influencing the soil. We have seen how cows may be nutritionists on the hoof. Weeds are not simply enemies but become harbingers of difference or change, gesturing to the farmer to look at variations in soil quality, or issues with nutrient deficiency or compaction.

Alterity

Conventional agricultural science has played a major "temptation" role in the narratives of people who have written and spoken about alternative agriculture over the past eighty years. The technologies and methods and also the institution of science itself, have come under persistent scrutiny and criticism. While conventional agriculture would appear to offer laborsaving and lucrative technologies, the stories say, these are in fact often misguided, unsustainable approaches to farming. In addition, many farmers, especially in the ecoagriculture network, have come to view agricultural science as a handmaiden to a government that is intent on destroying small family farms. Conventional agricultural science, as it is portrayed in the narratives of many alternative farmers, is at best incomplete, and is typically viewed as misguided, corrupted by powerful chemical industry and government interests, and overwhelmed with a reductionist bias that makes it difficult to think ecologically about a farm as an interacting whole.

Economic interests have a stranglehold on agricultural science, the story goes, such that any divergent farm practices are derided as backward. Virginia farmer and DIY proponent Joel Salatin states this in no uncertain terms:

Daily I am assaulted by the cultural elite as being "unscientific." What could be more unscientific than putting chickens out on pasture [they say]? Here in our neck of the woods, where the vertically integrated poultry industry got its start, I am known as a bioterrorist, because red-winged blackbirds, starlings and sparrows can touch our chickens—and thus, the reasoning goes, transport their

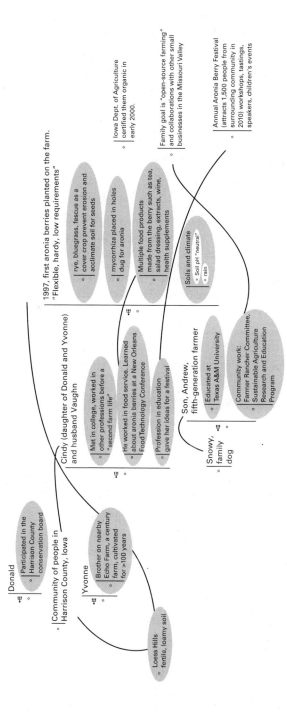

Figure 6.1
Characters in the making of Sawmill Hollow Farm, Iowa

diseases as they do to the immuno-deficient soundscience birds compressed in inhumane, fecal-factory, concentration-camp mausoleum houses. (Salatin 2004)

This attitude has a long history. In a 1946 publication, Sir Albert Howard worried about the scientific establishment's support for increased use of commercial chemicals in farming: "The amalgamation of the artificial manure industry, the Ministry of agriculture, the experiment stations, the agricultural colleges, the agricultural press, and the . . . agricultural committees is complete. All urge upon the farmer and the gardener the use of more and more chemicals almost as a moral duty" (Howard 1946, 7).

Steiner described conventional science as "trial and error" and "not rational" ([1924] 1993, 49).

Even the way the scientists phrase their statements about fertilizing shows that they don't have any idea of its significance in the household of nature. . . . [w]hen it comes to the most important questions, it is so very difficult to come to any kind of understanding with this modern science—and yet we must come to terms with it . . . I am not talking about experiments—as a rule, what science says about experiments is true, and they're very useful. It is the theorizing after the fact that's so bad. (63)

Writing over ten years after these words from Steiner, Howard similarly critiqued the process of conventional science, especially its tendency toward reductionism:

The instrument science and the subject (agriculture) at once lose contact. The workers in these institutes confine themselves to some aspect of their specialized field . . . the reports describe the activities of large numbers of workers all busy on the periphery of the subject and all intent on learning more and more about less and less . . . What would be the reaction of some Charles Darwin or Louis Pasteur of the future if circumstances had compelled them to remain in such an organization, working at some fragment of science? (Howard 1940, 189)

In the introduction to his 1986 autobiography, Walters explicitly challenges the value of conventional agricultural science, and repeats Howard's concern about the complicit relationships between business, government, and advice given to farmers:

Ecoagricultural outreach appeals to farmers who would equate their success with independence from a suspect system of government-supported agricultural research and development. The answer to crop pests is sound fertility management using . . . scientific farming principles that USDA, Extension and Land Grant colleges have refused to teach ever since the great discovery was made that fossil fuel companies have grant money. (Walters 1986, xiii)

At a biodynamics workshop in Random Lakes, Wisconsin, teacher and farmer Hugh Lovell stated bluntly, "Biodynamics gets away from having to accept what one is told to pay for inputs and having to take what's offered for outputs—a formula for getting screwed."

Breach—Keeping the Story Interesting

What keeps a story interesting is an unexpected twist to a plot, a "breach" of the anticipated path of a story that pleases the listener (Bruner 1987b). The metanarrative of alternative agriculture offers a distinctive breach of expectations around what is, and is not, rational and scientific. It is not conventional agriculture that is built on science after all, according to this narrative, but the alternative approaches. Conventional agriculture is "pseudoscience." Salatin minces no words in his critique of conventional agricultural production: "What are the new darlings of sound science? Irradiation, genetic engineering, more concentration, less domestic production, and a Walmart on every corner stocked to the hilt with Archer Daniels Midland, amalgamated, extruded, reconstituted, chlorinated, adulterated, manipulated, constipated pseudo-food" (Salatin 2004). The Acres U.S.A. web site (www.Acres.org) states succinctly:

Based on the work of scientists and farmers whose sophisticated approach to agriculture reveals chemical farming as obsolete and misguided, Acres U.S.A. shows its readers how to embrace the science of nature. Rather than batter nature into submission with bizarre chemistry that short-circuits natural processes, sustainable farmers feed the soil and bring it into balance. They gently coax nature into yielding her bounty, and they are rewarded with superior crops and lower input costs.

Echoing the sentiments of Sir Albert Howard, ecoagriculture authors Wheeler and Ward produce a very pointed critique of misguided science, repeating earlier criticisms of an overspecialized and overly quantitative approach to farming. Simplification and reductionism are just "not nature's way," Wheeler and Ward (1998, 11) insist. They argue: "Conventional agriculture views nature as a linear system or the whole is equal to the sum of its parts. Scientists take one aspect, the nitrogen needs of plants, for instance, and believe they can research only that variable . . . We have the different agronomic departments specialties . . . all existing within the university structure with each researching its own questions. Seldom do these departments communicate together" (8). And more pointedly: "Modern agronomy applied linear thinking and linear procedures to a non-linear (complex) system called life and got the wrong answers" (214). Thus, the story goes that "truth" about soil cannot be gained solely through a detailed laboratory analysis of chemical components (although that can be nice information to have). Conventional approaches to agriculture fail to embrace the importance of relations, dynamics, and connections among plants, soil, and animals, and therefore present an unbalanced and irrational perspective on farm management. A truly scientific approach to farming involves on-farm observations of the smell and feel of a soil and an awareness of a field's history and performance. This criticism does not require rejecting all conventional soil science. In fact, most alternative agriculture proponents accept and build on conventional soil science basics. They meld these basics with farmers' firsthand experiences, creating what they argue is a rational, practical, and more scientific understanding of a farm environment.

Hermeneutics and Gaps

As described in chapter 3, a key part of narrative analysis is a hermeneutic exercise in which we place narrative in a comparative social, historical, and political context. This exercise elucidates contemporary influences that can help explain the arc of a narrative, its characters, and their actions. Thus, we can take into account the serial economic, social, and environmental crises that have plagued agriculture and were particularly acute in the 1980s when so many farmers lost their farms, and which marked the beginning of the contemporary surge in interest in alternative farming. We can also consider the history of tensions between industrial scale, high-input agriculture and family-based operations, and the role of government support for technologies that favor larger-scaled enterprises (Busch 1994; Buttel 1986; Greider 2000; NRC 2001).

Hermeneutics can also reveal narrative gaps—issues of the day that are excluded from a story. For example, very few farmers dwell on the intense labor required in order to manage the panoply of dynamic elements on a farm. Although relief from grinding labor is a central piece of the argument many conventional farmers make for their adoption of new technologies, little is discussed in alternative farmer's stories about the sustainability of the labor commitments required in order to carry out management-intensive alternative processes. Self-exploitation, and reliance on cheap labor, a foundation stone of the critique of small-scale agriculture, remains unattended to in most alternative farmer narratives (Guthman 1998).

This gap grows considerably wider when we consider issues of gender and social justice. Attention to the critical roles of women and immigrant labor to the success of organic and other alternative farming efforts has been slow to emerge. For example, the articles in *Acres U.S.A.* offer little coverage of women as leaders in alternative agriculture, and typically portray successful farm families in a classic nuclear formation, with a male "head" of household and traditional divisions of labor. Even less discussed is the importance of immigrant and migrant labor. Many organic and other alternative farmers, in order to stay viable in competitive markets, rely increasingly on immigrant labor (Allen 1991; Allen et al. 2003). To the contrary, much of the discussion in *Acres* during the past three decades has a decidedly nationalistic flavor, with a myopic focus on "U.S. jobs for U.S. farmers," for example.

Many of these narratives continue to present a picture of the farmer as rugged individual, and although there is often a mention of the farming community and shared ecology, as in the story from the chokeberry farm, the networks of labor and other support that help sustain the economic viability of a farm remain underdeveloped.

Contextuality of Knowledge

An extension to this story is that as part of an intricate and subtle farm system, good farmers are an important source of knowledge in the development of alternative farming technology. In an almost inverse relationship to conventional agricultural science, alternative farmers rather than university or agribusiness researchers are frequently characterized as the source of new ideas about better ways to farm. Alternative farmer narratives construct sustainable farmers as innovative, receptive producers of new knowledge about farming. By becoming sensitive to nature and learning how to "read" the appearance of weeds, crops, and animals, farmers produce successfully and at the same time generate new knowledge that is critical to the ongoing development of the alternative farming movement. In addition, these farmers are portrayed as resolute, able to withstand peer pressure and to not fall prey to the false promises of higher yields and higher incomes that might be gained through increased off-farm inputs.

Sir Albert Howard helped set the stage for this perspective, exhorting his contemporaries to appreciate the skills of Indian peasant farmers: "With no help from science, and by observation alone, (the Indian cultivator) has in the course of ages adjusted his methods to the conservation of soil fertility in a most remarkable manner. He is by no means ignorant and backward, but among the most economical farmers in the world" (Howard 1940, 210). Steiner also described farmers as capable of other ways of knowing: "An educated person may say the farmer is stupid, but in fact that is not true, for the simple reason that the farmer is actually a meditator. He meditates on many, many things during the winter nights. And indeed he arrives at a way of acquiring spiritual knowledge. . . . It just happens that it is suddenly there. As he is walking through the fields, it's suddenly there. He knows something, and afterwards he tries it out" (Steiner [1924] 1993, 56).

Steiner was also very specific about what he saw as the shortcomings of emerging farming trends in the early part of the twentieth century: "In the course of this materialistic age of ours, we've lost the knowledge of what it takes to continue to care for the natural world. People fertilize scientifically now; and the grains and potatoes and everything else become ever worse . . . yet today there is only resistance to practical measures that derive from what can be gained in spiritual vision" (Steiner [1924] 1993, 10). A more recent proponent of biodynamics, the German scientist and farmer Herbert Koepf has written similarly: "As the pressures for short-term gains in production persist, the problems with toxicological risks, economics, and disrupted ecosystems become more and more complex. Thus, the farmer is placed in a conflict with nature and humanity as a whole . . . Though many are aware of the technological innovations adopted by modern agriculture, few are aware of the impact of these innovations on the daily thinking, motivation, and lifestyle of the farmer" (Koepf 1989, 2).

Individual farmer narratives underscore this emphasis on farmer knowledge. In his article on his farm's transition to organics, Olson describes other farmers in his network as a "good source of information because they know what works, and they have new ideas." About conventional farmers, however, he is less positive: "I could not sit down at this table and talk to a bunch of people about various sprays. I would just get up and walk out the door. They name off all these names and I couldn't care less" (Olson 2003, 8).

Another Wisconsin organic farmer echoes the sentiments about farmer-to-farmer communication and the importance of building knowledge:

We bought this farm in '77 or '78, and had to learn all the basics. I had no background and so had to learn how the soil works. Field days, visiting people were really important. Albrecht, Charles Walters and the Rodale Institute they all reflect the basic idea—a guy needs to sit down to figure out nutrients and other things. In conventional ag you see an emphasis on the input sector rather than on knowledge and on systems. [Alternative agriculture consultant] Gary Zimmer definitely has a product to sell. But he earned my respect when he got a farm in the late '80s and put a learning center on it, and put his ideas to work. I listen to him because I can see what he is doing. Farmer-to-farmer is best. That's why field days are such a beautiful thing.[4]

Or consider this statement from a consultant teaching at the 2001 Upper Midwest Organic Farming Conference's Organic University in Lacrosse, Wisconsin: "The science from the lab isn't always transferable. It's good just to dig a hole—use your nose and eyes . . . there's lots that's nice to know, but a few really basic critical things" (Mealhow 2001). These quotations reveal the emphasis in alternative farming networks on a farmer's way of knowing. Although the narrative-networks vary in terms of emphasis, personal experience with farming is a commonly-recognized and heralded source of wisdom, leading to a more distributed notion of expertise (Ingram 2007).

Insights from Narrative Analysis

By analyzing narrative elements of the stories farmers and others tell about alternative agriculture, we gain insight into the diversity and longevity of alternative farming narrative-networks, the methods of sharing ideas, and the strategies employed in order to sustain ideas and motivation in the face of resistance. Narrative has revealed the diversity of "agents" on a farm and how farmers understand interactions among these agents to form an ecological farm system. We also see the economic rationale: it is possible to manage soil fertility and crop nutrition, for example, so that your soil improves as your crops grow more abundantly. Thus, you are able to improve one's farm and guarantee its value in the future at the same time you reap enough market rewards to maintain economic viability.

These narratives also help us understand the cohesive power of a common enemy—in this case, the collusion of science, government, and big business to take control of agricultural production. Like a boundary object, or Hajer's storylines, this common alterity in the narrative brings together people from diverse orientations, perspectives, and backgrounds to create a common understanding and sense of community, and also provides support in making decisions that go against the mainstream.

These farmer narratives also produce important insights into the generation of an alternative rationality. As we learned in the case study on cross-border Sonoran Desert networks, knowledge creation processes can be linked to building ties and establishing trust. Sir Albert Howard, in the organic farming narrative-network, questions the validity of conventional agricultural science by describing a biased knowledge production network involving government agricultural policy and industrial input manufacturers. He counters the suspect nature of this knowledge with the idea of knowledge produced in the context of firsthand experiences manipulating diverse farm environments, weathering environmental and economic challenges, and creating a sustainable practice. Thus, rational approaches to farming must build on conventional science and include the field-tested, on-the-ground expertise of farmers. Where scientists do participate in alternative farming networks, their expertise becomes trustworthy as people are able to see firsthand the results of new ideas as they are implemented on a farm. The breach within the prototypical alternative farmer narrative is that conventional agricultural knowledge is not scientific, while alternative knowledge, based on experience in the field informed by both other farmers' experiences and the work of scientists is rational and trustworthy.

Through farmer narratives we can discern the very diverse ways that people have of understanding, envisioning, and interacting with agricultural nature. We hear farmers and others describing the importance of biology, chemistry, spirituality, energy, cows, microbes, and other aspects of farm environments in an almost exhausting panoply of options for a farm manager to consider. In contrast, the role of tempter in the redemption story of alternative agriculture is almost always played by conventional agriculture and the science behind it. In contrast to a classic characterization of the conservative farmer, many of these stories reveal the ongoing, daily creativity of people in constructing and reacting to diverse, dynamic environments. Learning from mistakes is a key theme; farmers frequently share stories of turning points, or mistakes, from which they learned how to improve.

A central mechanism for farmer learning is the anticipation that "nature" generally conceived, has its own story to tell. Narrative becomes a primary tool for how farmers organize what they learn from their experiments and how they work to remain sensitive to diverse characters that can influence the story of what happens. Farmers anticipate the stories of land: ancient climatic processes that developed the soil, ongoing climate shifts, mistakes and successes of previous farmers, impacts of wildlife as well as livestock as they moved across a pasture making choices about what to eat, where to gather. Helping organize some of this multiplicity are core ideas about ecological agricultural nature, which vary according to emphases placed on soil life, chemistry, or magnetic force, for example. A diversity of ideas has been developed and sustained by these networks. These are the "immutable mobiles," which can be realized, understood, deployed in more than one place. Every farmer's story reveals how these ideas are considered and deployed at a specific time and farm, and involves changing sensitivities and relationships with diverse farm characters, all of which reflect the intellectual and affective environmental work of a farmer. These farmers' stories offer an integrated, dynamic, and emergent picture of how humans can interact with their environment in complicated and creative ways.

Narrative analysis also enables us to get a sense of the ethical reasoning by which farmers come to view themselves as part of a system that will "work" if they are sensitive to the environment and act appropriately. That is, there is an obtainable goal for these farmers, in which they are taking full advantage of all that the diverse elements on a farm have to offer, and are also able to ethically care for animals and to guarantee a future for the farm as well as to sustain themselves in the present. This requires a turning inward to consider and work with that system, rather than looking outward for expensive answers and inputs. These stories echo the idea of the yeoman farmer, independent in thinking, thrifty, and nurturing toward the farm so that it remains productive into the future. They also construct a picture of people and farm nature working together in an ethical, mutually beneficial relationship. Alternative farming narrative-networks have had less to say about how labor and gender dynamics shape farm environments.

Narratives such as these indicate a deep level of suspicion on the part of many alternative farmers to government programs, with important implications for policy. They also reflect commitment to a view of a natural, moralistic connection and balance, in which proper ecological management of a farm will result in economic stability and viability. At the extremes, these ideas are used to reject the idea of government policy in general and to promote a libertarian approach to agricultural policy, as well as a nationalistic bias toward market development that many would find unethical and untenable in today's globalized economy. However, many alternative farmers do not reject government involvement but describe a place for government policy that assists new and transitioning farmers, helps farmers survive their vulnerabilities to extreme weather events like drought or flood, and develops new markets for alternative products.

A central goal for alternative farming support networks has been a reframing of the narrative of farming practice away from a simplified and technical discussion of inputs and outputs, toward a complex, nuanced, and ethically charged set of management approaches and decisions. This kind of complexity is notoriously difficult to regulate, and, clearly, top-down and one-size-fits-all policies can be the enemy of small, diversified, and regionally distinctive farming operations. The evolution of the organic farming regulations, artisan cheese-making standards, and other cases, however, indicate that with enough on-the-ground support for tasks such as inspections and technology development, local diversity does not have to be a regulatory liability. Successful policies, then, will have the regulatory and implementation muscle to accommodate the very diverse ways that the farm environment can be envisioned within an ecological approach, while also being able to enforce standards. These policies will also be adaptive, responding and valuing the generation of new knowledge by on-farm practitioners.

7

Expanding the Ecological Imagination

Introduction

What our environment might become, given where we are now, is a question clouded by narratives that cannot now exist and perhaps never did. The *Paradise Lost* narrative, for example, tends to falsely separate humans and nature and to characterize human impacts as largely destructive. Our aim in this book has been to explore a range of alternative environmental narratives and to offer a method for understanding the role of narratives in informing and guiding environmental action.

In our work, we find a powerful argument for the systematic use of narratives, as told by both putative managers and other community members, as "models" of social-ecological systems. Through stories, narrators link themselves and their actions to a perceived larger system. Through narrative we get a sense of how the whole is determined by the actions and perspectives of the parts—literally, how the plot emerges from events and the actions of characters.

The stories in our case studies do not present exactly happy endings. Sonoran Desert advocates, however poignant their story of connectedness may be, still live in the shadow of the larger political discourse of militarized borders, divisions, and illegality. Alternative farming has not profoundly cut into the hegemony of concentrated, corporate agriculture. And, the Turtle Islands program still stands on uncertain ground, seemingly caught in the political hiatus of a global downturn and changing political regimes.

Still, our case studies speak to the frontier work undertaken by people building relationships with their environments. People are creating new stories about their motivations, as well as the science, ethics, and values informing their environmental practices. By accessing narrative-networks, we gain perspective on human-environment relationships, which can afford new ways of understanding how to be part of ecosystems. This allows us to move away from grand narratives of human technological transcendence and conquest on the one hand, and strict preservation and wilderness on the other.

In the following discussion, we chart the main lessons we learned in this book. We look at how narrative-network analysis provides unique insights into the organization of networks, the motivations of participants, and the role of science in knowledge produced by network members. We turn to the issue of ecological democracy and consider whether and how narrative-networks improve democratic franchise, scope, and authenticity. We then revisit our framework for narrative analysis and what we have learned about its applicability in different settings. Finally, we trace broader implications of narrative analysis for policy and practice.

Themes and Findings

Narrative-network analysis reveals the quality of arrangements, complex motivations, and relational knowledge that sustain attachment to environmental causes.   Narrative-networks, as we have called them, are simultaneously a story and a grouping of actors. A narrative-network is dialectic, where the actual phenomenon we are studying arises from the intimate relationship of the two terms. That is, networks exist, fundamentally, as narratives. Our argument all along has been that stories are used not just to enlighten the listener but also to refresh the ties that bind the teller to the movement. Thus, narratives are part of the glue that binds networks.

Narratives expose the quality and substance rather than just the structure and the organization of networks. Narrative analysis provides us with an alternative and often richer mode of describing the pattern of relationships. In chapter 2, we used standard network analysis and diagrams to explore the structure of the Sonoran Desert network. We found it to be constructed of thinly connected and widely dispersed relationships. Yet when we analyzed the stories network members told us in chapter 4, a surprising degree of unity and connection emerged. While members of the Tohono O'odham Nation and conservationists at the University of Arizona we interviewed did not often mention each other as people who inspired their actions or with whom they worked regularly, the fellowship of being at home in the desert created an affinity and trust that facilitated collaboration among members of the two groups. Such ability to stay loosely connected through strong attachment to a common place has sustained this network even in times of political and policy disappointment. There are implications here for network theory, as it deemphasizes the "node" and brings attention to the emergent nature of the "linkage."

Our focus on linkage resonates with ideas that question conventional understandings of individual subjectivity, particularly a neoliberal subject, motivated by such conventions as economic rationality, flexibility, agency, and resistance. In contrast, the stories we heard reveal how people knit themselves into relationships of responsibility, dependency, and constraint. We learned how people create ties with other people and with nonhumans that define and delimit what they do, rather than offering infinite possibility or flexibility. Attention to narrative networks expands our analytical focus from isolated individual, or node, to the connections of an obligated community.

Stories reveal a sense of mutual attachment. For instance, we recount in chapter 5 how the relationships of the regulators on the Turtle Islands with the egg probers and harvesters follow interactive patterns impossible to codify. The composition of the network does not exist in any formal sense, but solely in practice, which in turn is only reflected in the accounts people tell. In a sense, if we wanted a rich description of a network, it is only to be found in the narratives that reflect and reinforce it.

Narratives also reveal the complexity of network engagement and the importance of collective and communicative rationality. In the stories people tell us, we find self, other, history, and place all bound up in individual and group narratives. The heterogeneity and plurivocity of narrative-networks can help explain their openness and ability to bridge divisions and sustain ties. The inclusion of the nonhuman in narrative-networks reveals the source of connections between people who share little else other than their attachment to a plant, animal, or rock formation. For the Sonoran Desert networkers, the desert speaks in Spanish, English and O'odham. William Albrecht's characterization of the cow as a chemist on the hoof guiding her own nutrition appealed to alternative farmers in different countries and economic circumstances. While biodynamic, eco-agriculture, and organic farmers engage in different subnarratives, their common view of nature as teacher has allowed them to collaborate.

Narrative can contain information about emotional, aesthetic, and moral as well as material aspects of networks. Falling in love with

Mexican culture or being stunned by the shapes and colors of the Pinacate Mountains, as was the case for people from the Sonoran Desert network we interviewed, are experiences that became deeper in the retelling and were amplified by sharing with others with similar feelings. The alternative farmers reported on in the last chapter tell stories that characterize cows in multidimensional ways and that also carry an ethical charge around perceived right and wrong ways to relate to them.

Only their own narratives can relate the full complexity of the motivations that drove the biologists assigned to the Pawikan Conservation Project (PCP) in their relationships with different groups of islanders in chapter 5. To do their work, they needed to fit in, even if that meant turning an occasional blind eye to poachers. To survive, they accepted transportation and access to goods sometimes available only from trawlers who were identified as despoilers of environmentally sensitive resources. Their strategy was not entirely instrumental because the desire to fit in blended with a sense that everyone, including the turtles, was mutually dependent. What from the outside might be viewed as unprofessional turned out to be the practices of sustainability that could not be replicated by other, more conventional arrangements.

Narrative-network analysis enlightens our understanding of relational knowledge creation. Since the rise of science and society studies over thirty years ago, the creation of scientific facts and findings has been understood as a networked process. We know much more about how laboratory scientists rely on interaction with their peers (Latour and Woolgar 1979). To be useful, applied science needs to be created in partnership with users, and science is transferred only when sources are viewed as trusted and legitimate (Cash et al. 2002; Feldman and Ingram 2009a). Narrative-network analysis can add insight into how networks among scientists are created, and can emerge in concert with those who have traditional or experiential knowledge. Also, such analysis sheds light on how and why trust emerges. According to our interviews with Sonoran Desert network participants, knowledge created and transferred in the field inspired them and created bonds not otherwise possible. The story of a shared experience where the excitement of discovery takes place can link people together long after the field trip is over. The biologists, ecologists, and residents we talked to repeated stories of their shared encounters with plant and animal species, objects, and ecological relationships.

The PCP regulators gained practical knowledge, inaccessible through standard scientific methods, from the egg probers on the Turtle Islands.

In an organizational sense best classified as game wardens, the egg probers acted as mentors and coaches. In turn, the site-specific knowledge the regulators gained facilitated not only their work but also how they fit into the community. This demonstrated, actionable knowledge created trust, which carried over and was projected to other circumstances encountered by the PCP.

Alternative farmer narratives reveal farmers developing a practical body of knowledge based on experience in the field combined with agricultural science. Field days allow people to see firsthand the results of new ideas as they are implemented on someone's farm. Chapter 6 also notes the collaborations of farmer-authors, scientists, and publishers working to develop, test, and distribute techniques to a broader farming audience. A wide array of writers on the Sonoran Desert plays a similar role in the narrative-network discussed in chapter 4. Scientific findings on the generative capability of released flows through the lower Colorado River to the Sea of Cortez expanded and energized the narrative-network and led to policy changes.

Narrative-networks can extend and improve ecological democracy.   Our strongest claim regarding networks and democracy is that the narratives that help build networks can reflect new ideas about the environment and provide new examples of coexistence, a tangible working out of new ways of relating to deserts, for example, turtles, or soil. These stories, which contain information about the moral and aesthetic motivations of people within environmental networks, offer fresh insight into workable conceptions of a more just and environmentally durable future.

The connection of narrative-networks to the project of ecological democracy is a possibility that we embrace with hope tempered by skepticism. Prescriptions for deepening democracy are plentiful in the social science literature, and new rights have been extended, new administrative procedures adopted, and electoral reforms executed, all in the name of democratization. The ability of entrenched power to thwart or subvert such reforms is awesome and discouraging. Further, there are many examples of exclusive networks and narratives that justify the marginalization of others. Yet, the three case studies in this book support the hope that narrative-networks can and sometimes do enable people to present organized challenges to mainstream power relationships and conventional environmental behavior (Karvonen 2011).

Ecological problems are also social, and problems of democracy and ecological degradation are, at their core, a reflection of human domination over other humans and nonhumans (Bookchin 1998; Dobson 1995; Dryzek 1997; Eckersley 1992; Plumwood 1998). Perhaps more than any other scholar, John Dryzek (1999) has helped us comprehend the conditions for extending ecological democracy, which he views as an open-ended project. He writes: "The more political arrangements are pushed in a democratic direction, the more can environmental justice in particular and ecological values in general expect to benefit. Such enlargement can come in the form of either the size of the democratic franchise, the scope of issues falling under democratic control, or the authenticity of that control" (267).

Narrative-networks provide such opportunities in all three ways.

Size of franchise   It is impossible to extend voting rights to trees and coyotes whose language humans do not understand, and less than satisfactory for scientists and other experts to divine their preferences and act as surrogates. Yet, as our case studies have demonstrated, narrative-networks can extend the ways in which humans "hear" the nonhuman by reflecting varied, complex relationships. Events such as the sudden appearance of a wildlife species in suburbia require different stories to surface and narratives to change in ways that enlarge the number and kinds of relevant actors (Bennett 2010).

The size of the franchise is enlarged by the inclusion of diverse non-humans in human networks. In the Sonoran Desert, people spoke about other species in terms that sound very much like members of a family growing up or growing old around the desert. On the Turtle Islands, we find a type of kinship, too, but one where humans and nonhumans are bound in an effort toward coexistence. We find affection for turtles here, but more as a sense of one's future being inextricably tied to the other. On these islands, people bind themselves to the turtles out of necessity. The alternative farming study reveals ways in which farmers understand their connections to the diverse environments around them (the cattle, the soil microbes, the crops). These farmers strive to know about a farm in an intimate, complex way. One product of this narrative-network is a personal and practical, yet scientifically defensible, body of knowledge about nature that extends the franchise beyond farmers alone to include a large, diverse farm ecology.

While the narratives in all cases portray different species as "teachers" or "guides," perfect knowledge of these species is understood to remain beyond the grasp of humans. The narrative-networks we have studied portray ecological elements as surprising, idiosyncratic, and defined by complex relationships that thwart absolute predictability. This extension of indeterminacy to the nonhuman opens the franchise beyond that typically afforded by managerial sciences that base recommendations on previously established studies of species behavior.

Enlargement of the scope of alternatives   Narrative-networks promise to enlarge the scope of issues and alternatives to address them. Narrating or storytelling reflects a discourse of imagination in which people can explore what may be discredited by politics and institutions as unnatural, unscientific, dangerous, or backward. Narratives and narrative analysis have the possibility of expanding the range of choices and engaging different perspectives essential to the creation of alternative ecologies. By studying the narratives of these alternative networks, we find rich new ways of depicting situations and strategies for governance. In each of the cases explored in this book, narratives challenge conventional practice and bolster network participants' courage to be different.

For instance, while mainstream discourse portrays most things Mexican as violent, threatening, and alien, the Sonoran Desert network practices a brand of tri-nationality that engages Anglos, Native Americans, and Mexicans on equal terms. Even though their perspective is explicitly rejected in recent, as well as historical, laws that bifurcate cultural homelands and cut through historic wildlife ranges and corridors, the Sonoran Desert narrative-network soldiers on, singing a surprisingly optimistic tune. The narrative-network avoids portraying proponents of the mainstream narrative in negative terms for fear of empowering them beyond the possibility of challenge. Instead, their stories dwell on the visible evidence of the fruits of collaboration in new agreements on the lower Colorado River and other successes reported in chapter 4, keeping alive the possibility of larger change.

In the case of the Turtle Islands, we see the acting out of context-specific ecological preservation. The case fuels the idea that general management blueprints are suspect and should not be imposed everywhere (Berkes 2007; Lejano and Shankar 2012). The local mode of management departed radically from the conventional approach to ecological reserves, which places certain geographical areas as off-limits to human habitation or use. In line with the local narrative of mutual accommodation, residents and managers worked out a rough percentage allocation of harvesting permits and eggs left in nurseries. This process was implemented in a flexible, case-by-case way: when family needs surfaced, such as weddings, exceptions were made. Anti-poaching laws were not so much officially as culturally enforced, leaving to elders and fellow harvesters the sanctioning job. The dictum of everyone being in it together imposed limits that were surprisingly effective, and levels of turtle egg conservation were reached that were not replicated once more strict and bureaucratized management was imposed.

Challenging the discourse of industrial, corporate agriculture, the narrative of alternative agriculture embraces a range of different relationships between farmers and the crops, animals, and soil they cultivate. Rather than relying on seed and fertilizer suppliers or agricultural extension agents for farming knowledge, networks of alternative agriculturalists shared information with each other, connected by a redemption narrative of returning to the liberating lessons of "nature." Repeatedly rebuffed in mainstream educational and political arenas alternative agriculturalists pursued their own pathways to develop and share information and to develop markets for their products. Importantly, alternative agriculture narratives propounded an alternative view of agricultural science situated in direct experience and modes of communication. Alternative farming narrative-networks developed and circulated a large body of knowledge, often across international boundaries, that developed and sustained alternative farming experiment and practice for decades, and helped respond to growing public interest when it began to emerge in the 1980s and 1990s.

Deepening the authenticity of democratic discourse Dryzek (1990, 1997) recommended communicative reason as a supplement to instrumental reason and economic rationality as means toward more democratic deliberation. Communicative reason requires open and fair access to spheres where free and accessible deliberation takes place. As the case studies in this book have shown, paying attention to the narratives of networks can contribute to communicative reason to the extent that they provide opportunities to engage under different conditions and power dynamics. Of course, narratives can exclude as easily as they can bind. But narration can also allow individuals to contribute to unfolding stories about themselves and the environment. Ecological imagination allows new plots to emerge. Processes of listening, incorporating, and telling stories open up the types of interactions available to support democratic deliberation. Narration also broadens the kinds of evidence beyond that typically entertained in conventional political and scientific discourse.

The Promise and Challenge of Narrative Analysis

Narrative analysis emerged from the broader field of literary theory and criticism and has had only limited application in the social sciences. One of the impediments to wider use of narrative analysis has been the unavailability of an agreed upon framework that captures the power of narrative to inform research on environmental behavior. The narrative framework we lay out in figure 3.3 specifies key attributes of the narrative-networks that were tested in the three case studies that follow and that hold promise for wider application.

Emplotment is about how a story is connected out of disparate events and actions into an overall logic that binds together the members of a narrative-network. We look for the literal juxtaposing of different elements as a way to understand how people make connections. Very often stories will tap into universal themes that have transcended time, language, and cultural differences. For instance, the "homecoming" plot that binds together the Sonoran Desert narrative-network echoes the arduous and tortured travels of *The Odyssey*. While network members were attached to the landscape, what they found most magnetic varied: the sparse and hardy vegetation able to adjust to little rain, abundant marine life in the Sea of Cortez, endangered species like the pronghorn and jaguar, centuries-old villages of Native American desert dwellers. Finding, returning to, and protecting home, according to the story, requires struggles, a high tolerance of challenging conditions, and an ability to be patient. But the rewards, although not immediately apparent, are very great as the attractions of home are to be found nowhere else on earth.

The "we are all in this together" plot of the Turtle Islands case is reminiscent of the "everything is related to everything else" mantra of ecology. Yet the story is much more than all things find their appropriate niches. The mutual adjustments and implicit bargaining that takes place between PCP officers, egg probers, egg harvesters, poachers, and trawlers is as complicated and fraught with mishap as a Dickens novel. The complicated maneuvering among actors, all expected to somehow fit in, includes the turtles that are supposed to serve human needs along with their own. Characters move toward and then away from each other, never sure of their footing and very much tuned in to the moves of their partners. Patterns of interaction are embedded in this context, and the moral of the tale is that no idealized model of endangered species regulation can fit particular circumstances.

Emplotment in the alternative farming network is a "salvation" story. Farmers have gone astray following conventional agricultural practice and have ended up in an economic squeeze of spiraling fertilizer, pesticide, and other costs. The health and sustainability of their farms has also been undermined. The road to salvation turns away from technological pathways laid out by government agencies and international agribusiness conglomerates. Instead it turns toward the guidance offered by the subtle and complex natural farm environment. Common and persistent temptation is presented by conventional practices that promise easier management and quick economic returns, but that inevitably lead to the deterioration of the soil and other resources on which a successful farm depends.

Characterization has a clear payoff as an element of narrative analysis. Just as vivid characterization can make a novel more compelling, so too does characterization give a narrative-network broader salience. There are some common roles that can be found in each case study, like that of storyteller, mentor, or guide, although in each case these roles are exemplified very differently. It would be unwise to draw any conclusions about the importance of storytellers to the robustness of narrative-networks without examining many more cases. However, it would seem that the presence of storytellers could be positively associated with narrative diffusion beyond the locales of initial creation.

Sir Albert Howard, Rudolf Steiner, and others play the role of master storytellers in the case of alternative agriculture. The storytellers became influential because they articulated common experiences of many alternative farmers as they worked in the field. Sharing these stories is also critical to the maintenance of a network. Through writings such as *An Agricultural Testament* (Howard 1940), the U.S. publisher J. I. Rodale learned about and then disseminated many of Howard's ideas in the magazine *Organic Gardening and Farming*. Another journalist and publisher, Charles Walters Jr., used his newsmagazine *Acres U.S.A.* to diffuse alternative agriculture ideas. This publication spread the research of William A. Albrecht on soil nutrients. Rudolf Steiner's work on biodynamics, originally set forth in a series of lectures, was reproduced in print, which played a key role in the circulation of his ideas.

The guides, mentors, and storytellers in the Sonoran Desert case both shaped the narrative and facilitated the engagement of adherents, some exerting influence over decades. There are at least two generations of mentors. The first was in the 1960s and 1970s, and the second includes the contemporary generation. Graduate students of these mentors are now key participants in the Arizona-Sonoran transboundary environmental network. Face-to-face contact and fieldwork play important roles in the narrations of mentors. A deep commitment to place was often mentioned as growing out of these field experiences in which what was shared was not just about flora and fauna but also emotional attachments (Laird Benner and Ingram 2011).

While egg probers acted as mentors in the Turtle Islands case, the knowledge was site-specific and was not written down. Until relatively recently, the complex, site-specific pattern of negotiated management that existed among characters including PCP officers, egg probers, egg harvesters, poachers, and trawlers on the Turtle Islands had not been recognized (Lejano and Ingram 2007). The absence of articles, books, or other narrative "recordings" is likely one reason for the failure of the narrative-network to gain stature in the Philippines or for this type of site-specific management to be diffused to other places.

The heterogeneity of human and nonhuman characters in narrative-networks may well be associated with their ability to transcend barriers between groups usually separated by politics, race, class, education, and other divisions. People who have in common relationships with nonhuman species and places may be able to better set aside other differences. Be it the desert around which conservationists gather, the turtles that sustain a local way of life, or the land that organic farmers plow, nonhuman elements acted as boundary agents in these narrative-networks.

Sonoran pronghorn, turtles, and cows play central motivating characters in our narratives. The declines in the populations of pronghorn and turtles triggered human action and intervention. Individuals in government wildlife agencies were engaged in each case, although in the case of the turtles the first line of engagement came from local residents who depended upon egg harvesting and the local experts, the egg probers. In each case, the focus was upon improving the life chances of the respective animal populations. The responses of pronghorns and the turtles to trial-and-error attempts by the humans husbanding their welfare provided guides to what worked.

In the case studies of the pronghorns and the turtles, humans characterized their own roles as successful based largely on evidence of networked cooperation among themselves, and, to a lesser extent evidence of recovery of the endangered species. Pronghorn managers started a captive breeding program that raised population totals and allowed releases into the wild. While the border fence and other construction motivated by human security destroyed the binational habitat of the pronghorn, managers told positive stories about their involvement as evidence in chapter 4, characterizing peoples' ability to work together as "amazing." Turtle egg harvesters have a somewhat different relationship with the turtles than managers have with pronghorn since their livelihood is directly tied to the turtles. Perhaps because of this more essential relationship, humans and turtles are characterized as brothers in a linked endeavor to survive and prosper. The science involved in captive breeding of the pronghorn reflects a more technical engagement than does the egg probing and the miming by humans of the dance of the turtles as they emerge from the mounds where they were born to find their way to the sea. In both cases caretakers give themselves prominent roles in the survival of endangered animals. These relationships energize human participants and are the hub around which the network and narrative are built.

Domesticated cows are plentiful rather than scarce nevertheless the evidence they provide of when and how they prosper is just as central to the narrative-networks of alternative farming. "Following the cow," as farmers are exhorted to do, steers alternative farmers toward practices that are portrayed as better for the web of animals, farmers, and consumers.

Other nonhuman characters in the case studies include jaguars and birds in the case of the Sonoran Desert and cultivated plants in the case of alternative agriculture. Concerns with their survival and prosperity promote the active engagement of a variety of actors who might otherwise be separated by professional allegiances, geography, political boundaries, and other divisions. The networks of information-sharing for alternative farmers span the globe, for example, as graziers in the midwestern United States shared affinities and experiences with those in New Zealand. The public-private partnership built to create an operating jaguar reserve in the Mexican borderlands was designed not by some idealized institutional form, but instead by the cats themselves as they wandered in places and ways not anticipated by human managers. The narratives portray happy stories in large part because human relationships were positive and cooperative, and, of course, the species in question continued to exist and in some cases thrive.

Alterity clarifies affinity within networks as members often construct their identity against an "other." The "other" can exist as a real or imagined threat. The insights gained through the application of this element of the framework are clear in all three case studies, although in different ways. In the Sonoran Desert, everyone is or could be a member. Sonoran Desert networkers treat outside people as potential members and refuse to negatively characterize those who do not subscribe to the homecoming story. While political and policy opponents construct narratives that portray Mexicans and border crossers as lawless and criminals, their own story creates no parallel enemies. The upbeat and optimistic attitude conveys a welcoming and inclusive story appropriate to the essential notion of homecoming. In this case, the "other" inspires a story that steadfastly refuses to negatively stereotype as the conventional narrative does, and supports persistent optimism about the possibility for future environmental gains.

In the Turtle Islands case, the story begins with the PCP as potential outsiders, with their urgent need to belong. But the narrative portrays life on the island as taking place under a persistent cloud of threat. The trawlers threaten to destroy the habitat with their heavy equipment, although they are part of the ongoing negotiation of getting along together. In the background are international treaties and conventions signed by the Philippine government that view conservation as a set of clear and consistent rules and endorse categories like preserves, sanctuaries, and no-take zones that have little flexibility in the face of local need and variation. Locals viewed officials from Manila with suspicion inasmuch as the authority of the central government always threatened to impose itself on the locally negotiated systems on the island. The narrative of survival on the islands, and the need to coexist, becomes all the more compelling given the degree of otherness vis-à-vis the center.

The revelatory power of analyzing alterity is well illustrated in the alternative farming case. Conventional agriculture and government programs play roles as major "tempters," which farmers can resist by listening to other farmers in the network and working to be sensitive to the diverse elements of the farm around them. Supposed laborsaving and crop-boosting technologies promoted by the mainstream are shortcuts to disaster, according to the narrative, which reinforces the notion that redemption is a harder road in the short term, perhaps, but the only way to truly succeed at farming. The alternative farming network involves an extremely diverse group of people reflecting a spectrum of different religious and political orientations that are polarizing in wider society. The common "other" in this narrative, however, provided a necessary point of agreement and an opening for the discovery of additional commonalities. This broadly held suspicion of government and industry collusion, for example, was critical to the grassroots involvement in protesting what many saw as the corruption of organic values in the development of draft federal organic regulations.

Breach of convention is a category in the framework aimed at identifying twists and turns in the narrative that are curious and unanticipated, making the narrative, and thus the network, more interesting and compelling. It may come as an informal, relational turtle management program that evolved in defiance of conventional bureaucratic logic. It may come as a kind of ironic twist such as when a new law passed in Manila challenged existing arrangements on the Turtle Islands and the mayor tore up the enforcement directive. Without this climax, the story might never have diffused beyond a particular time and place. Attention to breach reinforces the power of alterity in the narrative. For example, Sonoran Desert advocates, in a breach of a typical negative response, discuss even the border fence in positive terms: arguing that it is serving environmental interests by spurring the investment of funds into monitoring and research. Breach is also useful in the alternative farming case. From the outside, the network might be perceived as antiscience, yet surprisingly the narrative asserts that alternative agriculture is based on science. Moreover, the story goes that the alternative approach is less biased by special interest, more grounded in the real experience of farming, is more coherent and comprehensive, and is less reductionist than that supporting conventional agriculture. The success of alternative farming networks over the decades has surely been in part due to their strategic use of existing science and their openness to collaborations with scientists—even if some dwell more on the margins of accredited science than others.

Context and gap consider political, social, historical, economic, and environmental contexts informing the narrative-network, including other narratives. This effort is important to understanding not just what has shaped a story but also what is left out of the narrative under analysis and why. All narratives include strategic gaps. Stories from the margins of environmental discourse often ignore issues that drive more mainstream discourses. For instance, the Sonoran Desert story systematically ignores the garbage and violence along the border imposed by undocumented immigrants. Similarly, the alternative agriculture narrative downplays the significant labor requirements of management-intensive alternative practices, even though "laborsaving" management is a major concern of mainstream farming. The locally based Turtle Islands narrative seems as blind to the stories of the international conservation of endangered species regime as international and national conservationists were to the progress being made through locally negotiated management. Because the narrative never caught on at other levels, and therefore no empathy and support developed, the arrangement was doomed.

Challenges of narrative analysis   While the narrative analysis performed in this book has proven fruitful, the pursuit of narrative analysis is not a simple proposition. Obtaining rich accounts and engaging in analysis requires long hours of organizing and interpreting sometimes exceedingly lengthy transcripts. A one-hour interview results in many pages of transcript, which then take hours to analyze. Narrative can be challenging to represent and summarize. One sometimes has to fight the urge to include five pages of verbatim transcript. Sometimes the only way to show meaning that emerges from narratives is to show the narratives themselves. We end up judiciously picking through choice quotations and passages, summarizing in some places, paraphrasing others—all the time cognizant of the loss of richness and the risks of interpretation when we do this.

The question comes up: "How do you know that a certain story, or your representation of a group's narrative, is accurate?" In other words, how did we know that the accounts we were told were told in good faith, or were good representations of the narrator's experience (rather than something constructed upon demand—this is Bourdieu's problem of synopticism)? In addition, how can we assure ourselves that our subsequent reconstruction of a narrative for the network was faithful both to the individual's story as well as the dynamic and identity of the network?

A critical part of the answer to this question was our long-term involvement with the people of each case study, which strengthens our confidence when it comes to determining common themes and similarities across individual narratives. By seeing how individual narratives intersect and resonate with each other, we essentially use a mode of triangulation to develop narratives that reflect those of many people in a network. We look for coherence between stories, both logically and dramatically. The events or motivations expressed within individual accounts or across them should be things we can logically connect as being compatible with each other, or if not logically, at least in terms of affect (e.g., transference of deep emotion from one's youth to a way of understanding the desert).

Broader Implications for Research and Action

Contribution to Resilience and Sustainability Research
Our work offers new directions for research on resilience and sustainability. Walker et al. (2004) define resilience as "the capacity of a system to absorb disturbance and reorganize while undergoing change so as to

still retain essentially the same function, structure, identity, and feedbacks" (2). This literature has succeeded in training our sights on processes of adaptation or even transformation—or as Gunderson and Holling (2002) refer to it, panarchy—of the system. The research has striven to refine systems models to include these social or institutional processes of adaptation and change, struggling to combine the social-cultural elements with physical models of environment.

Our work suggests that, before we even attempt to capture system resilience and sustainability in physical models and computer simulations, these phenomena necessarily need to show up first and foremost on the plane of narrative. If adaptation and transformation are to become everyday realities, they need to become incorporated into the narratives by which policy actors describe their situation. When one inquires how a social-ecological system has transformed and how it has managed to thrive despite adverse environmental change, we are essentially seeking out a story of change and survival. In our plane of description, the "systems model" is the narrative, and the analytical device that links diverse elements in the system to each other is that of emplotment. Narrative is the device that allows such integrative description—what Stokols, Lejano, and Hipp (2012) call the "transactional relationships among interacting natural and semiotic systems." While most of the resilience research struggles to describe system changes, including sociocultural and semiotic, in the "state-space" of matter and energy, narrative encompasses all these in the state-space of meaning (Lejano and Stokols 2012).

Researchers have discovered the potential merits of social network theory for resilience research (e.g., Bodin and Crona 2009). Just as this strand of research offers classic network analysis for studying resilient (and vulnerable) systems, we offer methods from narrative analysis. Narrative analysis is, for many of the same reasons, as immediately relevant to the considerable theoretical and case study work on the commons. Ostrom and colleagues have written about exciting new approaches, involving multiple methodologies, being brought to bear on commons research (Poteete, Janssen, and Ostrom 2010). To add to this evolving discussion, we hasten to add that, perhaps more than any other device, it is the use of narrative and its analytics that can shed the most light on the "stuff" of collective action and the ties that bind diverse actors in a commons. Likewise, it is through narrative that we gain access to the seemingly ineffable reasons behind the conflicts that tear the commons apart (Lejano and Leong 2012).

The focus on narrative also addresses the sometimes inevitable tendency of resilience research to revolve around a technical analytical exercise. For us, the search for resilience is not primarily a technical problem among those affected by environmental change but a search for a new, shared narrative. The instrument of scenario planning, which is becoming more and more useful for sustainability work, often works out as a technical exercise (e.g., Van Drunen, van't Klooster, and Berkhout 2011), but scenarios are, first and foremost, forward-looking narratives generated by communities of practice. When Gerlak and Heikkila (2011) ask what are the process and product of collaborative learning, our response is simple: narration and narrative. Our work has led us to appreciate the capacity of some institutions to allow joint storytelling, where, as Lyotard (1979) might describe, speaker and hearer alike belong to a community of narrators.

Contribution to Public Policy Research

Public policy analysis already incorporates many insights from network analysis, and narrative-network analysis further extends possibilities. The literature on policy process allows for a greater focus on the action of networks outside the pale of formal policymaking. Sabatier and Jenkins-Smith (1993) talk about the growth of policy subsystems, a niche for new networks. Also, social constructions of target populations in policy designs (Schneider and Ingram 1997) may well be linked to characterizations in narrative-networks.

The focus on narratives has implications for what we know about the policy process, the role of policy entrepreneurs, the salience of ideas, and windows for policy change—but they take on narrative form. For example, the act of the policy entrepreneur, especially as Callon (1986) describes the process of *interessement*, becomes that of spokesperson—gathering and retelling individual narratives, particularly those of the excluded and nonhuman actants. A useful exercise would be to attempt to relate phases in the narrative process to those classically identified in the policy process, the latter including work by Lasswell (1951), Pressman and Wildavsky (1973), and Kingdon (1984). A useful reference on policy processes can be found in Howlett, Ramesh, and Perl 2009. The following is a summary of some general correlates between narrative and policy processes. Although such processes (as depicted in table 7.1) are neither linear nor well differentiated, we suggest these ties offer promising directions for research.

We immediately realize, however, as Grindle and Thomas (1991) note, that real policy processes are neither linear nor well differentiated from

Table 7.1
Summary of general correlates between narrative and policy process

Narrative process	Policy process	Description
Disenchantment with grand narrative	Problem identification	Resentment over current policy gains ground, as a countermovement is born.
Growth of individual narratives	Formulation of alternatives	Individuals start telling their story, start envisioning change for themselves.
Storytellers' narration of new narratives	Agenda-setting	Influential actors express and formalize these sentiments in public forums.
Convergence into metanarrative	Policy adoption	The countermovement settles on a policy direction, identifies new policy.
Transmission of narrative	Policy implementation	Transmission of the new policy idea becomes part of enacting it in the field.

policy implementation; so too do we realize that narrative processes are interactive, irregular, and to some extent always somewhat liminal. Narratives are not set in stone (but then, neither is policy)—rather, they survive through the process of ongoing narration, and narratives evolve with each new telling of them. The loose but important ties between narrative and policy processes seem to be a promising direction for further investigation. Similarly, we can envision more work on delineating how multiple "streams" of events and sociopolitical conditions come together to form windows of opportunity for new narratives to become salient in the public eye.

Our turn to stories that policy actors share supports giving closer attention to the informal, everyday realities of institutional life. Among policy scholars, there has been an ongoing redirection of attention away from the formal and structural dimensions of institutions to their informal and relational elements (e.g., Innes and Booher 2010). By formal, we mean classifications of basic institutional forms (i.e., market, state, public/private partnerships). We also mean the traditional ways by which we describe institutions (i.e., organizational structure, lines of authority, rules, and bylaws). Without letting go of the formal and structural, the literature has given additional import to implementation, practice, organizational culture, and the everyday improvisations that actors make when going about their work.

Contributions of Literary Theory to Environmental Research

Much of early environmental scholarship focused on the formal dimensions of law and public policy, in part a legacy of the first wave of environmental statutes in the 1970s. Implementation studies that came somewhat later also focused on formal elements of policy, even though they showed that idealistic laws often did not work on the ground. More contemporary social movement analysis, while widening the focus outside the Beltway, the agency, and the political party, still focuses on the ostensible policy goals of movements (Meyer, Jenness, and Ingram 2005). The more recent turn to governance, which is the decentralization of power and responsibility beyond the state to include nongovernmental organizations, corporations, neighborhood organizations, and other actors including individuals, continues to focus on formal arrangements rather than more informal networks. The narrative approaches used in this book, by lending an ear to the everyday stories people tell, give us entry into less formal, emergent relationships.

Networks can be characterized in relational, rather than structural, terms (Lejano 2008). The use of narrative analysis allows us to describe these relationships in complex ways, utilizing the very stories that people tell in the same way that a novel provides an evolving account of the relationships between its characters. It also affords us an alternative (and sometimes more complex) mode of describing the pattern of relationships (which network analysis calls a structure) in terms of emplotment. Structural analysis allows us to depict patterns of interaction across actors, but plots allow other dimensions such as the differing understandings of the network (and events) by different actors, history and culture, personality and emotion, and other elements that make up the web of relationships and that are difficult to capture through notions of structure. As such, our approach lends itself to recent inquiry into the role of stories in institutional life (e.g., Wirgau 2012).

This narrative turn deemphasizes the role of the rational, self-interested individual subject. Classic European philosophy from Descartes to Kant emphasizes the autonomous individual as a critical center of analysis. Certainly, natural resources economics stresses individual self-interest as a dominant motivator of action. However, the figure of the individual person is seriously challenged by an emerging postmodern relationality that insists that we recognize individuals as dynamic creations of kinship, class, the subconscious, biology, and shaped by all sorts of network relations and sociocultural assemblages. Increased awareness of the myriad influences, both human and environmental, that mold individual action has fueled network analysis. Our work looks beyond the patterns of nodes and linkages that characterize much of network analysis to consider the qualities of the connections that bind and shape networks.

The use of narrative gives us access to logics (for action and collectivization) that depart from the strictures of individual rationality. While many critics have sought to demonstrate other important motivations behind behavior, it is only when we examine the stories people tell that we find these other logics faithfully described. Furthermore, these are not logics that stand independently of one another. In the stories people tell us, we find self, other, history, and place all bound up in individual and group narratives. It is in narrative that we find a new way to explain and describe the roots of community and collective action.

In a larger sense, our efforts seek new ways of studying social interactions of all kinds, a technique that blends detailed interviews with what we can learn from a literary sensibility. Our approach has involved an integration of social science and the humanities, a necessary complement to what we can learn about human-environment relations from the natural and policy sciences. We hope we have shown how analyses of environmental networks from the standpoint of the humanities can provide a useful way of understanding human behavior, and offer narrative networks as one step toward transdisciplinary research that can explore different facets of the world.

Linking Narratives to Practice

Narrative analysis is helpful not only in understanding the social-ecological landscape, but also in providing tools that planners, policymakers, and managers can put to practical use.

Lesson #1 Narrative has implications for planning and policy analysis. Consider a master plan, environmental impact statement, management report, or other summary analysis of a situation. These are, of course, narratives, but narratives should allow for plurivocity. Do these plans allow for different voices to tell their individual story? The lesson for policymakers and public managers is that forums for decision making should allow members of different and varied publics a chance to simply tell their story. Often, members of the public feel very constrained by the two or three minutes afforded them in typical public hearings or the formal, legalistic forum of notice-and-comment rule making. There are few opportunities for collaborative deliberation or alternate forms of material or experiential expression (Davies et al. 2012). Scholars like Forester call for a variety of forums, including informal arrangements, where planners and policymakers can seek out interested parties and spend ample time simply listening (Forester 1999).

Lesson #2 Many commentators have shown that management approaches need to be tailored to the specific context, instead of adopting a common, universalistic approach (cf. Ostrom, Janssen, and Anderies 2007; Pahl-Wostl et al. 2011). A narrative approach allows us to bring out what it is about non-blueprint approaches that make them effective and allow us to better describe them. A close examination of the narratives of regulators and turtle egg harvesters suggests why standard ecological reserves would not work well on the Turtle Islands (Lejano and Ingram 2007). Narrative analysis allows us to better describe the kind of system that did work.

Lesson #3 Narrative reveals how identity is marked by both constancy and change, and that contrary to conventional assumptions about individual self-interest, people often come to define themselves in relation to a complex world of humans and other beings and things. This has implications for institutional or program design. Is there flexibility and openness to local difference? Are ecological management programs allowed to adapt or do they lock themselves into fixed organizational structures and routinized practices? Is there a sense of relationships growing and deepening as the program develops, not just for humans, but for relationships with animals and place? In this sense, adaptive management is like a process of joint storytelling, where the past drives the narrative onward into new territory. In a narrative framework, the past is not simply regarded as sunk cost, and new ways of doing do not simply displace the old—rather, they all lend to the evolving metanarrative. This also goes for the way we define or position ourselves vis-à-vis other species—these, too, are evolving relationships, and we have to allow for change.

Lesson #4 Deliberative processes need to be expanded to include elements, especially nonhuman objects that narratives reveal. We join a number of other scholars (cf. Bennett 2010; Eckersley 1992; Latour 2004a; Plumwood 1993) in recognizing the limitations of a human/nonhuman divide. This means changing the way we design deliberative forums. The individual and collective act of narration perhaps requires processes and conventions not covered by Habermas's notion of communicative rationality as an agonistic process. Writing about political and ecological communication, Dryzek (1998) attempts to rescue communicative rationality from Habermas by recognizing agency in nature and underwriting respect for natural processes. He argues, "Just as democrats would condemn humans who would silence other humans, so we should condemn humans who would silence nature" (590). "Communicative reason can be extended to include non-human entities" (591).

Lesson #5 Although our case studies focused on intimate stories, the implications for narrative in motivating broader-based political action should not be missed. While the factors that have supported the impressive development of the organic agriculture industry are complex, for example, there is little doubt that the strength of the organic farming narrative network was crucial to developing and sustaining core ideas and messages, which later fed into a larger movement. We join social movement scholars who have also recognized the key role of narrative in motivating large groups of people to act.

There are elements of narration that should guide us in creating forums for participation. Narratives broaden our ability to "hear" non-humans, as they have been engaged with by people and have enabled people to entertain new ideas and actions (Stengers 2010). A purposeful attempt to collect a more complete narrative with multiple voices allows for different dimensions of actors to emerge. For instance, the collection and dissemination of stories about wolves being reintroduced to the wild can expand their characterization beyond predator to include their attractiveness to naturalists and tourists, how ranchers have found strategies to coexist, and their role in ecological health (Treves, Wallace, and White 2009). Leopold's narrative of extinguishing the "green fire" in the eyes of the dying wolf in *The Sand County Almanac* has played a key role in a long restoration campaign. While this book did not set out to prescribe new deliberative practices that might promote narrative plurivocity in policy arenas, we underscore the importance of such avenues of future inquiry. How to reform existing institutions (e.g., public hearings, environmental impact assessments, dispute resolution) toward greater narrative richness is an open question.

The overarching contribution of this book to environmental advocacy and practice is to point out the critical ways that attention to story can expand our ecological imagination and enrich environmental policy. Narrating a good story to which many subscribe and contribute is worthy work.

Notes

2 A Theory of "More than Social" Networks

1. Biophysical ecology shapes empire and tribe alike . . . self-similarity in social action, across levels and size reflects continuing impetus from the biophysical. Whether in work or demography or daily life, left untied to biophysical process, social organization tends to freeze up and to lose and possibility for change" (White 1992, 20).

2. Ariadne's thread is generally a method of solving a problem through a series of contingent, ordered steps accompanied by a record of the investigation (the thread) such that the steps may be retraced.

3 The Turn to Narrative Analysis

1. Note that narratologists sometimes distinguish *fabula*, which is the logical sequence of events, and *plot*, which is the story as actually presented by the author or narrator. For example, while the fabula may present the chronological sequence of events in Faulkner's novel *The Sound and the Fury*, the plot would present the story as actually told in the novel, flashbacks and all.

4 Narrative, Network, and Conservation on the Arizona-Sonora Border

1. The relative size of the red dots in this figure 4.3 is different from those portrayed in figure 2.1 because in figure 4.3 the size of dots relates to numbers of outgoing ties only.

2. An archive of video and audio interviews entitled *Sonoran Desert Voices: A Lasting Legacy Preserving the Cultural and Environmental Heritage of the U.S.-Mexico Border* is available at the International Sonoran Desert Alliance in Ajo, Arizona, and at several other locations. Due to various technical limitations, not all the people we interviewed are included in the archive and not all of those interviewed are portrayed in the network diagram.

6   Narratives of Nature and Science in Alternative Farming Networks

1. Retail sales of organic foods grew from $3.6 billion in 1997 to $21.1 billion in 2008, supported by an expanding diversity of organic products. Over half of the purchases in 2008 were in conventional supermarket and big box outlets (Dimitri and Oberholtzer 2009).

2. Interview by Mrill Ingram with John Hall, director of Michael Fields Agricultural Institute, East Troy, Wisconsin, February 2001.

3. Charles Walters and others refer to this network as "ecoagriculture."

4. Interview by Mrill Ingram with David Engel, Viroqua, Wisconsin, February 2001.

References

Albrecht, William. 1958. *Soil Fertility and Animal Health*. Webster City, IA: Fred Hahne Printing.

Albrecht, William. 1975. *The Albrecht Papers, Vol. I—Foundation Concepts*, ed. Charles Walters. Metairie, LA: Acres U.S.A.

Allen, Barbara. 2003. *Uneasy Alchemy: Citizens and Experts in Louisiana's Chemical Corridor Disputes*. Cambridge, MA: MIT Press.

Allen, Patricia. 1991. "The Social Side of Sustainability, Class, Gender and Race." *Science as Culture* 2 (13): 569–590.

Allen, Patricia, Margaret Fitzsimmons, Michael Goodman, and Keith Warner. 2003. "Shifting Plates in the Agrifood Landscape: The Tectonics of Alternative Agrifood Initiatives in California." *Journal of Rural Studies* 19 (1): 61–75.

Bal, Mieke. 2009. *Narratology: Introduction to the Theory of Narrative*. 3rd ed. Toronto: University of Toronto Press.

Barad, Karen. 2003. "Posthumanist Performativity: Toward an Understanding of How Matter Comes to Matter Signs." *Journal of Women in Culture and Society* 28 (3): 801–831.

Barnes, John. 1954. "Class and Committees in a Norwegian Island Parish." *Human Relations* 7:39–58.

Barthes, Roland. 1974. *S/Z: An Essay*. Trans. Richard Miller. New York: Hill and Wang.

Basurto, Xavier and Elinor Ostrom. 2009. "Beyond the Tragedy of the Commons." *Economia delle di Energia e dell'Ambiente* 1: 35–60.

Beal, Tom. 2012. "Border a Frequent Barrier for Scientists." *Arizona Daily Star*, April 22, sec. C.

Benford, Robert, and David Snow. 2000. "Framing Processes and Social Movements: An Overview and Assessment." *Annual Review of Sociology* 26:611–639.

Bennett, Jane. 2010. *Vibrant Matter: A Political Ecology of Things*. Durham, NC: Duke University Press.

Berardo, Ramiro, and John Scholz. 2008. "Self-Organizing Policy Networks: Risk, Partner Selection and Cooperation in Estuaries." http://polisci.fsu.edu/csdp/documents/BerardoScholzReviseFinal.pdf.

Berkes, Fikret. 1999. *Sacred Ecology: Traditional Ecological Knowledge and Resource Management*. New York: Taylor & Francis.

Berkes, Fikret. 2007. "Community-Based Conservation in a Globalized World." *Proceedings of the National Academy of Sciences of the United States of America* 104 (39): 15188–15193.

Berkes, Fikret. 2009. *Sacred Ecology*. 2nd ed. New York: Routledge.

Berkes, Fikret, Johan Colding, and Carl Folke, eds. 2003. *Navigating Social Ecological Systems: Building Resilience for Complexity and Change*. Cambridge, UK: Cambridge University Press.

Berkes, Fikret, and Carl Folke. 1998. "Linking Social and Ecological Systems for Resilience and Sustainability." In *Linking Social and Ecological Systems: Management Practices and Social Mechanisms for Building Resilience*, ed. Fikret Berkes and Carl Folke, 1–25. Cambridge, UK: Cambridge University Press.

Berry, Wendell. 2012. "Wendell E. Berry Lecture—It All Turns on Affection." http://www.neh.gov/about/awards/jefferson-lecture/wendell-e-berry-lecture.

Billig, Michael. 1996. *Arguing and Thinking*. Cambridge, UK: Cambridge University Press.

Blatter, Joachim, and Helen Ingram. 2001. *Reflections on Water: New Approaches to Transboundary Conflicts and Cooperation*. Cambridge, MA: MIT Press.

Blomquist, William, Edella Schlager, and Tanya Heikkila. 2004. *Common Waters, Diverging Streams: Linking Institutions and Water Management in Arizona, California, and Colorado*. Washington, DC: Resources for the Future.

Bodin, Orjan, and Beatrice Crona. 2009. "The Role of Social Networks in Natural Resources Governance: What Relational Patterns Make a Difference." *Global Environmental Change* 19:366–374.

Boelens, Rutgerd, David Getches, and Armando Guevara-Gil, eds. 2010. *Out of the Mainstream: Water Rights, Politics and Identity*. London: Earthscan.

Boje, David. 1991. "The Storytelling Organization: A Study of Story Performance in an Office-Supply Firm." *Administrative Science Quarterly* 36 (1): 106–126.

Boje, David. 1995. "Stories of the Storytelling Organization: A Postmodern Analysis of Disney as 'Tamara-Land.'" *Academy of Management Journal* 38 (4): 997–1035.

Boland, Richard, Jr., and Ramkrishnan Tenkasi. 1995. "Perspective Making and Perspective Taking." *Communities of Knowing Organization Science* 6 (4): 350–372.

Bookchin, Murray. 1998. "Society and Ecology." In *Debating the Earth: The Environmental Politics Reader*, ed. John Dryzek and David Schlosberg, 415–428. Oxford: Oxford University Press.

Boyce, Mary. 1995. "Collective Centering and Collective Sense-Making in the Stories and Storytelling of One Organization." *Organization Studies* 16 (1): 107–137.

Brandon, Kent, Kent H. Redford, and Steven Sanderson. 1998. *Parks in Peril People, Politics, and Protected Areas*. Washington, DC: Island Press.

Bremond, Claude. 1973. *Logique du Recit*. Paris: Seuil.

Brentano, Franz. 1874. *Psychology from an Empirical Standpoint* [Psychologie vom empirischen Standpunkt]. Trans. Antos C. Rancurello, D. B. Terell, and Linda McAlister. London: Routledge.

Brockington, Dan, Rosaleen Duffy, and Jim Igoe. 2008. *Nature Unbound: Conservation, Capitalism and the Future of Protected Areas*. London: Earthscan.

Brown, Andrew. 2006. "A Narrative Approach to Collective Identities." *Journal of Management Studies* 43 (4): 731–753.

Brown, F. Lee, and Helen Ingram. 1987. *Water and Poverty in the Southwest*. Tucson: University of Arizona Press.

Brown, John, and Paul Duguid. 1991. "Organizational Learning and Communities-of-Practice: Toward a Unified View of Working, Learning, and Innovation." *Organization Science* 2 (1): 40–57.

Broyles, Bill, and Mark Haynes. 2010. *Desert Duty*. Austin: University of Texas Press.

Brugnach, Marcela, Art Dewulf, Claudia Pahl-Wostl, and Tharsi Taillieu. 2008. "Toward a Relational Concept of Uncertainty: About Knowing Too Little, Knowing Too Differently, and Accepting Not to Know." *Ecology and Society* 13 (2): 30. http://www.ecologyandsociety.org/vol13/iss2/art30/.

Brugnach, Marcela, and Helen Ingram. 2011. "Ambiguity: The Challenge of Knowing and Deciding Together." *Environmental Science & Policy* 15 (1): 60–71.

Bruner, Jerome. 1987a. *Actual Minds, Possible Worlds*. Cambridge, MA: Harvard University Press.

Bruner, Jerome. 1987b. "Life as Narrative." *Social Research* 71:691–710.

Bruner, Jerome. 1990. *Acts of Meaning*. Cambridge, MA: Harvard University Press.

Bruner, Jerome. 1993. "The Autobiographical Process." In *The Culture of Autobiography: Constructions of Self-Representations*, ed. Robert Folkenflik, 38–56. Stanford: Stanford University Press.

Burt, Ronald. 2004. "Structural Holes and Good Ideas." *American Journal of Sociology* 110 (2): 349–399.

Busch, Lawrence. 1994. "The State of Agricultural Science and the Agricultural Science of the State." In *From Columbus to ConAgra*, ed. Alessandro Bonano et al., 69–84. Lawrence: University Press of Kansas.

Buttel, Frederick. 1986. "Agricultural Research and Farm Structural Change: Bovine Growth Hormone and Beyond." *Agriculture and Human Values* 3 (4): 88–98.

Butz, E. 1971. "Crisis or Challenge?" *Nation's Agriculture*, July–August, 19.

Calderon-Aguilera, Luis E., and Karl W. Flessa. 2009. "Just Add Water? Transboundary Colorado River Flow and Ecosystem Services in the Upper Gulf of California." In *Conservation of Shared Environments: Learning from the United*

States and Mexico, ed. Laura López Hoffman, Emily McGovern, Robert Varady, and Karl Flessa, 154–169. Tucson: University of Arizona Press.

Callon, Michel. 1986. "Some Elements of a Sociology of Translation: Domestication of the Scallops and the Fishermen of St Brieuc Bay." In *Power, Action and Belief: A New Sociology of Knowledge*, ed. John Law, 196–223. London: Routledge & Kegan Paul.

Camillo, Francesca. 2011. "Aronia Renaissance Iowa Organic Farm Brings Berry Renewed Popularity." *Acres U.S.A.* 41 (1): 34–37.

Campbell, Lisa. 1998. "Use Them or Lose Them? Conservation and the Consumptive Use of Marine Turtle Eggs at Ostional, Costa Rica." *Environmental Conservation* 24 (4): 305–319.

Campbell, Lisa, Jennifer Silver, Noella Gray, Sue Ranger, Annette Broderick, Tatum Fisher, Matthew Godfrey, et al. 2009. "Co-management of Sea Turtle Fisheries: Biogeography versus Geopolitics." *Marine Policy* 33:137–145.

Carson, Rachel. 1962. *Silent Spring*. New York: Houghton Mifflin.

Casey, Edward. 1993. *Getting Back into Place: Toward a Renewed Understanding of the Place-World*. Bloomington: Indiana University Press.

Cash, David, William Clark, Frank Alcock, Nancy Dickson, Noelle Eckley, David Guston, Jill Jäger, and Ronald Mitchell. 2003. "Knowledge Systems for Sustainable Development." *Proceedings of the National Academy of Sciences of the United States of America* 100 (14): 8086–8091.

Cash, David, William Clark, Frank Alcock, Nancy Dickson, Noelle Eckley, and Jill Jager. 2002. "Salience, Credibility, Legitimacy and Boundaries: Linking Research, Assessment and Decision Making." KSG Working Papers Series RWP 02–046. John F. Kennedy School of Government, Harvard University.

Castells, Manuel. 1996. *The Rise of the Network Society, Vol. 1: The Information Age: Economy, Society and Culture*. Oxford and Malden, MA: Blackwell Publishers.

Cawley, R. McGreggor. 1993. *Federal Land, Western Anger: The Sagebrush Rebellion and Environmental Politics*. Lawrence: University Press of Kansas.

Chester, Charles. 2006. *Conservation across Borders: Biodiversity in an Interdependent World*. Washington, DC: Island Press.

Christie, Patrick, and Allan White. 2006. "Creating Space for Interdisciplinary Marine and Coastal Research: Five Dilemmas and Suggested Resolutions." *Environmental Conservation* 38 (2): 172–186.

CNN. 2010. "Arizona's Brewer: Most Illegal Immigrants Are 'Drug Mules,'" June 25. http://articles.cnn.com/2010-06-25/us/arizona.immigrants.drugs_1_drug-cartels-drug-trafficking-smuggling?_s=PM:US

Coleman, Eliot. 1989. *The New Organic Grower*. Chelsea, VT: Chelsea Green.

Coleman, James. 1990. *Foundations of Social Theory*. Cambridge, MA: Harvard University Press.

Collins, Mary Elizabeth, Kate Cooney, and Sarah Garlington. 2012. "Compassion in Contemporary Social Policy: Applications of Virtue Theory." *Journal of Social Policy* 41 (2): 251–269.

Conca, Ken. 2006. *Governing Water: Contentious Transnational Politics and Global Institution Building*. Cambridge, MA: MIT Press.

Cooke, Bill, and Uma Kothari. 2001. *Participation: The New Tyranny?* London: Zed Books.

Cooren, Francis, and James Taylor. 1997. "Organization as an Effect of Mediation: Redefining the Link between Organization and Communication." *Communication Theory* 7 (3): 219–260.

Cope, Meghan, and Frank Latcham. 2009. "Narratives of Decline: Race, Poverty, and Youth in the Context of Postindustrial Urban Angst." *Professional Geographer* 61 (2): 150–163.

Cortner, Hanna, and Margaret Moote. 2009. *The Politics of Ecosystems Management*. Washington, DC: Island Press.

Cortner, Hanna, Margaret Shannon, Mary Wallace, Sabrina Burke, and Margaret Moote. 1999. "Changing Natural Resource Paradigms in the United States: Finding Political Reality in Academic Theory." In *Handbook of Global Environmental Policy and Administration*, ed. Dennis Soden and Brent Steele, 459–474. New York: Marcel Dekker.

Cronon, William. 1996. *Uncommon Ground: Rethinking the Human Place in Nature*. New York: W. W. Norton & Co.

Cudney-Bueno, Richard, and Xavier Basurto. 2009. "Lack of Cross-Scale Linkages Reduces Robustness of Community-Based Fisheries Management." *PLoS ONE* 4 (7): 1–8.

Currie, Graeme, and Andrew Brown. 2003. "A Narratological Approach to Understanding Processes of Organizing in a UK Hospital." *Human Relations* 56 (5): 563–586.

Czarniawska, Barbara. 1997. *A Narrative Approach to Organization Studies*. Thousand Oaks, CA: Sage.

Davey, Monica. 2010. "Fight Against Asian Carp Threatens Fragile Great Lakes Unity." *New York Times*, January 2.

Day, Richard. 2001. "Ethics, Affinity and the Coming Communities." *Philosophy and Social Criticism* 27 (1): 21–38.

Day, Richard. 2004. "From Hegemony to Affinity: The Political Logic of the Newest Social Movements." *Cultural Studies* 18 (5): 716–748.

Davies, Sarah R., Cynthia Selin, Gretchen Gano, and Ângela Guimarães Pereira. 2012. "Citizen Engagement and Urban Change: Three Case Studies of Material Deliberation." *Cities* 29 (6): 351–357.

de Bruijn, Johan, and Ernst ten Heuvelhof. 1995. "Policy Networks and Governance." In *Institutional Design*, ed. David L. Weimer, 161–179. Boston, MA: Kluwer Academic Publishers.

Dedeurwaerdere, Tom. 2011. "The Contribution of Network Governance to Sustainable Development. A Case Study on Sustainability Impact Assessment." http://perso.cpdr.ucl.ac.be/dedeurwaerdere/SIApaper_final.pdf.

Deleuze, Gilles, and Felix Guattari. [1980] 1987. *A Thousand Plateaus: Capitalism and Schizophrenia*. Trans. Brian Massumi. London: Athlone Press.

De Neufville, Judith, and Stephen Barton. 1987. "Myths and the Definition of Policy Problems: An Exploration of Home Ownership and Public-Private Partnerships. *Policy Sciences* 20:181–206.

Dewulf, Art, Marcela Brugnach, Helen Ingram, and Katrien Termeer. 2009. "The Co-Production of Knowledge about Water Resources: Framing, Uncertainty and Climate Change." Paper for the 7th International Science Conference on the Human Dimensions of Global Environmental Change, April 26–30, UN Campus, Bonn, Germany.

Dietz, Thomas, Elnor Ostrom, and Paul Stern. 2003. "The Struggle to Govern the Commons." *Science* 302:1907–1912.

Dimitri, Carolyn, and Lydia Oberholtzer. 2009. "Marketing U.S. Organic Foods: Recent Trends from Farms to Consumers." *Economic Information Bulletin*, no. 58. http://www.ers.usda.gov/publications/eib-economic-information-bulletin/eib58.aspx.

Dobson, Andrew. 1995. *Green Political Thought: An Introduction*. London: Routledge.

Dodgson, Mark. 1993. "Organizational Learning: A Review of Some Literatures." *Organization Studies* 14 (3): 375–394.

Domantay, Jose. 1953. "The Turtle Fisheries in Turtle Islands." *Bulletin of the Fisheries Societies of the Philippines* 3 (4): 3–27.

Doremus, Holly. 2004. "The Purposes, Effects and Future of the Endangered Species Act's Best Available Science Mandate." *Environmental Law* 34 (2): 397–450.

Douglas, Mary. 1966. *Purity and Danger: An Analysis of the Concepts of Pollution and Taboo*. London: Routledge & Kegan Paul.

Downs, Anthony. 1972. "Up and Down with Ecology-the Issue-Attention Cycle." *Public Interest* 28:38–50.

Dryzek, John. 1990. *Discursive Democracy: Politics, Policy, and Political Science*. Cambridge, UK: Cambridge University Press.

Dryzek, John. 1997. *The Politics of the Earth: Environmental Discourses*. Oxford: Oxford University Press.

Dryzek, John. 1998. "Political and Ecological Communication." In *Debating the Earth: The Environmental Politics Reader*, ed. John Dryzek and David Schlosberg, 13–30. Oxford: Oxford University Press.

Dryzek, John. 1999. "Global Ecological Democracy." In *Global Ethics and Environment*, ed. Nicholas Low, 264–282. London: Routledge.

Dryzek, John. 2008. "Policy Analysis as Critique." In *The Oxford Handbook of Public Policy*, ed. Michael Moran, Martin Rein, and Robert Goodin, 193–203. Oxford: Oxford University Press.

Eckersley, Robyn. 1992. *Environmentalism and Political Theory: Toward an Ecocentric Approach*. Albany: SUNY Press.

Ehrlich, Paul. 1968. *The Population Bomb*. New York: Ballantine Books.

Ezcurra, Exequiel. 2007. "The Desert Inside Us." In *Dry Borders: Great Natural Reserves of the Sonoran Desert*, ed. Richard Felger and Bill Broyles, xi–xiii. Salt Lake: University of Utah Press.

Ezcurra, Exequiel. 2009. "The Keepers of this Land." In *Conservation of Shared Environments: Learning from the United States and Mexico*, ed. Laura López Hoffman, Emily McGovern, Robert Varady, and Karl Flessa, xiii–xiv. Tucson: University of Arizona Press.

Fairfax, Sally, and Darla Guenzler. 2001. *Conservation Trusts*. Lawrence: University of Kansas Press.

Fairfax, Sally, Lauren Gwin, Mary Ann King, and Leigh Raymond. 2005. *Buying Nature: The Limits of Land Acquisition as a Conservation Strategy*. Cambridge, MA: MIT Press.

Fairfax, Sally K., Louise Nelson Dyble, Greig Tor Guthey, Lauren Gwin, Monica Moore, and Jennifer Sokolove. 2012. *California Cuisine and Just Food*. Cambridge, MA: MIT Press.

Feldman, David, and Helen Ingram. 2009a. "Making Science Useful to Decision Makers: Climate Forecasts, Water Management and Knowledge Networks. *Weather, Climate and Society* 1 (1): 9–13.

Feldman, David, and Helen Ingram. 2009b. "Multiple Ways of Knowing Water Resources: Enhancing the Status of Water Ethics." *Santa Clara Journal of International Law* 7 (1): 1–20.

Feldman, Martha, Anne Khademian, Helen Ingram, and Anne Schneider. 2006. "Ways of Knowing and Inclusive Management Practices." *Public Administration Review* 66:89–99.

Felger, Richard, and Bill Broyles. 2007. *Dry Borders: Great Natural Reserves of the Sonoran Desert*. Salt Lake City: University of Utah Press.

Fine, Gary A., and Brooke Harrington. 2004. "Tiny Publics: Small Groups and Civil Society." *Sociological Theory* 22 (3): 341–356.

Fischer, Frank. 1993. "Policy Discourse and the Politics of Washington Think Tanks." In *The Argumentative Turn in Policy Analysis and Planning*, ed. Frank Fischer and John Forester, 22–42. Durham, NC: Duke University Press.

Fischer, Frank. 2003. *Reframing Public Policy: Discursive Polities and Deliberative Practices*. Oxford: Oxford University Press.

Fischer, Frank, and John Forester, eds. 1993. *The Argumentative Turn in Policy Analysis and Planning*. Durham, NC: Duke University Press.

Fisher, Walter. 1987. "Technical Logic, Rhetorical Logic, and Narrative Rationality." *Argumentation* 1:3–21.

Fludernik, Monika. 2007. "Identity/Alterity." In *Cambridge Book of Narrative*, ed. D. Herman, Cambridge, UK: Cambridge University Press.

Folke, Carl. 2006. "Resilience: The Emergence of a Perspective for Social—Ecological Systems Analyses." *Global Environmental Change* 16:253–267.

Ford, Jeffrey. 1999. "Organizational Change as Shifting Conversations." *Journal of Organizational Change Management* 12 (6): 480–500.

Forester, John. 1999. *The Deliberative Practitioner.* Cambridge, MA: MIT Press.

Forester, Tom. 1987. *High-Tech Society: The Story of the Information Technology Revolution.* Cambridge, MA: MIT Press.

Forster, Edward Morgan. 1927. *Aspects of the Novel.* London: Harcourt, Brace, and Co.

Foucault, Michel. 1969. *Archeology of Knowledge.* New York: Routledge.

Freeman, Linton. 2000. "Visualizing Social Networks." *Journal of Social Structure* 1 (1). http://www.cmu.edu/joss/contents/articles/volume1/Freeman.html.

Freeman, Mark. 2001. "From Substance to Story: Narrative, Identity, and the Reconstruction of the Self." In *Narrative and Identity*, ed. Jens Brockmeier and Donald Carbaugh, 283–298. Philadelphia, PA: John Benjamins Publishing Company.

Frege, Gottlob. 1948. "Sense and Reference." *Philosophical Review* 57 (3): 209–230.

Friend, Richard, and David Blake. 2009. "Negotiating Trade-Offs in Water Resources Development in the Mekong Basin: Implications for Fisheries and Fiery-Based Livelihoods." *Water Policy* 11 (1): 13–30.

Fritsch, Oliver, and Jens Newig. 2008. "Participatory Governance and Sustainability: Early Findings of a Meta-analysis of Stakeholder Involvement in Environmental Decision-Making." In *Reflexive Governance for Global Public Goods*, ed. Eric Brousseau and Tom Dedeurwaerdere, 181–204. Cambridge, MA: MIT Press.

Funtowicz, Silvio, and Jerome Ravetz. 1990. *Uncertainty and Quality in Science for Policy.* Netherlands: Kluwer Academic Publishers.

Furmansky, Dyana Z. 2009. *Rosalie Edge, Hawk of Mercy: The Activist Who Saved Nature from the Conservationists.* Athens: University of Georgia Press.

Gadamer, Hans-Georg. 1975. *Truth and Method.* 2nd ed. London: Sheed and Ward.

Gaventa, John, and Gregory Barrett. 2010. "So What Difference Does It Make? Mapping the Outcomes of Citizen Engagement." Institute for Development Studies Working Paper 347. Brighton: University of Sussex.

Gaynor, Tim. 2012. "Migrant Trash Piles Up at Remote U.S.-Mexico Border Areas." Reuters, January 29. http://www.reuters.com/article/2012/01/29/us-immigration-usa-trash-idUSTRE80S0QB20120129.

Genette, Gerard. 1980. *Narrative Discourse.* Trans. Jane Lewin. Oxford: Blackwell.

Geertz, Clifford. 1973. *The Interpretation of Cultures.* New York: Basic Books.

Gentner, Dedre, and Albert Stevens, eds. 1983. *Mental Models.* Hillsdale, NJ: Lawrence Erlbaum Associates Inc.

Gerlak, Andrea, and Tanya Heikkila. 2011. "Building a Theory of Learning in Collaboratives: Evidence from the Everglades Restoration Program." *Journal of Public Administration: Research and Theory* 21 (4): 619–644.

Gibbs, Lois. 1982. *Love, Canal: My Story*. New York: Grove Press.

Gibbs, Mark. 2008. "Network Governance in Fisheries." *Marine Policy* 32 (1): 113–119.

Gilligan, Carol. 1982. *In a Different Voice: Psychological Theory and Women's Development*. Cambridge, MA: Harvard University Press.

Goffman, Erving. 1959. *Presentation of Self in Everyday Life*. New York: Doubleday.

Goffman, Erving. 1974. *Frame Analysis: An Essay on the Organization of Experience*. London: Harper and Row.

Goldstein, Bruce, Anne Taufen Wessells, Raul Lejano, and William Butler. 2012. "Transformative Urban Resilience through Collaborative Storytelling." Forthcoming in *Urban Studies*.

Goodall, Jane. 1998. *In the Shadow of Man*. New York: Addison-Wesley.

Granovetter, Mark. 1973. "The Strength of Weak Ties." *American Journal of Sociology* 78 (6): 1360–1380.

Granovetter, Mark. 1985. "Economic Action and Social Structure: The Problem of Embeddedness." *American Journal of Sociology* 91 (3): 481–510.

Greider, William. 2000. "The Last Farm Crisis." *The Nation*, November 2.

Greimas, Algirdas. 1966. *Sémantique Structural*. Paris: Presse Universitaires de France.

Grindle, Merilee, and John Thomas. 1991. *Public Choices and Policy Change: The Political Economy of Reform in Developing Countries*. Baltimore, MD: Johns Hopkins University Press.

Gross, Matthias. 2010. *Ignorance and Surprise: Science, Society, and Ecological Design*. Cambridge, MA: MIT Press.

Guevara-Gil, Amando. 2010. "Water Rights and Conflicts in the Inter-Andean Watershed: The Achamayo River Valley, Junin, Peru." In *Out of the Mainstream: Water Rights, Politics and Identity*, ed. Rutgerd Boelens, David Getches, and Amando Guevara-Gil, 183–196. London: Earthscan.

Gunderson, Lance, and C. S. Holling. 2002. *Panarchy: Understanding Transformations in Human and Natural Systems*. Washington, DC: Island Press.

Guston, David. 2001. "Boundary Organizations in Environmental Policy and Science: An Introduction." *Science, Technology & Human Values* 26 (4): 399–408.

Guthman, Julie. 1998. "Regulating Meaning, Appropriating Nature: The Codification of California Organic Agriculture." *Antipode* 30 (2): 135–154.

Haas, Peter. 2004. "Addressing the Global Governance Deficit." *Global Environmental Politics* 4 (4): 1–15.

Habermas, Jurgen. 1984. *Reason and the Rationalization of Society, Vol. 1: The Theory of Communicative Action*. Trans. Thomas McCarthy. Boston, MA: Beacon Press.

Habermas, Jurgen. 1987. *The Critique of Functional Reason, Vol. 2: The Theory of Communicative Action*. Trans. Thomas McCarthy. London: Heinemann.

Hajer, Maarten. 1993. "Discourse Coalitions and the Institutionalization of Practice: The Case of Acid Rain in Great Britain." In *The Argumentative Turn in Policy Analysis and Planning*, ed. Frank Fischer and John Forester, 43–77. Durham, NC: Duke University Press.

Hajer, Maarten. 1995. *The Politics of Environmental Discourses*. New York: Oxford University Press.

Hannan, Michael, and John Freeman. 1977. "The Population Ecology of Organizations." *American Journal of Sociology* 82 (5): 929–964.

Haraway, Donna. 1991. *Simians, Cyborgs and Women: the Reinvention of Nature*. London: Free Association Books.

Hayden, Julian, Bill Broyles, and Diane Boyer. 2011. *Field Man: Life as a Desert Archeologist*. Tucson: University of Arizona Press.

Hays, Samuel P. 1989. *Beauty, Health and Permanence: Environment, Environmental Politics in the United States 1955–1985*. Cambridge, UK: Cambridge University Press.

Heimer, Carol. 1992. "Doing Your Job and Helping Your Friends: Universalistic Norms about Obligations to Particular Others in Networks." In *Networks and Organizations: Structure, Form, and Action*, ed. Nitin Nohria and Robert Eccles, 143–164. Boston, MA: Harvard Business School Press.

Heimer, Carol. 2001. "Solving the Problem of Trust." In *Trust in Society*, ed. Karen S. Cook, 40–88. New York: Russell Sage Foundation.

Herman, David. 2007. "Introduction." In *The Cambridge Companion to Narrative*, ed. David Herman, 3–21. Cambridge, UK: Cambridge University Press.

Heydebrand, Wolf. 1989. "New Organizational Forms." *Work and Occupations* 16 (3): 323–357.

Hillier, Jean. 2009. "Assemblages of Justice: The 'Ghost Ships' of Graythorp." *International Journal of Urban and Regional Research* 33 (3): 640–661.

Hoekenga, Christine. 2012. "An Ode to Hiking with Scientists." Tucson Citizen. http://tucsoncitizen.com/tucson-outdoors/2012/04/20/an-ode-to-hiking-with-scientists/.

Holland, Dorothy, and Naomi Quinn, eds. 1987. *Cultural Models in Language and Thought*. Cambridge, UK: Cambridge University Press.

Howard, Albert. 1940. *An Agricultural Testament*. London: Oxford University Press.

Howard, Albert. 1946. *The War in the Soil*. Emmaus, PA: Rodale Press.

Howard, Albert. [1947] 1972. *The Soil and Health A Study of Organic Agriculture*. New York: Schocken Books.

Howell-Martens, Klaas. 2001. "From Amber Waves to Market." Presentation at the Upper Midwest Organic Farming Conference, February 24–26, La Crosse, WI.

Howlett, Michael, M. Ramesh, and Anthony Perl. 2009. *Studying Public Policy: Policy Cycles and Policy Subsystems*. 3rd ed. Ontario, Canada: Oxford University Press.

Husserl, Edmund. [1900] 1970. *Logical Investigations* [Logische Untersuchungen]. Trans. John N. Findlay. New York: Routledge.

Ingram, Helen, Nancy Laney, and David Gillilan. 1995. *Divided Waters: Bridging the US-Mexico Border*. Tucson: University of Arizona Press.

Ingram, Helen, Lenard Milich, and Robert Varady. 1995. "The Sonoran Pimeria Alta: Shared Environmental Problems and Challenges." *Journal of Southwest* 37 (1): 102–122.

Ingram, Mrill. 2007. "Biology and Beyond: The Science of Back-to-Nature Farming in the U.S." *Annals of the Association of American Geographers. Association of American Geographers* 97 (2): 298–312.

Ingram, Mrill. 2010. "Keeping Up with the E.coli: Considering Human-Nonhuman Relationships in Natural Resources Policy." *Natural Resources Journal* 50 (2): 371–392.

Ingram, Mrill, and Helen Ingram. 2005. "Credible Edibles: The Development of Federal Organic Regulations." In *Routing the Opposition: Social Movements and Public Policy*, ed. David Meyer, Valerie Jenness, and Helen Ingram, 121–148. Minneapolis: University of Minnesota Press.

Innes, Juddith, and David Booher. 2010. *Planning with Complexity: An Introduction to Collaborative Rationality for Public Policy*. New York: Routledge.

Jones, Michael, and Mark McBeth. 2010. "A Narrative Policy Framework: Clear Enough to Be Wrong?" *Policy Studies Journal* 38 (2): 329–353.

Kamieniecki, Sheldon, and Steven Cohen. 2005. *Strategic Planning in Environmental Regulation: A Policy Approach that Works*. Cambridge, MA: MIT Press.

Kempton, Willett A., James S. Boster, and Jennifer A. Hartley. 1995. *Environmental Values in American Culture*. Cambridge, MA: MIT Press.

Karvonen, Andrew. 2011. *Politics of Urban Runoff: Nature, Technology, and the Sustainable City*. Cambridge, MA: MIT Press.

Kingdon, John. 1984. *Agendas, Alternatives, and Public Policies*. Boston, MA: Little, Brown & Co.

Klijn, Erik-Hans, and Joop Koppenjan. 2000. "Public Management and Policy Networks: Foundations of a Network Approach to Governance." *Public Management* 2 (2): 135–158.

Koepf, Herbert. 1989. *The Biodynamic Farm*. Hudson, NY: Anthroposophic Press.

Kooiman, Jan. 1993. "Governance and Governability: Using Complexity, Dynamics and Diversity." In *Modern Governance*, ed. Jan Kooiman, 35–50. London: Sage.

Kooiman, Jan. 2000. "Societal Governance: Levels, Models, and Orders of Social-Political Interaction." In *Debating Governance*, ed. Jon Pierre, 138–166. Oxford: Oxford University Press.

Kraft, Michael, and Sheldon Kamieniecki. 2007. *Business and Environmental Policy: Corporate Interests in the American Political System.* Cambridge, MA: MIT Press.

Kresan, Peter. 2007. "A Geologic Tour of the Dry Borders Region." In *Dry Borders: Great Natural Reserves of the Sonoran Desert*, ed. Richard Felger and Bill Broyles, 31–45. Salt Lake City: University of Utah Press.

Kvale, Steinar. 1996. *InterViews: An Introduction to Qualitative Research Interviewing.* Thousand Oaks, CA: Sage Publications.

Laird Benner, Wendy, and Helen Ingram. 2011. "Sonoran Desert Network Weavers: Surprising Environmental Successes on the U.S./Mexico Border." *Environment Magazine* 53 (1): 7–16.

Larson, Kelli, and Denise Lach. 2010. "Equity in Urban Water Governance through Participatory, Place-based Approaches." Natural Resources Journal 50 (Spring): 407–430.

Lasswell, Harold. 1951. "The Policy Orientation." In *The Policy Sciences*, ed. Daniel Lerner and Harold Lasswell, 3–15. Stanford: Stanford University Press.

Latour, Bruno. 1987. *Science in Action: How to Follow Scientists and Engineers Through Society.* Cambridge, MA: Harvard University Press.

Latour, Bruno. 1988. *The Pasteurization of France.* Cambridge, MA: Harvard University Press.

Latour, Bruno. 1993. *We Have Never Been Modern.* Trans. Catherine Porter. Cambridge, MA: Harvard University Press.

Latour, Bruno. 2004a. "How to Talk about the Body. The Normative Dimension of Scientific Studies." *Body & Society* 10 (2–3): 205–229.

Latour, Bruno. 2004b. *Politics of Nature.* Cambridge, MA: Harvard University Press.

Latour, Bruno. 2011. "Love Your Monsters." *Breakthrough Journal*, no. 2 (Fall). http://breakthroughjournal.org/content/authors/bruno-latour/love-your -monsters.shtml.

Latour, Bruno, and Peter Weibel. 2005. *Making Things Public: Atmospheres of Democracy.* Cambridge, MA: MIT Press.

Latour, Bruno, and Steve Woolgar. 1979. *Laboratory Life: The Social Construction of Laboratory Life.* Beverly Hills, CA: Sage Publications.

Lejano, Raul. 2006. *Frameworks for Policy Analysis: Merging Text and Context.* New York: Routledge Press.

Lejano, Raul. 2008. "The Phenomenon of Collective Action: Modeling Institutions as Structures of Care." *Public Administration Review* 68 (3): 491–504.

Lejano, Raul, and Helen Ingram. 2007. "Place-Based Conservation: Lessons from the Turtle Islands." *Environment: Science and Policy for Sustainable Development* 49 (3): 24–28.

Lejano, Raul, and Helen Ingram. 2009. "Collaborative Networks and New Ways of Knowing." *Environmental Science & Policy* 12 (6): 653–662.

Lejano, Raul, and Helen Ingram. 2012. "Modeling the Commons as a Game with Vector Payoffs." *Journal of Theoretical Politics* 24 (1): 66–89.

Lejano, Raul, Helen Ingram, John Whiteley, Daniel Torres, and Sharon Agduma. 2007. "The Importance of Context: Integrating Resource Conservation with Local Institutions." *Society & Natural Resources* 20 (2): 1–9.

Lejano, Raul, and Ching Leong. 2012. "A Hermeneutic Approach to Explaining and Understanding Public Controversies." *Journal of Public Administration Research & Theory* 22 (4): 793–814.

Lejano, Raul, and Alma Ocampo-Salvador. 2006. "Comparative Analysis of Two Community-based Fishers' Organizations." *Marine Policy* 30 (6): 726–736.

Lejano, Raul, and Savita Shankar. 2012. "The Contextualist Turn and Mechanisms of Institutional Fit." *Policy Sciences.* http://link.springer.com/article/10.10 07%2Fs11077-012-9163-9.

Lejano, Raul and Daniel Stokols. 2012. "The Social Ecology of Value." Working manuscript.

Lejano, Raul, and Anne Taufen Wessells. 2006. "Community and Economic Development: Seeking Common Ground in Discourse and in Practice." *Urban Studies* 43 (9): 1469–1489.

Leopold, Aldo. 1962. *Sand County Almanac and Sketches Here and There.* New York: Oxford University Press.

Levesque, Suzanne. 2000. "From Yellowstone to Yukon: Combining Science and Advocacy to Shape Public Opinion and Policy." Diss., University of California at Irvine.

Lorimer, Hayden. 2006. "Herding Memories of Humans and Animals." *Environment and Planning. D, Society & Space* 24:497–518.

Lyotard, Jean-Francois. 1979. *The Postmodern Condition: A Report on Knowledge.* Minneapolis: University of Minnesota Press.

MacIntyre, Alasdair. 1984. *After Virtue: A Study in Moral Theology.* 2nd ed. Notre Dame, IN: University of Notre Dame Press.

March, James, and Johan Olsen. 1989. *Rediscovering Institutions: The Organizational Basis of Politics.* New York: Free Press.

Marglin, Stephen. 2008. *The Dismal Science: How Thinking Like an Economist Undermines Community.* Cambridge, MA: Harvard University Press.

Marsden, Peter V. 1990. "Network Data and Measurement." *Annual Review of Sociology* 16:435–463.

Martin, J. 1982. "Stories and Scripts in Organizational Settings." In *Cognitive Social Psychology*, ed. Albert Hasdorf and Alice Isen, 255–305. New York: Elsevier North-Holland.

Martinez, Oscar. 1988. *Troublesome Border*. Tucson: University of Arizona Press.

Mazmanian, Daniel, and Michael Kraft. 1999. *Toward Sustainable Communities: Transitions and Transformations in Environmental Policy*. Cambridge, MA: MIT Press.

McCarthy, John D., and Mayer N. Zald. 1977. "Resource Mobilization and Social Movements: A Partial Theory." *American Journal of Sociology* 82 (6): 1212–1241.

Mealhow, Gene. 2001. "Organic University." Presentation at the Upper Midwest Organic Farming Conference, February 24–26, La Crosse, WI.

Meinzen-Dick, Ruth. 2007. "Beyond Panaceas in Water Institutions." *Proceedings of the National Academy of Sciences of the United States of America* 104 (39): 15200–15205.

Merchant, Carolyn. 2007. *American Environmental History: An Introduction*. New York: Columbia University Press.

Meyer, David, Valerie Jenness, and Helen Ingram, eds. 2005. *Routing the Opposition: Social Movements, Public Policy, and Democracy*. Minneapolis: University of Minnesota Press.

Mitroff, Ian, and Ralph Kilmann. 1975. "Stories Managers Tell: A New Tool for Organizational Problem Solving." *Management Review* 64: 18–28.

Morgan, Dewayne. 2002. "Biodynamic Agriculture: How I Made the Transition." *Acres U.S.A.* 32 (2). http://www.acresusa.com/toolbox/reprints/biodynamic _febmar02.pdf.

Moran, Michael. 2002. "Review Article: Understanding the Regulatory State." *British Journal of Political Science* 32 (2): 391–413.

Musilim, S. 2003. *Minutes of the Regular Session of the Sangguniang Bayan of Turtle Islands*. Tawi-Tawi, Philippines: Turtle Islands City Council.

National Research Council (NRC). 2001. *Publicly Funded Agricultural Research and the Changing Structure of U.S. Agriculture*. Washington, DC: National Academy Press.

Nehrlich, Brigitte. 2010. "'Climategate': Paradoxical Metaphors and Political Paralysis." *Environmental Values* 19:419–442.

Neuendorf, Kimberly. 2001. *The Content Analysis Guidebook*. Thousand Oaks, CA: Sage Publications.

Newton, Lina. 2008. *Alien, or Immigrant: The Politics of Immigration Reform*. New York: New York University Press.

Noe, Alva. 2009. *Out of Our Heads: Why You Are Not Your Brain, and Other Lessons from the Biology of Consciousness*. New York: Hill and Wang.

Nohria, Nitin, and Robert Eccles. 2000. "Face to Face: Making Network Organizations Work." In *Networks and Organizations: Structure, Form and Action*, ed. Nitin Nohria and Robert Eccles, 288–308. Boston, MA: Harvard Business School Press.

Norgaard, Kari. 2011. *Living in Denial: Climate Change, Emotions, and Everyday Life*. Cambridge, MA: MIT Press.

Nowotny, Helga, Peter Scott, and Michael Gibbons. 2001. *Rethinking Science: Knowledge and the Public in an Age of Uncertainty*. Cambridge, UK: Polity.

Nussbaum, Martha. 1990. *Love's Knowledge Essays on Philosophy and Literature*. New York: Oxford University Press.

Odum, Eugene. 1953. *Fundamentals of Ecology*. Philadelphia: W. B. Saunders Company.

Ogunseitan, Oladele. 2005. "Topophilia and the Quality of Life." *Environmental Health Perspectives* 113 (2): 143–148.

Olson, Mancur. 1968. *The Logic of Collective Action*. New York: Shocken Books.

Olson, Paul. 2003. "Biological Agriculture, Making Farming Fun Again." *Acres U.S.A.* staff report, November, 1–24.

Ostrom, Elinor. 1990. *Governing the Commons: The Evolution of Institutions for Collective Action*. Cambridge, UK: Cambridge University Press.

Ostrom, Elinor. 2001. "Environment and Common Property Institutions." In *International Encyclopedia of the Social & Behavioral Sciences*, ed. Neil Smelser and Paul Baltes, 4560–4566. Oxford: Pergamon.

Ostrom, Elinor, Marco Janssen, and John Anderies. 2007. "Going Beyond Panaceas." *Proceedings of the National Academy of Sciences of the United States of America* 104 (39): 15176–15178.

O'Toole, Laurence. 1997. "Treating Networks Seriously: Practical and Research-Based Agendas in Public Administration." *Public Administration Review* 57 (1): 45–52.

Pahl-Wostl, Claudia, Paul Jeffrey, Nicola Isendahl, and Marcela Brugnach. 2011. "Maturing the New Water Management Paradigm: Progressing from Aspiration to Practice." *Water Resources Management* 25 (3): 837–856.

Patriotta, Gerardo. 2003. "Sensemaking on the Shop Floor: Narratives of Knowledge in Organizations." *Journal of Management Studies* 40 (2): 349–376.

Pentland, Brian. 1999. "Building Process Theory with Narrative: From Description to Explanation." *Academy of Management Review* 24 (4): 711–724.

Pentland, Brian, and Martha Feldman. 2007. "Narrative Networks: Patterns of Technology and Organization." *Organization Science* 18 (5): 781–795.

Peterson, Garry. 2010. "Expansion of Social Ecological Systems Science." Resilience Science. http://rs.resalliance.org/2010/04/16/expansion-of-social ecological -systems-science/.

Pielke, Roger, Jr. 2004. "When Scientists Politicize Science: Making Sense of Controversy over the Skeptical Environmentalist." *Environmental Science & Policy* 7:405–417.

Plumwood, Val. 1993. *Feminism and the Master of Nature*. London: Routledge.

Plumwood, Val. 1998. "Inequality, Ecojustice and Ecological Rationality." In *Debating the Earth: The Environmental Politics Reader*, ed. John Dryzek and David Schlosberg, 559–584. Oxford: Oxford University Press.

Polletta, Francesca. 1998. "'It Was like a Fever . . .' Narrative and Identity in Social Protest." *Social Problems* 45 (2): 137–159.

Poteete, Amy, Marco Janssen, and Elinor Ostrom. 2010. *Working Together: Collective Action, the Commons, and Multiple Methods in Practice*. Princeton, NJ: Princeton University Press.

Powell, Walter. 1990. "Neither Market nor Hierarchy: Network Forms of Organization." *Research in Organizational Behavior* 12:295–336.

Pressman, Jeffrey, and Aaron Wildavsky. 1973. *Implementation: How Great Expectations in Washington Are Dashed in Oakland: Or, Why It's Amazing that Federal Programs Work at All, This Being a Saga of the Economic Development Administration as Told by Two Sympathetic Observers Who Seek to Build Morals on a Foundation of Ruined Hopes*. Berkeley: University of California Press.

Prince, Gerald. 1990. "On Narratology (Past, Present, Future)." *French Literature Series* 17:1–14.

Propp, Vladimir. 1968. *Morphology of the Folktale*. 2nd ed. Trans. Laurence Scott. Austin: University of Texas Press.

Quiggin, John. 2010. *Zombie Economics: How Dead Ideas Still Walk among Us*. Princeton, NJ: Princeton University Press.

Repetto, Robert, ed. 2006. *Punctuated Equilibrium and the Dynamics of U.S. Environmental Policy*. New Haven: Yale University Press.

Rhodes, Rod A. 1981. "The New Governance: Governing without Government." *Political Studies* 44:652–667.

Ricoeur, Paul. 1973. "The Model of the Text: Meaningful Action Considered as Text." *New Literary History* 5 (1): 91–117.

Ricoeur, Paul. 1976. *Interpretation Theory: Discourse and the Surplus of Meaning*. Fort Worth: Texas Christian University Press.

Ricoeur, Paul. 1981a. *Hermeneutics and the Human Sciences: Essays on Language, Action and Interpretation*. Trans. John B. Thompson. Cambridge, UK: Cambridge University Press.

Ricoeur, Paul. 1981b. "Narrative Time." In *On Narrative*, ed. William J. Thomas Mitchell, 165–186. Chicago: University of Chicago Press.

Ricoeur, Paul. 1984. *Time and Narrative*. Vol. 1. Trans. Kathleen McLaughlin and David Pellaver. Chicago: Chicago University Press.

Ricoeur, Paul. 1992. *Oneself as Another*. Trans. Kathleen Blamey. Chicago: University of Chicago Press.

Roe, Emery. 1994. *Narrative Policy Analysis: Theory and Practice*. Durham, NC: Duke University Press.

Roy, Arundhati. 1999. *The Greater Common Good*. Bombay: India Book Distributor.

Ryan, Marie-Laure. 2007. "Toward a Definition of Narrative." In *The Cambridge Companion to Narrative*, ed. David Herman, 22–35. Cambridge, UK: Cambridge University Press.

Rycroft, Robert. 2003. *Self-Organizing Innovation Networks: Implications for Globalization*. Occasional Paper Series. CSGOP-03-07. Washington, DC: The GW Center for the Study of Globalization.

Sabatier, Paul. 1999. *Theories of the Policy Process*. Boulder, CO: Westview Press.

Sabatier, Paul, Will Focht, Mark Lubell, Zev Trachtenberg, Arnold Vedlitz, and Marty Matlock. 2005. *Swimming Upstream: Collaborative Approaches to Watershed Management*. Cambridge, MA: MIT Press.

Sabatier, Paul, and Hank Jenkins-Smith, eds. 1993. *Policy Change and Learning: An Advocacy Coalition Approach*. Boulder, CO: Westview Press.

Sabel, Charles. 1994. "Learning by Monitoring: The Institutions of Economic Development." In *Handbook of Economic Sociology*, ed. Neil Smelser and Richard Swedberg, 137–165. Princeton, NJ: Princeton University Press and Russell Sage Foundation.

Salatin, Joel. 1998. "Generating Soil Fertility on Farm." *Acres U.S.A.*, May, 1.

Salatin, Joel. 2004. "Sound Science Is Killing Us." *Acres U.S.A.* 34 (4): 1–3.

Sandercock, Leonie. 2003. "Out of the Closet: The Importance of Stories and Storytelling in Planning Practice." *Planning Theory & Practice* 4 (1): 11–28.

Schmidt, Jeremy, and Martha Dowsley. 2010. "Hunting with Polar Bears: Problems with the Passive Properties of the Commons." *Human Ecology* 38:377–387.

Schmidt, Vivien A. 2008. "Discursive Institutionalism: The Explanatory Power of Ideas and Discourse." *Annual Review of Political Science* 11:303–326.

Schneider, Anne, and Helen Ingram. 1997. *Policy Design for Democracy*. Lawrence: University of Kansas Press.

Schön, Donald, and Martin Rein. 1994. *Frame Reflection: Toward the Resolution of Intractable Policy Controversies*. New York: Basic Books.

Searle, John. 1969. *Speech Acts: An Essay in the Philosophy of Language*. Cambridge, UK: Cambridge University Press.

Segee, Brian, and Ana Córdova. 2009. "A Fence Runs through It: Implications of Recent U.S. Border Security Legislation." In *Conservation of Shared Environments*, ed. Laura Lopez-Hoffman, Emily McGovern, Robert Varady, and Karl Flessa, 241–256. Tucson: University of Arizona Press.

Sen, Amartya. 1977. "Rational Fools: A Critique of the Behavioral Foundations of Economic Theory." *Philosophy & Public Affairs* 6:317–344.

Sen, Amartya. 2005. "Why Exactly Is Commitment Important for Rationality?" *Economics and Philosophy* 21:5–14.

Sethi, Meera, and Adam Briggle. 2011. "Making Stories Visible: The Task for the Bioethics Commission." *Issues in Science and Technology*. http://www.issues.org/27.2/sethi.html.

Shanahan, Elizabeth, Michael Jones, and Mark McBeth. 2011. "Policy Narratives and Policy Processes." *Policy Studies Journal* 39 (3): 535–559.

Sheridan, Thomas. 1998. "Another Country." In *La Vida Notreno: Photographs of Sonora, Mexico*, ed. David Burckhalter, 13–37. Albuquerque: University of New Mexico Press.

Sheridan, Thomas. 2012. *Arizona: A History*. Tucson: University of Arizona Press.

Snow, David, E. Burke Rochford, Jr., Steven Worden, and Robert Benford. 1986. "Frame Alignment Processes, Micromobilization, and Movement Participation." *American Sociological Review* 51:464–481.

Snow, David, Louis Zurcher, and Sheldon Ekland-Olsen. 1980. "Social Networks and Social Movements: A Microstructural Approach to Differential Recruitment." *American Sociological Review* 45:787–801.

Somers, Margaret. 1994. "The Narrative Constitution of Identity: A Relational and Network Approach." *Theory and Society* 23:605–649.

Soper, Kate. 1995. *What Is Nature: Culture, Politics and the Non-Human*. Oxford: Basil Blackwell.

Starr, Susan, and James Grieseme. 1989. "Institutional Ecology, Translations and Boundary Objects: Amateurs and Professionals in Berkeley's Museum of Vertebrate Zoology, 1907–39." *Social Studies of Science* 19:387–420.

Steiner, Rudolf. [1924] 1993. *Spiritual Foundations for the Renewal of Agriculture*. Kimberton, PA: Bio-Dynamic Farming and Gardening Association, Inc.

Stengers, Isabelle. 2010. *Cosmopolitics I*. Trans. R. Bononno. Minneapolis: University of Minnesota Press.

Stiglitz, Joseph. 2002. *Globalization and Its Discontents*. New York: Norton.

St. Martin, Kevin. 2001. "Making Space for Community Resource Management in Fisheries." *Annals of the Association of American Geographers. Association of American Geographers* 91 (1): 122–142.

Stokols, Daniel, Raul Lejano, and John Hipp. 2013. "Enhancing the Resilience of Human-Environment Systems: A Social Ecological Perspective." *Ecology and Society* 18 (1): 1–12.

Stone, Deborah. 1989. "Causal Stories and the Formation of Policy Agendas." *Political Science Quarterly* 104 (2): 281–300.

Susskind, Lawrence, Alejandro Camacho, and Todd Schenk. 2012. "A Critical Assessment of Collaborative Adaptive Management in Practice." *Journal of Applied Ecology* 49 (1): 47–51.

Sustainable Agriculture Research & Education (SARE). 2005. http://www.sare.org/Learning-Center/Books/The-New-American-Farmer-2nd-Edition/Text-Version/North-Central-Region/Rich-Bennett-Napoleon-OH.

Sze, Julie. 2007. *Noxious New York: The Racial Politics of Urban Health and Environmental Justice*. Cambridge, MA: MIT Press.

Tancredo, Tom. 2003. Remarks in the *Congressional Record-House*, vol. 149, pt. 4, February 25.

Thachankary, Tojo Joseph. 1992. "Organizations as 'Texts': Hermeneutics as a Model for Understanding Organizational Change." *Research in Organizational Change and Development* 6:197–233.

Treves, Adrian, Randle Jurewicz, Lisa Naughton-Treves, and David Wilcove. 2009. "The Price of Tolerance: Wolf Damage Payments after Recovery." *Biodiversity and Conservation* 18 (4): 4003–4021.

Treves, Adrian, R. Wallace, and S. White. 2009. "Participatory Planning of Interventions to Mitigate Human-Wildlife Conflicts." *Conservation Biology* 23 (6): 1577–1587.

Trewavas, Anthony. 2001. "Urban Myths of Organic Farming." *Nature* 410 (March 22): 409–410.

Turnhout, Esther. 2009. "The Effectiveness of Boundary Objects: The Case of Ecological Indicators." *Science & Public Policy* 36 (5): 403–412.

Van Drunen, Michiel, Susan van't Klooster, and Frans Berkhout. 2011. "Bounding the Future: The Use of Scenarios in Assessing Climate Change Impacts." *Futures* 43:488–496.

Walker, Brian, C. S. Holling, Stephen Carpenter, and Ann Kinzig. 2004. "Resilience, Adapatability and Transformability in Social Ecological Systems." *Ecology and Society* 9 (2): 5. http://www.ecologyandsociety.org/vol9/iss2/art5/.

Walters, Charles. 1986. *A Life in the Day of an Editor*. Metairie, LA: Acres U.S.A.

Wargo, John. 2009. *Green Intelligence:Creating Environments That Protect Human Health*. New Haven, CT: Yale University Press.

Wasserman, Stanley, and Katherine Faust. 1994. *Social Network Analysis*. Cambridge, UK: Cambridge University Press.

Weick, Karl. 1995. *Sensemaking in Organizations*. Thousand Oaks, CA: Sage.

Wenger, Etienne. 1998. *Communities of Practice: Learning, Meaning, and Identity*. Cambridge, UK: Cambridge University Press.

Wesselink, Anna, and Jeroen Warner. 2010. Reframing Floods: Proposals and Politics. *Nature and Culture* 5 (1): 1–14.

Whatmore, Sarah. 2002. *Hybrid Geographies: Natures Cultures Spaces*. London: Sage.

Wheeler, Philip, and Ronald Ward. 1998. *The Non-Toxic Farming Handbook*. Metairie, LA: Acres U.S.A.

White, Harrison C. 1992. *Identity and Control: A Structural Theory of Social Action*. Princeton, NJ: Princeton University Press.

Wickson, Fern. 2008. "Narratives of Nature and Nanotechnology." *Nature Nanotechnology* 3:313–315.

Wildavsky, Aaron. 1973. "If Planning Is Everything, Maybe It's Nothing." *Policy Sciences* 4:127–153.

Wirgau, Jessica. 2012. "Quality and Access: Bureaucratic Autonomy and the Role of Storylines at the National Endowment for the Arts." *Administration & Society*. http://aas.sagepub.com/content/early/2012/05/09/0095399712438380.abstract.

Wolfe, Cary. 2010. *What Is Posthumanism?* Minneapolis: University of Minnesota Press.

Woodin, Ann. 1984. *Home Is the Desert*. Tucson: University of Arizona Press.

Wylie, John. 2005. "A Single Day's Walking: Narrating Self and Landscape on the SouthWest Coast Path." *Transactions of the Institute of British Geographers* 30 (2): 234–247.

Wynne, Brian. 1992. "Uncertainty and Environmental Learning—Reconceiving Science and Policy in the Preventive Paradigm." *Global Environmental Change* 2 (2): 111–127.

Youngberg, Garth. 1978. "Alternative Agriculturists: Ideology, Politics, and Prospects." In *The New Politics of Food*, ed. Don Hadwiger and William Browne, 227-246. Lexington, MA: Lexington Books.

Zaffos, Joshua. 2006. "An Ecosystem Wanting for Wolves." *High Country News*, January 23.

Index

American and Comparative Environmental Policy

Sheldon Kamieniecki and Michael E. Kraft, series editors

Judith A. Layzer, *Natural Experiments: Ecosystem-Based Management and the Environment*

Daniel A. Mazmanian and Michael E. Kraft, editors, *Toward Sustainable Communities: Transition and Transformations in Environmental Policy*, second edition

Henrik Selin and Stacy D. VanDeveer, editors, *Changing Climates in North American Politics: Institutions, Policymaking, and Multilevel Governance*

Megan Mullin, *Governing the Tap: Special District Governance and the New Local Politics of Water*

David M. Driesen, editor, *Economic Thought and U.S. Climate Change Policy*

Kathryn Harrison and Lisa McIntosh Sundstrom, editors, *Global Commons, Domestic Decisions: The Comparative Politics of Climate Change*

William Ascher, Toddi Steelman, and Robert Healy, *Knowledge in the Environmental Policy Process: Re-Imagining the Boundaries of Science and Politics*

Michael E. Kraft, Mark Stephan, and Troy D. Abel, *Coming Clean: Information Disclosure and Environmental Performance*

Paul F. Steinberg and Stacy D. VanDeveer, editors, *Comparative Environmental Politics: Theory, Practice, and Prospects*

Judith A. Layzer, *Open for Business: Conservatives' Opposition to Environmental Regulation*

Kent Portney, *Taking Sustainable Cities Seriously: Economic Development, the Environment, and Quality of Life in American Cities*, second edition

Raul Lejano, Mrill Ingram, and Helen Ingram, *The Power of Narrative in Environmental Networks*